Comparing Federal Systems

THIRD EDITION

Ronald L. Watts

Institute of Intergovernmental Relations
Published for the School of Policy Studies, Queen's Universi'
McGill-Queen's University Press
Montreal & Kingston • London • Ithaca

Library and Archives Canada Cataloguing in Publication

Watts, Ronald L.
    Comparing federal systems / Ronald L. Watts. — 3rd ed.

Includes bibliographical references.

ISBN 978-1-55339-188-3

    1. Federal government. 2. Comparative government. I. Queen's University
(Kingston, Ont.). School of Policy Studies II. Title.

JC355.W28 2008   321.02   C2008-901113-9

Contents

List of Tables

List of Figures

Foreword to the First Edition

For many observers, the Canadian debate over the reform of our federal systems has fallen into predicable patterns. Decades of argument about the central issues facing the federation seem to have etched deep grooves in our collective consciousness, subtly guiding successive rounds of discussion along familiar — and unsuccessful — lines. Yet, as Ron Watts emphasizes, Canadian debates underestimate the wonderful flexibility inherent in the central idea of federalism and the rich variety of federal arrangements that exist around the world. The central message of his monograph is that a comparative perspective can expand our understanding of the possibilities before us.

To broaden our vision, Professor Watts draws on his unique breadth of knowledge of federal systems. He explores the complexities of federations in advanced industrial nations such as the United States, Switzerland, Australia, Austria and Germany, multilingual federations such as India and Malaysia, emerging federations such as Belgium and Spain, and federations that have failed such as Czechoslovakia and Pakistan. In exploring this diverse set of countries, he focuses on the ways in which they cope with the kinds of tensions that dominate Canadian headlines every day.

Ron Watts is Principal Emeritus and Professor Emeritus of Political Studies at Queen's University, and is a Fellow of the Institute of Intergovernmental Relations. He has devoted a lifetime of study to the comparative analysis of federal systems, and is an international leader in the field. He has also served as an advisor to governments on many occasions. In 1978–79, he was a Commissioner on the Task Force on Canadian Unity (the Pepin-Robarts Commission); and in 1991–92, he served the federal government as Assistant Secretary to Cabinet for Federal-Provincial Relations (Constitutional Affairs). Since 1991 he has been President of the International Association of Centers for Federal Studies.

The Institute of Intergovernmental Relations, which is the only centre dedicated exclusively to federal studies in Canada, provides a forum for research and debate over critical questions confronting the Canadian and other federations.

This study is part of the Institute's series of research monographs that examines a broad range of issues on federalism and is a companion piece to the recent study by Peter M. Leslie, *The Maastricht Model: A Canadian Perspective on the European Union*. All contributions to this series are peer reviewed.

The research for this publication was supported by the Privy Council Office of the Government of Canada. However, the views expressed are those of the author and do not necessarily represent those of the Government of Canada or the Institute of Intergovernmental Relations.

Harvey Lazar
Director
January 1997

Preface to the Third Edition and Summary

Many observers have noted that during the past decade there has been increasing interest throughout the world in adopting federal political institutions. Indeed, there are at present some two dozen countries encompassing over 40 percent of the world's population that exhibit the fundamental characteristics of a federation. A distinctive feature about this current popularity of federalism in the world is that the application of the federal idea has taken an enormous variety of forms and that there have emerged new and innovative variants.

In these circumstance and at a time when the future of the Canadian federation was very much in question, the first edition, published in 1996 under the title *Comparing Federalism in the 1990s*, was written with a view to looking at the theory and operation of federal systems elsewhere in the world for both the positive and the negative lessons they might provide Canadians. That edition focused upon a selected group of twelve federations chosen for their particular relevance to issues that were currently prominent in Canada and for the lessons they might provide. Four categories of federations were selected. The first was that of federations in developed industrial societies including the United States (1789), Switzerland (1848), Canada (1867), Australia (1901), Austria (1920) and Germany (1949). The second category consisted of two federations in Asia which, in spite of all their problems, have had a remarkable record of accommodating their intensely multilingual, multicultural and multiracial populations: India (1950) and Malaysia (1963). The third category was represented by two recently emerged and emerging federations in developed industrial societies: Belgium (1993) and Spain (1978). These two have adopted innovative approaches to the application of the federal idea, the former in relation to bicommunal arrangements and the latter in terms of an asymmetrical approach to accommodating its Autonomous Communities. The fourth category consisted of two bicommunal federations that had failed — Czechoslovakia and Pakistan — providing insights into the pathology of federations.

Three years after the first edition was published, with copies of that edition sold out, the opportunity was taken to update the text generally in a second edition entitled *Comparing Federal Systems*. It is now eight years since that edition first appeared, and given the many developments that have occurred internationally it has seemed appropriate once again to update the text, hence this third edition. Moreover, since the demand, not just in Canada but elsewhere, has led to the need for repeated reprinting of the second edition (five to date), this new edition is now directed less specifically at a Canadian audience and more widely at the lessons that can be learned from the experiences of federations throughout the world. With this in mind, two new chapters have been added: chapter 3, which reviews the factors and processes leading to the formation of federations, and chapter 4, which outlines the character of the constituent units within federations. As well, the range of federations specifically considered has been expanded, both in the text and in the tables, particularly with the inclusion of references to the Latin American federations and also to a number of others. The tables have all been extensively updated, and the list of suggested readings has been enlarged to take account of numerous significant books and articles that have appeared since the second edition was published.

The introductory chapter considers some broad issues, including the relevance and limits of comparatives studies, the history of federalism and its particular relevance today, conceptual issues relating to the notion of federalism, and identification of issues in the design and operation of federations.

The second chapter provides a brief overview of the contemporary federations considered in this study and outlines the distinctive features of each.

The third chapter reviews the different factors and processes that have led to the creation of federations. There is no single factor that explains all examples. In each case a range of factors has served as catalysts for some balance in the pressures for both political integration and regional autonomy.

The fourth chapter considers the constituent units that have served as the building blocks within federations. Significant variations are noted in the size and number of these units, in the degree to which they express distinct linguistic, ethnic or religious communities, and the existence of minorities within them. Different arrangements for federal capitals are also noted.

The fifth chapter examines how the objective of balancing unity and diversity within different federal societies has been reflected in the internal distribution of powers and the scope of responsibilities assigned to each sphere of government in different federations. A finding that emerges is the great variety among federations, both in the form and in the allocation of specific responsibilities in them.

Chapter 6 focuses upon the distribution of financial resources within federations. This is an important aspect since it enables or constrains what the different arenas of government within each federation can do in exercising their constitutionally assigned legislative and executive responsibilities. The allocations of revenues and expenditures in different federations is compared. This indicates the virtually inevitable existence of vertical and horizontal imbalances and the need for intergovernmental transfers to correct these. There is considerable variation in the extent to which conditional or unconditional transfers are employed and in the use of schemes of equalization transfers. An important aspect considered as well is the processes and institutions used for adjusting the financial arrangements and the variety of forms that these have taken.

The processes that federations have adopted for achieving more general flexibility and adjustment through intergovernmental collaboration are considered in chapter 7. It includes a consideration of the relative merits of cooperative and competitive federalism and their implications for democratic accountability. It would appear that a blend of intergovernmental cooperation and competition is in the long run most desirable.

The issue of symmetry and asymmetry among the constituent units within a federation is addressed in chapter 8. A distinction is made between political asymmetry and constitutional asymmetry among the constituent units within a federation, and examples of each are identified. In some federations constitutional asymmetry, or at least the advocacy of it, has induced counter-pressures for symmetry, suggesting that there may be limits beyond which extreme asymmetry may become dysfunctional. Nevertheless, in a number of federations the recognition of some significant constitutional asymmetry has provided an effective way of accommodating major differences in the interests and pressures for autonomy among constituent units.

A notable feature of the contemporary world is the membership of a number of federations within even wider federal organizations. Chapter 9 therefore considers the significance of multilevel federal systems resulting from the increasing emphasis both upon supra-federation organizations and upon the role of local governments.

The representative institutions of federal governments are compared in chapter 10 with particular attention given to the difference between those based on the principle of the separation of powers between executives and legislatures and those based on the fusion of the executive and the legislature through the adoption of responsible parliamentary executives. These differences have affected the particular character of intergovernmental relations, the process for giving voice to regional interests in federal policy making, the character of their political parties, and the role of federal second chambers.

A characteristic feature of federations generally is an emphasis upon constitutional supremacy as the ultimate source defining federal and state or provincial jurisdiction. A number of issues relating to the status of constitutions within federations are considered in chapter 11, including the status of their constitutions as supreme law, the processes of judicial review and the role of the courts, constitutional amendment procedures, the role of constitutional bills of rights, and constitutional provisions for secession.

Chapter 12 examines centralization and non-centralization in various federations. While identifying the conceptual problems inherent in attempting to measure relative decentralization and autonomy, an effort is made to assess the degree of decentralization in different federations.

Chapter 13 turns to the pathology of federations. It includes an examination of the sources of stress in federations and the special problem of bicommunal federations with particular reference to the failures of Czechoslovakia and Pakistan. The chapter also gives consideration to the processes and consequences of the disintegration of federations. It notes that where separation occurs, despite professions in advance about the desirability of continued economic linkages after separation, in practice emotions aroused at the time of separation have usually meant that for a considerable subsequent period economic ties have fallen far below expectations.

The concluding chapter considers the importance of public acceptance of the basic values and processes required for federal systems to operate effectively: explicit recognition of multiple identities and loyalties, and an overarching sense of shared purposes and objectives. It also emphasizes the enormous variety of ways in which the federal idea can be applied to meet particular conditions, and the value of proceeding by pragmatic and incremental adjustments. Rigid and unbending federations that fail to make the substantial adjustments necessary in changing circumstances, however, are prone to crack and disintegrate. Finally, it considers the relationship between the values of federalism and liberal democracy.

Ronald L. Watts
December 2007

Acknowledgements

I would especially like to thank April Chang for invaluable research assistance in the preparation of the third edition, particularly the complete revision of the tables, updating information, and the preparation of the index, and John McLean for earlier assistance with both the first and second editions. I would like to express my gratitude to George Anderson, who encouraged the writing of the first edition and who now as President of the Forum of Federations encouraged and helped the preparation of this third edition by financial assistance from the Forum. Douglas Brown read earlier drafts of the first edition and provided helpful comments, as did James Hurley and David Péloquin. Uwe Leonardy and Harihar Bhattacharyya made helpful suggestions for revisions in the second edition. Thomas Fleiner and his colleagues at the Institute of Federalism in Fribourg, Switzerland, assisted by their interpretation of the significance of the total revision of the Swiss constitution in 1999. George Anderson, David Cameron, Cheryl Saunders and John Kincaid reviewed the text of the third edition. I am grateful to all those who have provided advice, but of course, responsibility for any errors or misrepresentations remains mine alone.

I am also grateful to Patti Candido and Mary Kennedy for their assistance in the preparation of all these editions even to the extent of interrupting vacation time. Eric Leclerc and Hillary Ryde spent many hours preparing the text of this third edition, and Carlotta Lemieux undertook the onerous task of copyediting. In addition, I acknowledge the work of Mark Howes and Valerie Jarus of the School of Policy Studies Publications Unit at Queen's University for all three editions.

Ronald L. Watts
December 2007

Chapter 1

Introduction

1.1 THE RELEVANCE OF COMPARISONS OF FEDERAL SYSTEMS

In the early years of the 21st century the world appears to be in the midst of a paradigm shift from a world of sovereign nation-states to a world of diminished state sovereignty and increased interstate linkages of a constitutionally federal character. Indeed, there are at present some twenty-five countries encompassing over 40 percent of the world's population that each exhibits the fundamental characteristics of a functioning federation. There would appear to be some value, therefore, in looking at the theory and operation of federations for both the positive and the negative lessons that might be learned from their experience.

At the outset it should be noted that the comparison of federations requires some caution. There is no single pure model of federation that is applicable everywhere. Rather, the basic notion of involving the combination of *regional self-rule* for some purposes and *shared-rule* for others within a single political system so that neither is subordinate to the other has been applied in different ways to fit different circumstances.[1] Federations have varied and continue to vary in many ways: in the character and significance of the underlying economic and social diversities; in the number of constituent units and the degree of symmetry or asymmetry in their size, resources and constitutional status; in the scope of the allocation of legislative, executive and expenditure responsibilities; in the allocation of taxing power and resources; in the character of federal government

---

[1] The epigram of federation as "regional self-rule plus shared rule" was introduced by Daniel J. Elazar. See Elazar, *Exploring Federalism* (Tuscaloosa, Al: University of Alabama Press, 1987).

institutions and the degree of regional input to federal policy making; in the procedures for resolving conflicts and facilitating collaboration between interdependent governments; and in procedures for formal and informal adaptation and change.

One cannot, therefore, just pick models off a shelf. Even where similar institutions are adopted, different circumstances may make them operate differently. A classic illustration of this is the operation of the similar formal constitutional amendment procedures in Switzerland and in Australia. Both involve referendums for ratification of constitutional amendments requiring double majorities, i.e., a majority of the federal population and majorities in the majority of the constituent units. In Switzerland over 110 formal constitutional amendments met this requirement between 1891 and 1999 (over three-quarters of those initiated by Parliament and submitted to referendum), but in Australia of 42 attempts since 1901 only 8 have succeeded.

As long as these cautions are kept in mind, there is a genuine value in undertaking comparative analyses. Indeed, many problems are common to virtually all federations. Comparisons may therefore help us in several ways. They may help to identify options that might otherwise be overlooked. They may allow us to foresee more clearly the consequences of particular arrangements advocated. Through identifying similarities and differences they may draw attention to certain features of our own arrangements whose significance might otherwise be underestimated. Furthermore, comparisons may suggest both positive and negative lessons; we can learn not only from the successes but also from the difficulties or failures of other federations and of the mechanisms and processes they have employed to deal with problems.

1.2 A BRIEF HISTORY OF FEDERALISM

While the United States, which adopted a federal constitution in 1787, is often regarded as the first modern federation, the history of federalism is much older.

The first documented federal system came into being among the ancient Israelite tribes over 3200 years ago.[2] Of similar antiquity were the confederations of the Bedouin tribes and the Native confederacies in North America. The early leagues of the Hellenic city-states in what is today Greece and Asia Minor were designed to aggregate communal democracies to foster trade and secure defence.[3]

---

[2] Daniel J. Elazar, *Federalism: An Overview* (Pretoria: HSRC, 1995), p. 19.

[3] E.A. Freeman, *History of Federal Government in Greece and Italy*, ed. J.B. Bury (London & New York: Macmillan, 1893).

The Roman Republic established asymmetrical arrangements whereby Rome became the federate power and weaker cities were attached to it as federal partners.[4]

The medieval period saw self-governing cities in what is now northern Italy and Germany, and cantons in Switzerland linking in loose confederations for trade and defence purposes. The Swiss confederation established in 1291 lasted despite some disruptions until 1798 and was renewed 1815–47. In the late sixteenth century an independent confederation, the United Provinces of the Netherlands, was established during a revolt against Spain. Both the Swiss and Netherlands confederations were affected by the Reformation, which sharpened internal divisions. This period also saw the first writing on explicitly federal theory, exemplified by the *Politica Methodice Digesta* of Althusius and subsequently by the efforts of German theorists to provide a grounding for a restored and modernized Holy Roman Empire. Several of the British settlements in North America, particularly in New England, were based on federal arrangements growing out of Reformed Protestantism.

Following the American Revolution the newly independent states established a confederation in 1781. Its deficiencies, however, led to its transformation in 1789, following the Philadelphia Convention of 1787, into the first modern federation. Switzerland, after a brief civil war, transformed·its confederation into a federation in 1848. Canada became the third modern federation in 1867. In 1871 the North German Federation of 1867 was expanded to include south German states. Not long after, in 1901, Australia became a full-fledged federation. In addition, during the nineteenth century a number of Latin American republics — Venezuela, Mexico, Argentina and Brazil — adopted federal structures in imitation of the U.S. federation, but these proved unstable, suffering periods of autocratic and military rule.

The second half of the twentieth century saw a proliferation of federations as well as other federal forms to unite multi-ethnic communities in former colonial areas and in Europe. New federations or quasi-federations, not all of which have survived, were founded in Asia, for example, in Indochina (1945), Burma (1948), Indonesia (1949), India (1950), Pakistan (1956), Malaya (1948 and 1957) and then Malaysia (1963); in the Middle East, for example, in the United Arab Emirates (1971); in Africa, for example, Libya (1951), Ethiopia (1952), Rhodesia and Nyasaland (1953), Nigeria (1954), Mali (1959), the Congo (1960), Cameroon (1961), and Comoros (1978); and in the Caribbean, for example, the West Indies (1958). Among the federations founded or restored in central and eastern Europe were those of Austria (1945), Yugoslavia (1946), Germany (1949) and Czechoslovakia (1970).

---

[4] Elazar, *Federalism*, p. 20.

Between 1960 and the late 1980s, however, it became increasingly clear that federal systems were not the panacea that many had imagined them to be. Many of the post-war federal experiments experienced difficulties and a number of them were temporarily suspended or abandoned outright. These experiences suggested that, even when undertaken with the best of motives, there are limits to the appropriateness of federal solutions or particular federal forms in certain circumstances.

Despite these developments there was a revival of interest in federal political solutions in the 1990s. Belgium (which transformed its constitution into a full-fledged federal one in 1993), South Africa (which in 1996 confirmed with modifications a constitutional hybrid of federal and unitary features originally instituted in the interim constitution of 1994) and Spain (which as a result of the operation of the 1978 constitution has, in practice, become increasingly a federation in all but name) have been moving towards new and often innovative federal and quasi-federal forms. In South America, following earlier failures, Brazil (1988), Argentina (1994) and Venezuela (1999) adopted new federal constitutions, and Mexico from 2000 on made efforts to bring greater reality to its federalism. Following the breakup of the USSR, Russia adopted a new federal constitution in 1993. With the restoration of civilian rule, Nigeria in 1999 established a new federal constitution. There have also been efforts to resolve severe conflicts by federal experiments in Bosnia and Herzegovina (1995), Sudan (2005), Iraq (2005) and the Democratic Republic of Congo (2006). Furthermore, federal solutions have also been mooted, although not yet achieved, in Sri Lanka, the Philippines and Nepal. In Italy too there has been an evolution towards the adoption of a federal system. The United Kingdom has adopted new devolutionary arrangements for Scotland, Wales and Northern Ireland. Progress towards greater integration in what has become the European Union has also heightened interest in federal ideas. Political leaders, leading intellectuals and even some journalists increasingly refer to federalism as a liberating and positive form of political organization.

1.3 THE CONTEMPORARY RELEVANCE OF FEDERALISM

Thus, federalism is far from being an obsolete nineteenth-century form of government inappropriate in the contemporary world as some have argued. In fact, in the past decade and a half it is the concept of the nation-state, developed in the seventeenth century, that more and more people have been coming to regard as obsolete. Observers have noted that we appear to be moving from a world of sovereign nation-states to a world of diminished state sovereignty and increased interstate linkages of a constitutionally federal character. There are at present, among the 192 politically sovereign states recognized by the United Nations, 25 that are functioning federations in their character, claim to be federations or exhibit the major characteristics of federations. They contain about two billion people, or 40 percent of the world population, and they encompass some 510 constituent or federated units. In addition to these federations, there have emerged new variants in the application of the federal idea. Just one of many examples is the European Union where individual federations, unions and unitary states have "pooled their sovereignty" (as they express it) in a hybrid structure which has come to involve elements of confederation and federation.

There are a number of reasons for the contemporary international trends both to increased pooling of sovereignty among states in various federal forms and also to increased devolution within countries. First, modern developments in transportation, social communications, technology and industrial organization have produced pressures at one and the same time for larger political organizations and for smaller ones. The pressure for larger political units has been generated by the goals shared by most Western and non-Western societies today: a desire for progress, a rising standard of living, social justice, and influence in the world arena, and by a growing awareness of worldwide interdependence in an era whose advanced technology makes both mass destruction and mass construction possible. The desire for smaller, self-governing political units has arisen from the desire to make governments more responsive to the individual citizen and to give expression to primary group attachments — linguistic and cultural ties, religious connections, historical traditions and social practices — which provide the distinctive basis for a community's sense of identity and yearning for self-determination. Given these dual pressures throughout the world, more and more peoples have come to see some form of federalism, combining a shared government for specified common purposes with autonomous action by constituent units of government for purposes related to maintaining their regional distinctiveness, as allowing the closest institutional approximation to the complex multicultural and multidimensional economic, social and political reality of the contemporary world.

Second, and closely related, is the recognition that an increasingly global economy has itself unleashed economic and political forces strengthening both international *and* local pressures at the expense of the traditional nation-state. Global communications and consumership have awakened desires in the smallest and most remote villages around the world for access to the global marketplace of goods and services. As a result, governments have been faced increasingly with the desires of their people to be both *global* consumers and *local* citizens at the same time. Tom Courchene has labelled this trend "glocalization."[5] Thus, the nation-state itself is simultaneously proving both too small and too large to serve

---

[5] Thomas J. Courchene, "Glocalization: The Regional/International Interface," *Canadian Journal of Regional Science*, 18:1 (1995): 1–20.

all the desires of its citizens. Because of the development of the world market economy, the old-fashioned nation-state can no longer deliver many of the benefits its citizens value, such as rising living standards and job security. Self-sufficiency of the nation-state is widely recognized as unattainable and nominal sovereignty is less appealing if it means that, in reality, people have less control over decisions that crucially affect them. At the same time, nation-states have come to be too remote from individual citizens to provide a sense of democratic control and to respond clearly to the specific concerns and preference of their citizens. In such a context federalism with its different interacting levels of government has provided a way of mediating the variety of global and local citizen preferences.

Third, the spread of market-based economies is creating socioeconomic conditions conducive to support for the federal idea. Among these are the emphasis on contractual relationships; the recognition of the non-centralized character of a market-based economy; entrepreneurial self-governance and consumer rights consciousness; markets that thrive on diversity rather than homogeneity, on interjurisdictional mobility and on competition as well as cooperation; and the recognition that people do not have to like each other in order to benefit each other. There has been a long association between federations and market economies and as Kincaid has noted federal countries have been more likely than non-federal countries to have a market economy.[6]

Fourth, changes in technology have been generating new and more federal models of industrial organization with decentralized and "flattened hierarchies" involving non-centralized interactive networks. This in turn has produced more favourable attitudes towards non-centralized political organization.

Fifth, increasing public attention, especially in Europe, has been given to the principle of "subsidiarity," the notion that a "higher" political body should take up only those tasks that cannot be accomplished by the "lower" political bodies themselves. There are some problems with the concept: it is difficult to translate into legal terms, it has a clearly hierarchical character, and it implies that ultimately it is for the "higher" body to decide at which level tasks should be performed. Nevertheless, the decentralist thrust of the subsidiarity principle has been instrumental in encouraging wider interest in a "citizen-oriented federalism."

Yet another factor has been the resilience of the classical federations in the face of changing conditions. The constitutions of the United States (1789), Switzerland (1848), Canada (1867) and Australia (1901) are among the longest

---

[6] John Kincaid, "Federalism and Democracy: Comparative Empirical and Theoretical Respectives", paper presented at workshop on "Federalism and Democracy", Centre for Federal Studies, University of Kent, Canterbury, April 2-6, 2006.

continuously surviving of any in the world today. In spite of problems experienced over the past three decades, these four federations along with Germany, another federation, have displayed a degree of flexibility and adaptability.

Also contributing to the appeal of federation as a model has been the consistent placing of 8 federations within the top 21 of the some 174 sovereign states in the annual United Nations ranking in terms of economic welfare, respect for rights and quality of life.[7] Indeed in 2006, Australia ranked third, Canada sixth, USA eighth, Switzerland ninth, Belgium thirteenth, Austria fourteenth, Spain nineteenth and Germany twenty-first as "the world's most liveable countries." The example of the progressive widening and deepening of the European Union has also provided an influential model for closer collaboration among states.

For all these reasons, the federal idea is now more popular internationally than at any time in history. This suggests that state builders should be wary of rejecting the advantages that so many elsewhere see in federal solutions.

A distinctive feature about the current popularity of federalism in the world is that the application of the federal idea has taken a great variety of forms. The degrees of centralization or decentralization differ across federations, as do their financial arrangements, the character of their federal legislative and executive institutions, institutional arrangements for facilitating intergovernmental relations, judicial arrangements for umpiring internal conflicts, and procedures for constitutional amendment. Among interesting recent developments and innovations has been the acceptance in an increasing number of instances of some degree of asymmetry in the relationship of member units to federations or to supranational organizations. Significant examples in practice include Belgium, India, Malaysia, Russia, Spain and, following the Maastricht Treaty, the European Union. Another has been the trend for federations themselves to become constituent members of even wider federations or supranational organizations. Examples are Germany, Belgium and Austria within the European Union.[8] It is also worth noting that the three members of the North American Free Trade Agreement (NAFTA) — Canada, the USA and Mexico — are each themselves federations. Thus, there has been an emerging trend towards three or even four (not just two) levels of federal organization to reconcile supranational, national, regional and local impulses and thereby to maximize the realization of citizen preferences.

---

[7] United Nations Development Programme, *Human Resources Report* (New York: Oxford University Press, 2006). The paper by John Kincaid, op. cit., found a positive empirical association generally between federal countries and relatively high Human Development Index, human rights and democracy scores as compared to non-federal countries.

[8] To complicate the picture further, Benelux, one of whose members is itself a federation (Belgium), represents a confederation within the wider confederal European Union.

1.4 DEFINITION OF TERMS AND OF PRINCIPLES OF FEDERALISM

There has been much scholarly debate about the definition of federalism. Generally, in this debate the term "federalism" has been widely used both as a normative idea and as a descriptive category for a certain category of political institutions. For the sake of clarity, however, I shall distinguish the three terms: "federalism," "federal political systems," and "federations." In this distinction, "federalism" is used basically not as a descriptive but as a normative term and refers to the advocacy of multi-tiered government combining elements of shared-rule and regional self-rule. It is based on the presumed value and validity of combining unity and diversity, i.e., of accommodating, preserving and promoting distinct identities within a larger political union. The essence of federalism as a normative principle is the value of perpetuating both union and non-centralization at the same time.

"Federal political systems" and "federations" are used as descriptive terms applying to particular forms of political organization. The term "federal political systems" refers to a broad category of political systems in which, by contrast to the single central source of political and legal authority in unitary systems, there are two (or more) levels of government thus combining elements of *shared-rule* (collaborative partnership) through a common government and *regional self-rule* (constituent unit autonomy) for the governments of the constituent units. This broad genus encompasses a whole spectrum of more specific non-unitary forms, i.e., species ranging from "quasi-federations" and "federations" to "confederacies" and beyond. As in a spectrum, the categories are not sharply delineated but shade into one another at the margins.

Daniel Elazar has identified the following as specific categories within this range: unions, constitutionally decentralized unions, federations, confederations, federacies, associated statehood, condominiums, leagues and joint functional authorities.[9] (See table 1 for definitions of these terms.) Tables 2, 3, 4, 5, 6 and 7 list current examples of these federal forms. Furthermore, other political systems outside the general category of federal systems may incorporate some federal arrangements because political leaders and nation-builders are less bound by considerations of theoretical purity than by the pragmatic search for workable political arrangements. Such considerations may also lead to hybrids such as the European Union which, although originally a purely confederal arrangement, has in recent years incorporated some features of a federation.

---

[9] Elazar, *Federalism*, 2–7, 16, and Daniel J. Elazar, ed., *Federal Systems of the World*, 2nd ed. (Harlow: Longman Group, 1994), p. xvi.

Within the broad genus of federal political systems, "federations" represent a particular species in which neither the federal nor the constituent units of government are constitutionally subordinate to the other, i.e., each has sovereign powers derived from the constitution rather than from another level of government, each is empowered to deal directly with its citizens in the exercise of its legislative, executive and taxing powers, and each is directly elected by its citizens. Table 2 identifies 25 contemporary functioning examples. This book focuses primarily on analysing the design and operation of these as a form of government which at the beginning of the twenty-first century is proving to be so widespread.

The generally common structural characteristics of federations as a specific form of federal political system are the following:

- at least two orders of government, one for the whole federation and the other for the regional units, each acting directly on its citizens;
- a formal constitutional distribution of legislative and executive authority and allocation of revenue resources between the two orders of government ensuring some areas of genuine autonomy for each order;
- provision for the designated representation of distinct regional views within the federal policy-making institutions, usually provided by the particular form of the federal second chamber;
- a supreme written constitution not unilaterally amendable and requiring the consent for amendments of a significant proportion of the constituent units;
- an umpire (in the form of courts, provision for referendums, or an upper house with special powers); and
- processes and institutions to facilitate intergovernmental collaboration for those areas where governmental responsibilities are shared or inevitably overlap.

There are several important points to note. First, there is an important distinction between constitutional form and operational reality. In many political systems political practice has transformed the way the constitution operates. In Canada and India, for example, the initial constitution was quasi-federal, containing some central overriding powers more typical of unitary systems. But in Canada these powers have fallen into complete disuse and in India, although still employed, they have been moderated so that in both cases operational reality comes closer to that of a full-fledged federation. Other particularly notable examples of the impact of operational practice have occurred in Malaysia, Pakistan, Russia, South Africa, Spain and Venezuela. Table 3 summarizes the constitutional and operational character of 28 nominal federations plus the European Union. Thus, to understand federal systems generally and federations in particular it is necessary to study both their constitutional law and their politics and how these interact.

TABLE 1: The Spectrum of Federal Political Systems

Unions	Polities compounded in such a way that the constituent units preserve their respective integrities primarily or exclusively through the common organs of the general government rather than through dual government structures. New Zealand and Lebanon are examples. Belgium prior to becoming a federation in 1993 was an example (when central legislators served also with a dual mandate as regional or community councillors).
Constitutionally decentralized unions	Basically unitary in form, in the sense that ultimate authority rests with the central government but incorporate constitutionally protected sub-national units of government that have functional autonomy. See table 6 for examples.
Federations	Compound polities, combining strong constituent units and a strong general government, each possessing powers delegated to it by the people through a constitution, and each empowered to deal directly with the citizens in the exercise of its legislative, administrative and taxing powers, and each with major institutions directly elected by the citizens. Currently there are some 25 countries in the world that meet or claim to meet the basic criteria of a functioning federation, although in the cases of South Africa and Spain their constitutions have not adopted the label. See table 2 for functioning examples. In addition, efforts to create federations in post-conflict situations are currently underway in three countries (see table 3).
Confederations	These occur where several pre-existing polities join together to form a common government for certain limited purposes (for foreign affairs, defence or economic purposes), but the common government is dependent upon the will of the constituent governments, being composed of delegates from the constituent governments, and therefore having only an indirect electoral and fiscal base. Historical examples include Switzerland 1291–1798 and 1815–47, and the United States 1781–89. In the contemporary world, the European Union is primarily a confederation, although it has increasingly incorporated some features of a federation. See table 4 for other examples.
Federacies	This term, coined by Elazar (1987, pp. 7, 54–7) refers to political arrangements where a smaller unit or units are linked to a larger polity, but the smaller unit or units retain considerable autonomy, have a minimum role in the government of the larger one, and the relationship can be dissolved only by mutual agreement. Examples are the relationship of Puerto Rico and the Northern Marianas to the United States. See table 5 for other examples.
Associated states	These relationships are similar to federacies, but they can be dissolved by either of the units acting alone on prearranged terms established in the constituting document or a treaty. The relationship between New Zealand and the Cook Islands and Niue are examples. See table 5 for other examples.

... continued

TABLE 1 (*continued*)

Condominiums	Political units that function under the joint rule of two or more external states in such a way that the inhabitants have substantial internal self-rule. Examples have been Andorra, which functioned under the joint rule of France and Spain 1278–1993, Vanuatu, which operated under a British-French condominium 1906–80, and Nauru which was under a joint Australia–New Zealand–United Kingdom condominium 1947–68.
Leagues	Linkages of politically independent polities for specific purposes that function through a common secretariat, rather than a government, and from which members may unilaterally withdraw. See table 7 for examples.
Joint functional authorities	An agency established by two or more polities for joint implementation of a particular task or tasks. The North Atlantic Fisheries Organization (NAFO), the International Atomic Energy Agency (IAEA), and the International Labor Organization (ILO) are three of many examples. Such joint functional authorities may also take the form of trans-border organizations established by adjoining sub-national governments, e.g., the interstate grouping for economic development involving four regions in Italy, four Austrian Länder, two then-Yugoslav republics and one West German Land established in 1978, and the interstate Regio Basiliensis involving Swiss, German and French cooperation in the Basle area.
Hybrids	Some political entities combine characteristics of different kinds of political systems. Those which are predominantly federations in their constitutions and operation but which have some overriding federal government powers more typical of a unitary system may be described as "quasi-federations." Examples are Canada initially in 1867, which was basically a federation but contained some unitary elements which fell into disuse in the second half of the twentieth century. India, Pakistan and Malaysia are predominantly federations, but their constitutions include some overriding central emergency powers. South Africa (1996) has most of the characteristics of a federation but retains some unitary features. Germany, while predominantly a federation, has a confederal element in the Bundesrat, its federal second chamber, which is composed of instructed delegates of the Land governments. A hybrid combining much more fully the characteristics of a confederation is the European Union after the Maastricht Treaty. This is basically a confederation but has some features of a federation. Hybrids occur because statesmen are often more interested in pragmatic political solutions than in theoretical purity.

TABLE 2: Contemporary Functioning Federations (including quasi-federations)[1]

Federation	Current Constituent Units	Originally Founded[2]	Current Constitution[3]
Argentine Republic	23 provinces + 1 federal district	1853	1994
Australia, Commonwealth of	6 states + 1 territory + 1 capital territory + 7 administered territories	1901	1901
Austria, Federal Republic of	9 Länder	1920	1945
Belau, Republic of	16 states	1981	1981
Belgium, Kingdom of	3 regions + 3 cultural communities	1993	1993
Bosnia and Herzegovina	2 entities + 1 district	1995	1995
Brazil, Federative Republic of	26 states + 1 federal capital district	1891	1988
Canada	10 provinces + 3 territories + Aboriginal organizations	1867	1867+1982
Comoros, Union of the	3 islands	1978	2001
Ethiopia, Federal Democratic Republic of	9 ethnically based states + 2 chartered cities	1995	1995
Germany, Federal Republic of	16 Länder	1949	1949
India, Republic of	28 states + 7 union territories	1950	1996
Malaysia	13 states	1963	1963
Mexico (United Mexican States)	31 states + 1 federal district	1824	1917
Micronesia, Federated States of	4 states	1979	1986
Nigeria, Federal Republic of	36 states + 1 federal capital territory	1954	1999
Pakistan, Islamic Republic of	4 provinces + federally administered tribal areas + 1 capital territory	1973	1973
Russian Federation	86 subjects: republics and various categories of regions	1993	1993
St. Kitts and Nevis, Federation of	2 islands	1983	1983
South Africa, Republic of[4]	9 provinces	1996	1996
Spain, Kingdom of[4]	17 autonomous communities + 2 autonomous communities + 3 sovereign areas + 1 principality	1978	1978
Swiss Confederation	26 cantons	1848	2000
United Arab Emirates[5]	7 emirates	1971	1996
United States of America	50 states + 1 federal district + 2 federacies + 3 associated states + 3 local home-rule territories + 3 unincorporated territories + 130 Native American domestic dependent nations	1789	1789
Venezuela, Bolivarian Republic of	23 states + 1 federal district + 1 federal dependency consisting of 72 islands	1811	1999

[1] For the definition and examples of quasi-federations see table 1 under "Hybrids."
[2] Year originally founded as a federation.
[3] Current constitution with date of coming into force.
[4] South Africa and Spain, while predominantly federations in form, have not adopted the label "federation" in their constitutions.
[5] The constitution of the United Arab Emirates refers to it as a "federal state," but its structure is fundamentally confederal.

TABLE 3: Constitutional and Operational Character of Nominal Federations

Federation	Current Constituent Unit	Constitution	Operation 2007
United States	50 states + 1 federal district + 2 federacies + 3 associated states + 3 local home-rule territories + 3 unincorporated territories + 130 Native American domestic dependent nations	Federation (1789)	Federation
Switzerland	26 cantons	Federation (1848, 1999)	Federation
Canada	10 provinces + 3 territories + Aboriginal organizations	Quasi-federation (1867, 1982)	Federation
Australia	6 states + 1 territory + 1 capital territory + 7 administered territories	Federation (1901)	Federation
Austria	9 Länder	Federation (1920, 1945)	Federation
Germany	16 Länder	Federation (1949)	Federation
India	28 states + 7 union territories	Quasi-federation (1950)	Federation (some quasi-federal aspects)
Brazil	26 states + 1 federal capital district	Federation (1988)	Federation
Belgium	3 regions + 3 cultural communities	Federation (1993)	Federation
Spain	17 autonomous communities + 2 autonomous communities + 3 sovereign areas + 1 principality	Devolved Union (1978)	Federation in practice
Mexico	31 states + 1 federal district	Federation (1917)	Centralized Federation
Nigeria	36 states + 1 federal capital territory	Federation (1999)	Centralized Federation
Ethiopia	9 ethnically based states + 2 chartered cities	Federation (1995)	Centralized Federation

...continued

TABLE 3 (*continued*)

Federation	Current Constituent Unit	Constitution	Operation 2007
South Africa	9 provinces	Devolved Union (1996)	Quasi-federation
Russia	86 subjects: republics and various categories of regions	Federation (1993)	Quasi-federation
Argentina	23 provinces + 1 federal district + 6 regions	Quasi-federation (1994)	Quasi-federation
Malaysia	13 states	Quasi-federation (1963)	Centralized quasi-federation
Venezuela	23 states + 1 federal district + 1 federal dependency consisting of 72 islands	Federation (1999)	Centralized quasi-federation
Micronesia	4 states	Federation (1978)	Micro-federation
Belau	16 states	Federation (1981)	Micro-federation
St. Kitts-Nevis	2 islands	Federation (1985)	Micro-binary-federation
Comoros	3 islands	Federation (2001)	Micro-quasi-federation
Pakistan	4 provinces + federally administered tribal areas + 1 capital territory	Quasi-federation (1973)	Devolved unitary military regime
United Arab Emirates[1]	7 emirates	Confederation (1996)	Hybrid confederation-federation
European Union	27 independent, democratic member states	Hybrid (1993)	Hybrid confederation-federation
Bosnia and Herzegovina	2 entities + 1 district	Federation (1995)	International (EU) tutelage
Sudan[2]	25 states	Federal Constitution (2005)	In transition
Iraq[2]	18 governorates	Federal Constitution (2005)	In transition
Dem. Rep. of Congo[2]	25 provinces and capital	Federal Constitution (2006)	In transition

[1] The constitution of the United Arab Emirates refers to it as a "federal state," but its structure is fundamentally confederal.
[2] Federal experiments not fully operational and therefore not listed in table 2.

TABLE 4: Some Contemporary Confederations and Hybrids

Name	Constituent Units	Current Constitution[1]
Benelux	3 member states	1944 (1958)
Caribbean Community (CARICOM)	15 member states + 5 associate members + 7 observers	1973
Commonwealth of Independent States (CIS)	11 member states + 1 associate member	1991
European Union (EU)	27 member states	1993
United Arab Emirates (UAE)	7 emirates	1971 (1996)[2]

[1] Current constitution, with founding date and significant amendment in brackets (if applicable).
[2] The Constitution of the UAE refers to it as a "federal state," but in structure it is fundamentally confederal.

TABLE 5: Associated States and Federacies

Name	Form	Federated Power
Åland Islands	Federacy	Finland
Azores Islands	Federacy	Portugal
Bhutan, Kingdom of	Associated State	India
Cook Islands	Associated State	New Zealand
Faroe Islands	Federacy	Denmark
Greenland	Federacy	Denmark
Guernsey, Bailiwick of	Federacy	United Kingdom
Isle of Man	Federacy	United Kingdom
Jammu and Kashmir	Federacy	India
Jersey, Bailiwick of	Federacy	United Kingdom
Liechtenstein, Principality of	Associated State	Switzerland
Madeira Islands	Federacy	Portugal
Monaco, Principality of	Associated State	France
Netherlands Antilles	Associated State	Netherlands
Niue	Associated State	New Zealand
Northern Mariana Islands, Commonwealth of	Federacy	United States
Puerto Rico, Commonwealth of	Federacy	United States
San Marino	Associated State	Italy

TABLE 6: Decentralized Unions with Some Federal Features

Name	Constituent Units	Current Constitution[1]
Antigua and Barbuda	6 parishes + 2 dependencies	1981
Union of Burma	7 divisions + 7 states	1974 (suspended 1988)
Republic of Cameroon	10 provinces	1972 (1996)
People's Republic of China	23 provinces + 5 autonomous regions + 4 municipalities + 2 special administrative regions	1982
Republic of Colombia	32 departments + 1 capital region	1991
Republic of Fiji Islands	4 divisions + 1 dependency	1997
French Republic	22 regions	1958
Republic of Ghana	10 regions	1992
Georgia	9 regions + 2 autonomous republics	1995
Republic of Indonesia	30 provinces + 2 special regions + 1 special capital city district	1959
Italian Republic	15 regions + 5 autonomous regions	1947
Japan	47 prefectures	1947
Republic of Namibia	13 regions	1990
Kingdom of the Netherlands	12 provinces	1815 (2002)
Independent State of Papua New Guinea	20 provinces	1975
Portuguese Republic	18 districts + 2 autonomous regions	1976
Solomon Islands	9 provinces + 1 capital territory	1978
Democratic Socialist Republic of Sri Lanka	8 provinces	1978
Kingdom of Sweden	21 counties	1975
United Republic of Tanzania	26 regions	1977 (1984)
United Kingdom of Great Britain and Northern Ireland	4 countries + 5 self-governing islands	(1999)
Ukraine	24 provinces + 1 autonomous republic (Crimea) + 2 municipalities	1996
Republic of Vanuatu	6 provinces	1980

[1] Current constitution, with date of significant amendment in brackets (if applicable).

TABLE 7: Examples of Varieties of Federal Arrangements

Decentralized Union	Federation[1]	Confederation	Federacy	Associated Statehood	Condominium	League
Antigua-Barbuda	Argentina	Benelux	Denmark-Faroes	France-Monaco	Andorra: France and Spain (1278–1993)	Arab League
Cameroon	Australia	Economic Union	Finland-Åland	India-Bhutan	Vanuatu: U.K.-France (1906–80)	Association of South East Asian Nations (ASEAN)
China	Austria	Caribbean Community (CARICOM)	Greenland-Denmark	Italy-San Marino	Nauru: Australia-New Zealand-U.K. (1947–68)	Baltic Assembly
Colombia	Belau	Commonwealth of Independent States	India-Jammu and Kashmir	Netherlands-Netherlands Antilles		Commonwealth of Nations
Italy	Belgium	European Union	Portugal-Azores	New Zealand-Cook Islands		North Atlantic Treaty Organization (NATO)
Japan	Bosnia Herzegovina	United Arab Emirates[2]	Portugal-Madeira Islands	New Zealand-Niue		Nordic Council
Netherlands	Brazil		UK-Guernsey	Switzerland-Lichtenstein		South Asian Association for Regional Cooperation (SAARC)
Papua/New Guinea	Canada		UK-Jersey			
Solomon Islands	Comoros		UK-Isle of Man			
Tanzania	Ethiopia		US-Northern Marianas			
Ukraine	Germany		US-Puerto Rico			
United Kingdom	India					
Vanuatu	Malaysia					
	Mexico					
	Micronesia					
	Nigeria					
	Pakistan					
	Russia					
	St. Kitts-Nevis					
	South Africa					
	Spain					
	Switzerland					
	United States					
	Venezuela					

[1] Including quasi-federations as defined in table 1 under "Hybrids."
[2] The constitution of the United Arab Emirates refers to it as a "federal state," but its structure is fundamentally confederal.

Second, while knowledge about the structural character of a federal political system or a federation is important to gain an understanding of its character, equally important is the nature of its political processes. Significant characteristics of federal processes include a strong predisposition to democracy, since they presume the voluntary consent of citizens in the constituent units; non-centralization as a principle expressed through multiple centres of political decision making; open political bargaining as a major feature of the way in which decisions are arrived at; the operation of checks and balances to avoid the concentration of political power; and a respect for constitutionalism and the rule of law, since each order of government derives its authority from the constitution.

Third, federal processes may be territorial or consociational or both. While there are some examples of federations in which there are non-territorial constituent units recognized in the constitution, the most notable example being the Belgian Communities, the constitutional distribution of power among *territorial* units is by far the most common pattern among federations. In many federations the constitutional powers are distributed equally among the main category of constituent units. It is noteworthy, however, that in some federations there is some asymmetry in the relationship of the main constituent units (e.g., Canada, Malaysia, India, Spain and Russia). In some the main constituent units are classified into two or more categories with "territories" distinguished from the major constituent units by having less autonomy. (Table 2 indicates those federations that include such territories.)

Fourth, among the advantages claimed for federations compared with confederations as a form of political partnership are that federation permits a relatively decisive form of shared-rule able to carry out redistributive policies. Furthermore, because most of the federal institutions are based on direct election by the citizens (in contrast to confederations, federacies and associated states), federation as a form provides all citizens with an opportunity to participate fully through democratic processes in the legislative and executive operations of shared-rule. In this way it contributes to a sense of citizen-ownership of the institutions of shared-rule. While the political autonomy of the constituent units is limited to those spheres assigned to them by the constitution, unlike decentralized unitary systems these are fully safeguarded by a supreme constitution not unilaterally amendable by the federal government. The main disadvantage usually attributed to federations is their tendency to complexity, legalism and rigidity.

1.5 VARIATIONS IN FEDERATIONS

While certain structural features and political processes common to most federations can be identified, federations have exhibited many variations in the application of the federal idea. There is no single "ideal" or "pure" form of federation. Among the variations to meet particular circumstances that can be identified among federations are those in:

- the degree and distribution of cultural or national diversity that they attempt to reconcile;
- their creation by aggregation of constituent units, devolution to constituent units, or both processes;
- the number, relative size and symmetry or asymmetry of the constituent units;
- the distribution of legislative and administrative responsibility among governments;
- the allocation of taxing powers and financial resources;
- the roles of federal and constituent-unit governments in the conduct of international relations;
- the character and composition of their central federative institutions;
- the processes and institutions for resolving conflicts and facilitating collaboration between interdependent governments;
- the ratification of constitutional amendments by regional legislatures or referendums;
- the degree of political centralization or non-centralization and the degree of economic integration.

Furthermore, in some cases, while most of the defining characteristics and associated attributes of federations outlined in section 1.4 may be present, some of them may be missing. Yet other cases may involve hybrids combining unitary or confederal elements. Nevertheless, they may be regarded as predominately federations if in operation they exhibit some genuine constitutionally based autonomy in both orders of government.

Consequently, an important element in the comparative analysis of federations in this volume will be to identify and contribute to the understanding of the effectiveness or ineffectiveness of different kinds of federal arrangements and processes in different circumstances.

1.6 FEDERAL SOCIETIES, CONSTITUTIONS AND GOVERNMENTS

In comparing federations it is important to distinguish between federal societies, constitutions and governments. The motivations and interests leading to pressures both for political diversity and for common action within a society, the legal constitutional structure, and the actual operation, processes and practice of governments are all important aspects in the operation of federal systems. It is through studying the interaction of these that we may come to understand the nature of federal systems.

When political studies were concerned less with the analysis of political forces within society or of political and administrative behaviour and more with the study of legal and constitutional structures, authors examining federations tended to concentrate primarily on the legal framework within which federal and provincial or state governments carried on their activities. Since the 1950s, students of politics have come to realize, however, that a merely legalistic study of constitutions will not adequately explain political patterns within federal systems. Indeed, the actual operations and practices of governments within federal systems have, in response to the play of social and political pressures, frequently diverged significantly from the formal relationships specified in written legal documents.[10]

Scholars writing about federations in the second half of the twentieth century have been conscious of the importance of the social forces underlying federal systems. Even K.C. Wheare, whose pioneering comparative work, *Federal Government* (1946), is often described as institutional in approach, included a chapter on "Some Prerequisites of Federal Government" which was in some respects a sociology of federal systems.[11] W.S. Livingston, writing in 1956, went so far as to suggest that federal systems were a function not of constitutions but of societies:

> The essential nature of federalism is to be sought for, not in the shadings of legal and constitutional terminology, but in the forces — economic, social, political, cultural — that have made the outward forms of federalism necessary ... The essence of federalism lies not in the constitutional or institutional structure but in the society itself. Federal government is a device by which the federal qualities of the society are articulated and protected.[12]

In view of the importance of social forces in moulding federal political institutions and their operation, throughout this study there will be frequent references to their significance and influence.

But the view that federal institutions are merely the instrumentalities of federal societies, while an important corrective to purely legal and institutional analyses, is also too one-sided and oversimplifies the causal relationships. As authors such as Alan Cairns and Donald Smiley have pointed out, constitutions and institutions,

---

[10] For one effort to operationalize the idea of a federal political culture note Richard L Cole, John Kincaid and Alejandro Rodriguez, "Public Opinion in Federalism and Federal Political Culture in Canada, Mexico and the United States, 2004," *Publius: The Journal of Federalism*, 34: 3 (2004): 201-221.

[11] K.C. Wheare, *Federal Government* (London: Oxford University Press, 1946), ch. 3. See also his "Federalism and the Making of Nations," in A.W. Macmahon, ed., *Federalism, Mature and Emergent* (New York: Russell and Russell, 1955), pp. 28–43.

[12] W.S. Livingston, *Federalism and Constitutional Change* (Oxford: Clarendon Press, 1956), pp. 1–2.

once created, themselves channel and shape societies.[13] For example, in both the United States and Switzerland the replacement of confederal structures by federal institutions in 1789 and 1848 marked turning points enabling more effective political reconciliation of pressures for diversity and unity within those societies.

It must be recognized that the causal relationships between a federal society, its political institutions, and political behaviour and processes are complex and dynamic. The pressures within a society may force a particular expression in its political institutions, processes and behaviour; but these institutions and processes, once established, in turn shape the society by determining the channels in which these social pressures and political activities flow. Thus, the relationships between a society, its constitution and its political institutions are not static but involve continual interaction. In comparing federal systems and their design, we shall be concerned, therefore, not only with the influence of social forces upon the adoption, design and subsequent operation of federal constitutional structures, but with the influence that particular federal political superstructures and the related processes and political practices have had upon social loyalties, feelings and diversities. It is in the interplay of the social foundations, the written constitutions and the actual practices and activities of governments that an understanding of the nature and effectiveness of federal political systems is to be found. In comparing and assessing different federal systems, account therefore needs to be taken not only of how well the institutions in each system reflect the particular social and political balance of forces in that society, but also to what extent these institutions, once established, channel and influence the articulation of unity and diversity within the polity. Figures 1 and 2 illustrate this complex relationship.

The interaction of these various aspects is illustrated by the way in which different federations have evolved. Some that began with federal constitutions of a highly decentralized form have with time become more integrated and relatively centralized. The United States and Australia are classic examples. Others, beginning with more centralized or even quasi-federal constitutions have over time become more decentralized. Canada is a classic example of this pattern, but India, Belgium and Spain also illustrate this. Some formerly unitary political systems have also decentralized under internal pressures adopting in part, or even whole, federal institutions. Examples are Belgium, Spain, South Africa, the United Kingdom and Italy. In all these cases, the pattern of evolution has been the product of the mutual interaction of social forces and the political institutions.

---

[13] A. Cairns, "The Governments and Societies of Canadian Federalism, *Canadian Journal of Political Science*, 10:4 (1977): 695–725; D.V. Smiley, *The Federal Condition in Canada* (Toronto: McGraw-Hill Ryerson Ltd., 1987), pp. 3–11.

FIGURE 1: The Interaction of Federal Societies, Constitutions and
                    Governments

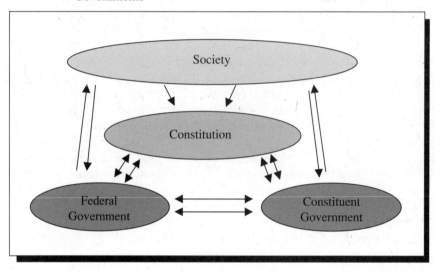

FIGURE 2: Federal Evolution through Time

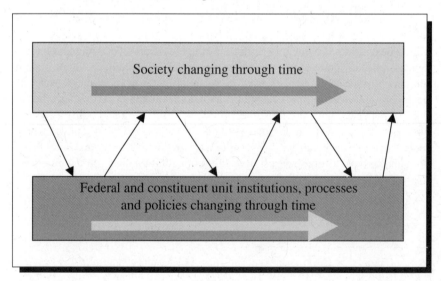

A predominant issue running through all these examples has been the effort to encourage a balance between the pressures for unity and diversity. Where diversity within a society is deep-rooted, the effort simply to impose political unity has rarely succeeded, and indeed has often instead proved counter-productive, creating dissension. The early experience of Canada before 1867 illustrates this, as has the much more recent experience in the USSR, Czechoslovakia, and even the United Kingdom. On the other hand, the recognition of diversity, by providing the different internal groups with a greater sense of security, has often contributed to reduced tension, as in Switzerland and more recently India and Spain. But by itself, greater autonomy may simply encourage separatism, a trend that in Belgium, Quebec and Scotland has drawn concern. It is clear that more regional autonomy may contribute to the accommodation of diversity, but by itself it is likely to be insufficient. It needs to be accompanied by the institutional encouragement of common interests that provide the glue to hold the federation together. Thus *both* the elements of "self-rule" for constituent units and "shared-rule" through common institutions, a combination that characterizes federal political systems, are essential to their long-run effectiveness in combining unity and diversity. This theme runs through this volume but will be explored further in chapter 13 on the pathology of federations.

1.7 ISSUES IN THE DESIGN AND OPERATION OF FEDERATIONS

This study, because its aim is to draw lessons from the experience of federations, will focus on the following issues in their design and operation:

1. The interrelation of social institutions, institutional structures and political processes and the interaction of these affecting each other. This theme, rather than being treated in a separate section, runs through all the sections of this study.

2. The common and varying features of federations:

    - the common objectives of combining unity and diversity
    - common institutional structures and processes in federations
    - variations in the institutional structures and processes of federations

    Consideration of the common and varying features of federations also runs through all the sections of this study.

3. Issues in the design of federations that affect their operation:

    - the character of the constituent units in terms of their number, absolute and relative sizes, and absolute and relative wealth (chapter 4)

- whether the drawing of constituent unit boundaries and constituent units should represent differences or cut across them (chapter 4)

- the distribution of functions in terms of the following:

  - the form of distribution, including the significance of exclusive, concurrent and residual authority assigned to each level (chapter 5)
  - the allocation of legislative and administrative responsibilities (chapter 5)
  - the scope of functions allocated to each level (chapter 5)
  - the allocation of financial resources (chapter 6)
  - structures and processes relating to intergovernmental relations within federations (chapter 7)
  - degrees of symmetry or asymmetry in the allocation of powers to constituent units (chapter 8)
  - degrees of decentralization and non-centralization (chapters 5, 6, 12)
  - degrees of autonomy or interdependence of governments (chapters 5, 6, 12)
  - identification of commonly regarded essential federal powers (chapter 12)

- the nature of the common federative institutions (chapter 10):

  - the distinction in this respect between federations and confederations
  - the distinction between parliamentary and non-parliamentary federations and their differing impact
  - special provisions for proportionate representation of constituent units in the federal executive, legislative institutions (particularly second chambers), public service and agencies
  - the role of constituent unit representatives in common decision making

- the role and status of the constitution (chapter 11):

  - as supreme law
  - the role of the courts and judicial review
  - the issue of balancing rigidity and flexibility
  - formal constitutional amendment processes
  - the role of referendums
  - safeguarding individual and collective rights

1.8 FEDERATIONS CONSIDERED IN THIS STUDY

Among the federations currently in the world, those on which attention will especially be focused are the "mature" federations that have operated effectively for at least a half-century or more. In this category are the United States (1789),

Switzerland (1848), Canada (1867), Australia (1901), Austria (1945), Germany (1949) and India (1950). Each of these relatively long-standing federations exhibits virtually all of the characteristics of a federation (described in section 1.4 above) and has displayed a prolonged period of relative federal stability. Unlike some of the more recent emergent federations, these mature federations have in their evolution developed both federal and state governments which have not only formally autonomous powers but which have exercised them fully in practice.

, A second category of federations that is of interest are those that might be described as "emergent." These are federations that have been established during the past fifty years and are still in the process of establishing their equilibrium. Two European federations in this category are Spain and Belgium. In Spain, the 1978 constitution has produced a continuing process of asymmetrical devolution which has resulted in a federation in everything but name. In Belgium, two decades of step-by-step devolution culminated in 1993 in the implementation of an explicitly federal constitution.

Among the emergent federations are three that have developed a relatively centralized "quasi-federal" character. These three provide interesting examples of the impact of a dominant political party on the operation of a federation. Malaysia (1963) is of interest because of its multiracial character and the formal asymmetry of powers allocated to its Borneo states. Russia (1993) is significant because of its swing from an almost confederal and extreme asymmetry in the treatment of its constitutional units in the Yeltsin years to the emphasis on central predominance in the Putin era. South Africa's quasi-federal constitution adopted in 1996 exhibits many interesting features designed to foster intergovernmental cooperation.

The Latin American federations, Mexico, Brazil, Argentina and Venezuela, all have had long histories of federal institutions stretching back to the nineteenth or early twentieth centuries, in each case heavily influenced by the model of the United States. But all four have experienced either lengthy periods of military and autocratic rule or of one-party dominance. Each of them has had a new federal rebirth in the past two decades, Mexico with the end of PRI party dominance, and the other three with new federal constitutions: Brazil in 1988, Argentina in 1994 and Venezuela in 1999. Mexico, Brazil and Argentina have developed somewhat less centralized regimes, but in Venezuela strong centralizing trends have been reinforced by the Chavez presidency. Each is still in the process of finding its equilibrium as a federation.

Two emergent federations have been marked particularly by instability and by frequent periods of military rule. Nigeria first became a federation in 1954 but emerged from its most recent period of military regime with the new constitution of 1999. It remains a troubled federation still seeking stability. Pakistan, after the secession of Bangladesh, adopted a new federal constitution in 1973, but like Nigeria it has suffered repeated periods of military rule, and while the 1973 constitution (heavily amended) remains nominally in force, a military president since 1999 has created a *de facto* decentralized but unitary government.

An emergent federation with particularly unique features has been Ethiopia (1995). Ethiopia is particularly interesting in the way in which the ethnic basis of the constituent units is emphasized, but to date the federal policy process has been mainly channelled by and through the ruling political party.

Among the 25 federations listed in table 2 are four micro-federations. Largely the product of decolonization, these "lilliput" federations, as Anckar has referred to them, are federations of small islands: Micronesia, Belau, St. Kitts and Nevis, and Comoros, with populations ranging from 630,000 in Comoros and 104,000 in Micronesia to 41,000 in St. Kitts and Nevis and 17,000 in Belau.[14]

The United Arab Emirates has mixed aspects of traditional and modern rule and consequently a number of unorthodox and unique federal arrangements which are in many respects more confederal in character, although the constitution describes it as a "federal state." The other distinctive example of a hybrid is the European Union, which is fundamentally confederal in character but includes a significant number of features more typical of federations. Therefore, where relevant, it will be alluded to in this volume.

In addition to these functioning federations and hybrids, four others are of special note because they represented post-conflict experiments. Bosnia and Herzegovina emerged out of the conflict accompanying the disintegration of Yugoslavia. It has a number of unique features arising from its complex structure consisting of two entities — one of which, the Bosniac-Croat Federation is itself a federation — and from its operation under international (first UN then EU) tutelage. Iraq and Sudan have adopted federal constitutions in efforts to resolve conflict situations, but continuing conflict has meant that in practice they remain non-functional as federations. The Democratic Republic of the Congo is another post-conflict federal experiment whose constitution came into effect (in 2006) following a prolonged period of ethnic strife and civil war. Because these latter three federations are still in transition and do not yet operate functionally, they are not listed in table 2, although they are noted in table 3.

Other cases to which attention will be paid in chapter 13 on the pathology of federations are the bicommunal federations of Pakistan (1947–71), Czechoslovakia (1948–92) and Serbia and Montenegro (1992–2006), each of which disintegrated into two successor states. The same chapter will also include references to other federations that have disintegrated, such as the USSR (1918–91), Yugoslavia (1946–91), the West Indies Federation (1958–62) and Rhodesia and Nyasaland (1953–63).

---

[14] D. Anckar, "Lilliput Federalism: Profiles and Varieties," *Regional and Federal Studies*, 13:3 (2003): 107–24.

The federations reviewed in this study encompass a wide range of variations. Seven cover vast continental land masses (two, Canada and the USA, in North America; two in South America, Brazil and Argentina; one, Russia, stretching from Europe to Asia; one occupying most of the Indian sub-continent; and one, Australia a continent in the South Pacific). Five, by contrast, are relatively compact federations in Europe (Switzerland, Austria, Germany, Spain and Belgium); and four are micro-federations uniting islands with tiny populations (Micronesia, Belau, St. Kitts and Nevis, and Comoros). Four (the USA, Switzerland, Canada and Australia) have existed continuously as functioning federations for more than a century, five (Austria, Germany, India, Malaysia and Nigeria) were restored or created in the first two decades after World War II, and the remainder have been recent restorations or creations. Four (Canada, Australia, India and Malaysia) have parliamentary systems on the majoritarian Westminster model, three (Germany, Spain, Belgium) have European parliamentary institutions, seven (United States, Mexico, Brazil, Argentina, Venezuela, Nigeria and Pakistan) have presidential forms of executive, one (Switzerland) has a collegial executive, and two (South Africa and Russia) have mixed presidential-parliamentary systems. Eight (Switzerland, India, Malaysia, Ethiopia, Nigeria, Belgium, Spain and Canada) have significant territory-based minority language groups, while others in varying degrees are relatively more homogenous. Three (Pakistan, Czechoslovakia, and Serbia and Montenegro) were bicommunal federations that subsequently split in two. Thus, these federations provide a considerable variety of geographic, historical, economic, political, social and interterritorial characteristics from which lessons may be drawn.

Chapter 2

Overview of Contemporary Federations

2.1 MATURE FEDERATIONS

UNITED STATES OF AMERICA (1789)

The United States of America, the first modern federation, adopted federation as the organizing principle for its structure of government in 1789 following the Philadelphia Convention of 1787. This resulted from the failure of a confederal form of government established under the Articles of Confederation of 1781. Originally comprising 13 states, the United States has evolved into a federation of 50 states plus 2 federacies, 3 associated states, 3 local home-rule territories, 3 unincorporated territories and over 130 Native American domestic dependent nations, with a total population of about 300 million. It survived a devastating civil war during the first century of its existence, but as the most enduring federation in the world, it is an important reference point in any comparative study of federations.

Among federations it is marked by a relatively homogeneous society. There are significant black and Hispanic minorities, but in no state do they constitute a majority. Nevertheless, there are regional variations in political culture and a considerable emphasis upon the value of state and local government.

In comparative terms, the federation is moderately decentralized. Jurisdiction assigned to the 50 states is symmetrical, although this does not apply to the relationship of the various federacies and associated states. The major feature of the distribution of powers is the arrangement whereby the constitution lists subject matters under federal authority — most of which are concurrent and some of which are made exclusively federal by prohibiting the states from legislating on them — and leaves the unspecified residual matters to the states.

The federal institutions are based on the principle of the separation of powers between executive and legislature with presidential-congressional institutions involving a system of checks and balances. Congress includes a Senate in which the states are equally represented with members elected directly (since 1912).

Over more than two centuries of operation, the United States as a federation has become increasingly integrated and the federal government more powerful. In recent decades the dominant role of the federal government and the extensive practice of unfunded mandates and federal pre-emption has been described as a trend from cooperative to coercive federalism.[1] At the same time, there have been political counter-pressures for more decentralization, although progress in this direction has been limited. The Bush administration has not propounded an explicit policy on federalism, but in practice its advocacy of legislation and constitutional amendments, fiscal policies, administrative actions and judicial policies has sacrificed federal considerations to specific objectives which have had centralizing impacts.[2]

Virtually all subsequently attempted federations have taken some account of the constitutional design and operation of the United States in developing their own federal structures, making it an important example.

THE SWISS CONFEDERATION (1848)

The Swiss Confederation, which had existed in various forms since 1291, broke down in the brief Sonderbund civil war of 1847; a new constitution in 1848, "the Federal Constitution of the Swiss Confederation," converted it into a federation. Switzerland, a small country of some 7 million people, now comprises 26 constituent units called cantons, of which 6 are designated "half cantons."

The Swiss federation is notable for its significant degree of linguistic and religious diversity, although the German Swiss continue to dominate in overall numbers and economic power. Its three official languages (German, French and Italian; a fourth, Romansh, is recognized as a "national language") and two dominant faiths (Roman Catholic and Protestant) represent territorial cleavages that cut across each other. Among German-speaking cantons, some are Roman Catholic and some are Protestant, and the French-speaking cantons are similarly divided. Consequently, on different issues, cantons form different alignments. Of the 26 cantons, 17 are unilingually German, 4 are unilingually French and one is Italian, 3 are bilingual German and French, and one, Graubunden, is trilingual (German, Italian and Romansh). In all, 14 cantons have Roman Catholic majorities and 12 have Protestant majorities, the Roman Catholic and Protestant majorities representing more than two-thirds of the cantonal population in 18 of the 26 cantons.

---

[1] John Kincaid, "From Cooperative to Coercive Federalism," *Annals of the American Academy of Politics*, 509 (1990): 139–52.

[2] T. Conlan and J. Dinar, "Federalism, the Bush Administration and the Transformation of American Conservatism," *Publius: The Journal of Federalism*, 27:3 (2007): 279–303.

A significant proportion of the constitutional distribution of powers is assigned to the federal government, with the residual powers to the cantons. However, there is in practice a high degree of decentralization because the constitution leaves the federal government highly dependent upon the autonomous cantons for the administration of a large proportion of its legislation. There is a relative symmetry in the jurisdiction of the cantons, although 6 of the 26 cantons are classified as "half cantons" and therefore each of these has only half the representation in the federal second legislative chamber, the Council of States (Standerat).

The principle of the separation of powers has been applied to the federal institutions, but the executive (the Federal Council) is a collegial body elected by the Swiss federal legislature for a fixed term and composed of seven councillors among whom the presidency rotates annually. The federal legislature is bicameral, composed of the National Council (Nationalrat) and the Council of States (Standerat); in the latter, cantons have two representatives each and half cantons one. The electoral system based on proportional representation has resulted in a multiparty system, but the fixed-term executive has provided stability, and the tradition has developed that it should encompass the four major political parties representing an overwhelming majority in the federal legislature. A characteristic of the Swiss political process has been the widespread use of referendums and initiatives. Another feature is that dual membership in the cantonal and federal legislatures is permitted so that about one-fifth of federal legislators are also members of cantonal legislatures. A long Swiss tradition of consensual politics has in the past decade come under increasing strain with the growth of Christoph Blocher's Swiss People's Party and its controversial policies. This has been illustrated by its virile anti-immigration campaign in the 2007 federal election.

In April 1999, three decades of sporadic efforts to achieve a comprehensive revision of the Swiss Constitution culminated in the approval in a referendum of the total revision of the constitution. In the referendum, the new constitution was supported by 59.2 percent of the voters, including majorities in 12 of the 20 cantons and in 2 of the 6 half cantons. Although a total revision of the constitution, the draft avoided substantial and controversial reforms. It took the form largely of modernizing the language rather than the content of the federal constitution. Even then, it resulted in a closer than expected vote, opposition coming largely from the small rural cantons of Switzerland fearing greater centralization, while the main cities all supported the new constitution. The new constitution, while largely a modernization of the previous one, nevertheless refined the fundamental rights of citizens and the relations between federal, cantonal and municipal authorities. The largest long-term issue currently on the agenda of the Swiss federation is its relationship with the European Union, which to date the Swiss voters have rejected joining. However, marginal steps have been made in European integration, with Swiss citizens voting in favour of joining the Schengen Treaty in June 2005.

In 2003, Parliament approved a reform of the fiscal equalization arrangements which disentangles respective responsibilities, invigorates cooperation among the

cantons with an institutionalized system of burden sharing, encourages cooperation in areas of joint responsibility, and creates a new system of direct fiscal
equalization.

Although small in terms of population and area, its multilingual and multicultural
character makes Switzerland a federation of particular interest.

CANADA (1867)

Second only to Russia in territorial size, Canada became a federation in 1867.
While Canadians use the term "Confederation," this refers to the process of bringing
provinces together into a federation in 1867 rather than the adoption of a confederal
structure. The federation grew out of efforts to overcome the political difficulties
and deadlocks within the United Province of Canada created by the Act of Union
of 1840. This was to be achieved by splitting it into the two new provinces of
Ontario with an English-speaking majority and Quebec with a French-speaking
majority, and by the addition of the maritime provinces of Nova Scotia and New
Brunswick both for trade and defence purposes. Originally a union of four
provinces, the federation has grown until it is now composed of ten provinces and
three northern territories, following the division in 1999 of the Northwest Territories. It has a population of over 30 million. A distinctive feature of the Canadian
federation is the continuing existence and vitality of a French Canadian majority
concentrated within one province. Approximately 80 percent of the French Canadian population live in Quebec, where they constitute over 80 percent of the
population. Throughout its history, the Canadian federation has been marked both
by the French-English duality and by a strong regionalism expressed through the
provinces. More recently, there has been increasing attention given to recogniz-
ing the place of the Aboriginal peoples within the federation.

The original 1867 constitution was marked by strong central powers, including
some powers enabling the federal government to override the provinces in certain
circumstances. Unlike the two federations that preceded it, the constitution specifically listed three forms of legislative powers: exclusively federal, exclusively
provincial, and concurrent, with the major residual powers assigned to the federal
government. Despite its originally centralized form, 140 years of pressures to
recognize duality and regionalism have made Canada a relatively decentralized
federation, both legislatively and administratively. The *Constitution Act, 1982*
added a Charter of Rights and Freedoms and new constitutional amendment procedures involving in most cases both the federal and provincial governments. The
original *Constitution Act, 1867* recognized the particular character of Quebec by
including some recognition of asymmetry in provisions relating to language, education and civil law, but efforts within the past four decades to recognized the
reality of Quebec's distinctiveness by increasing constitutional asymmetry have
been highly controversial.

The most innovative feature of the federation was that in contrast to the United States and Swiss federations, which emphasized the separation of the executive and legislature in their federal institutions, Canada was the first federation to incorporate a system of parliamentary responsible government in which the executive and the legislature are fused. This combination of federal and parliamentary systems was subsequently adopted in Australia and in many of the other federations considered in this study. The majoritarian character of the parliamentary federal institutions has had a significant impact on the dynamics of federal politics in Canada.

The March 2007 federal budget introduced sweeping changes to the system of equalization. This budget represented a move towards equal per capita cash payments for Canada's vertical fiscal transfers and the restoration of a formula-based equalization program for horizontal fiscal transfers.

In comparative terms the Canadian federation is of particular interest because of the way in which it has attempted to deal with the English-French duality of its society and because it was a pioneer in combining federal and parliamentary institutions.

THE COMMONWEALTH OF AUSTRALIA (1901)

The Australian federal constitution of 1901 united a number of self-governing British colonies. Today the federation consists of six states (of which the two most populous, New South Wales and Victoria, comprise 59 percent of the federal population) plus one capital territory, the Northern Territory, and seven administered territories, and has a total population of over 20 million.

Australia is a relatively homogenous society with a population of about 18 million people mostly descended from British and European settlers, but the geographic vastness and the concentration of populations in dispersed state capitals each serving its own hinterland have made federation a natural form of political organization.

The founders of the Australian federation rejected the Canadian model of a relatively centralized distribution of powers and followed the American model, enumerating a limited list of federal exclusive powers and a substantial list of concurrent powers, leaving unspecified residual powers to the state governments. In practice, however, the Australian federation has evolved into a relatively more centralized federation, particularly with respect to financial arrangements. In terms of jurisdiction, there is a symmetry among the six states. While adopting a different form of distribution of powers, the Australian federation did follow the Canadian precedent of combining federal and parliamentary institutions, responsible cabinet government operating at both federal and state levels. Nevertheless, it incorporated a relatively powerful directly elected Senate with equal representation of the states. The impact of the parliamentary system has, however, made the Senate more of a "party house" than a "regional house."

As a parliamentary federation, Australia has developed the institutions and processes of "executive federalism" more extensively than any other federation, with the possible exception of Germany. With its British heritage of parliamentary institutions and tradition of executive federalism, Australia as a federation illustrates the characteristics that flow from a marriage of federal and parliamentary institutions.

In 1999 growing republican sentiment culminated in a referendum to replace the monarchy, but this was marginally rejected.

The federal government introduced a value-added tax in 1999 to replace all others sales taxes and to serve as the basis of the fiscal equalization scheme. All the Goods and Services Tax (GST) revenue collected by the federal government is distributed to the states in an equalized form based on recommendations of the Commonwealth Grants Commission (CGC). This reform, as well as the operation of the CGC and the earlier Australian Loan Council (which coordinates borrowing by Commonwealth and state governments) has reinforced Australia as a pioneer in financial and equalization arrangements.

THE FEDERAL REPUBLIC OF AUSTRIA (1920)

Austria adopted a federal constitution in 1920, shortly after the demise of the Austro-Hungarian Empire. Modifications were made in 1929 and again in 1945, when the Austrian Republic was restored, but the fundamental character of the original constitution remained basically unchanged. Currently, with a population of 8 million, it comprises nine Länder.

Austria is culturally largely homogenous. German is the official language, although special constitutional provision is made for the use of Slovene and Croat languages in certain regions of the country.

Given a statist and hierarchical traditional political culture, the Austrian federation exhibits a highly centralized legislative jurisdiction, but with the administration of federal law extensively decentralized to the Länder. This administrative decentralization is seen in the 2001 public service reforms that established Land governments as the first and only point of access for citizens. Among federations, it is one of the most legislatively centralized, with the constituent units often serving mainly as "agents" and "subordinates" of the federal government, although they are assigned the residual legislative authority. Within the federation, the units are symmetrical in power and status.

Federal government institutions are parliamentary in character, the Chancellor and Cabinet being responsible to the Nationalrat, although there is a directly elected federal president who performs the functions of head of state. The federal legislature is bicameral. The members of the second chamber (the Bundesrat) are indirectly elected by the assemblies of the Länder with representation fairly closely proportional to population except for a minimum guarantee of three representatives for each Land.

The Austrian federation is of interest because it shows how far centralization and federal-state interdependence can be taken in the spectrum of federal arrangements. It is worthy of note that although recent efforts at reforming the federal system in 1989–94 and 2003–05 did not succeed, in 2007 another effort was launched to enhance the constitutional autonomy of the Länder and reduce the supervising powers of the federal government over the states in the implementation of federal laws. A committee of experts was appointed to make recommendations on these objectives.

THE FEDERAL REPUBLIC OF GERMANY (1949)

The German federation owes a great deal to the earlier experience of the German Empire (1871–1918), the Weimar Republic (1919–34) and the failure of the totalitarian centralization of the Third Reich (1934–45). West Germany in 1949 became the Federal Republic of Germany comprising 11 Länder. The reunification of Germany in 1990 provided for the accession of 5 new Länder. The federation now consists of 16 Länder with a total population of over 82 million.

The population of the German federation is linguistically homogenous, although a considerable gulf remains between the political cultures of the former West Germany and the former East Germany.

A notable characteristic of the German federation is the interlocked relationship of the federal and the state governments. The federal government has a very broad range of exclusive, concurrent and framework legislative powers, but the Länder have a mandatory constitutional responsibility for applying and administering a large portion of these laws. These arrangements are similar to those in Austria and Switzerland, although the Swiss cantons have legislative jurisdiction over a larger range of subject matters. A significant difference in the German federation, however, is that the Länder governments in Germany are more directly involved in the federal government decision-making process through the representation of their first ministers and designated cabinet ministers in the federal second chamber, the Bundesrat, which possesses a veto on all federal legislation affecting the Länder. (About 60 percent of federal legislation fell into this category until reforms in 2006 reduced this proporion). Thus the Bundesrat is a key institution in the interlocking federal-state relationship within the German federation. Within that framework, the Länder are marked by symmetry in their relative powers, although special financial arrangements have been particularly necessary for the five new eastern Länder.

Both the Federal and Land institutions are parliamentary in form. The Federal Chancellor and Cabinet are responsible to the Bundestag, but there is a formal head of state, the President of the Federal Republic, elected by an electoral college consisting of the Bundestag and an equal number of members elected by the legislatures of the Länder. The federal parliament is bicameral, with the second chamber composed of ex officio instructed delegates of the Land governments.

The German federation is of interest because of the manner in which the relationships between the federal and state governments interlock and because of the way in which the unique Bundesrat serves as a key institution in these interdependent processes. It is worth noting that recently the tightness of the interlocking arrangements has come under some criticism and review.

The first stage of reforms to the federal system came into force in September 2006 with the support of a "grand coalition" of political parties. The overarching goal of these reforms was to enhance the ability of both the Federation and the Länder to take autonomous decisions and to clarify the division of political powers.[3] It is estimated that these reforms will reduce the proportion of federal legislation requiring the assent of a majority in the Bundesrat from 60 to about 40 percent. The second stage of federalism reforms is planned to address the prevention and management of budget crises, the necessity of realigning revenue-raising capabilities with expenditure responsibilities, and consolidation of special political services and their impact on the financial relationship between the Federation and the Länder.

THE REPUBLIC OF INDIA (1950)

India became independent in 1947 and its parliament, serving also as a constituent assembly, drafted the new constitution that came into effect on 26 January 1950, establishing the federal Union of India. Its federal features followed closely the *Government of India Act, 1935,* under which the British government had attempted a federal solution to resolve the problems facing India at the time, an act which itself had been modelled on the *British North America Act, 1867,* which established the Canadian federation. Given the vast, populous and variegated nature of India and concerns with the threat of insecurity and disintegration, the Constituent Assembly concluded that the soundest framework was "a federation with a strong Centre." Today, the federation comprises 28 states and 7 union territories (one of the territories being the "National Capital Territory of Delhi" having a special status) with a total population of over one billion people.

India is a diverse multilingual society. Hindi, the official language, is spoken by about 40 percent of the population (mostly in the north) and there are 18 constitutionally recognized regional languages. Following the report of the States Reorganization Commission established in 1955, between 1956 and 1966 the states were reorganized largely on an ethno-linguistic basis and in one case (Punjab) on

---

[3] See Ralf Thomas Baus, Raoul Blindenbacher, and Ulrich Karpen, eds., *Competition versus Cooperation: German Federalism in Need of Reform: A Comparative Perspective* (Baden-Baden: Nomos Verlagsgesellschaft, 2007).

a religio-linguistic basis. Since then there have been some further revisions to the number of states.

While the founders sought to create a new kind of federation with sufficient central powers to ensure cohesion and hence with some unitary elements, the ethno-linguistic basis of many of the states and the powerful forces of regionalism within the Indian sub-continent have meant in practice a federation that is only partially centralized and that has powerful states. The constitution provides for three exhaustive lists of legislative powers — exclusive federal powers, exclusive provincial powers and concurrent powers (with federal paramountcy) — and for residual powers assigned to the Union government. There is a degree of asymmetry with respect to the state of Jammu and Kashmir, which has been given powers different from those of others states. Asymmetrical relationships have also applied to some of the smaller new states established in tribal areas. Formally, the Union government possesses very substantial powers, especially powers of intervention and pre-emption in emergencies, but it functions within an ethno-political and multiparty context that requires that those powers be used for the most part to preserve federalism in form and spirit. Increasingly, power-sharing as a way of reconciling conflict and the operation of coalition governments has come to predominate, despite some imperfections in the process.

The institutions of the Union and state governments are parliamentary in form with responsible cabinet governments at both levels. The head of state is a president, elected by an electoral college consisting of the elected members of both houses of parliament and the state legislatures. The formal heads of the states, the governors, are appointed by the Union government but, the chief ministers and their cabinets are responsible to their state legislatures.

Six developments in recent decades have been especially significant. One is that with the decline of the Congress party, which had dominated in the early years after independence, there has grown a multitude of regional parties, making necessary multiparty coalitions sensitive to regional interests within the federal government. The second was the passage of the Seventy-Third and Seventy-Fourth Amendments to the constitution in 1991 establishing local governments, the *panchyats* and municipalities, as constitutionally recognized basic "institutions of self-government." Third has been a decline in the frequency with which the Union government has exercised "emergency rule" in the states, a decline influenced by a ruling of the Supreme Court defining the limits of this power. Fourth has been the impact of two major influential commissions, the Sarkaria (1988) and the Venkatachelliah (2002) commissions, on the working of the constitution. Fifth has been the bringing into operation of the Inter-State Council, provided for in the original constitution to facilitate intergovernmental cooperation but implemented only following the recommendations of the Sakaria commission. Sixth has been the reinforcement of state finances progressively by the recent quinquennial Finance Commissions.

India as a federation is of particular interest because of the way in which it has used federal institutions and processes to hold together a linguistically diverse society for over half a century. In 1947 many doubted that the federation could endure for more than a decade in this vast, poor and deeply divided country, but India has defied the sceptics and sixty years later it is marked by a vibrant federation and a growing economy and role in the world.

2.2 EMERGENT FEDERATIONS

THE UNITED MEXICAN STATES (1917)

Historical pressures towards excessive centralization have heavily influenced the practice of federalism in Mexico. Although this country has technically operated as a federation since 1917, significant discretionary powers were vested in the central government, in practice allowing sub-national units little autonomy. This *de facto* centralization arose from the need to overcome the strong regional forces. A major source of centralization was the dominance of the Partido Revolucionaro Institucional (PRI) party, which from its creation in 1929 to 2000 exercised virtually hegemonic control at all levels of government. It has only been since the loosening of PRI dominance in the past decade that Mexico has begun to function federally.

The 1917 constitution established a "federal, democratic and representative republic, composed of free and sovereign states in regard to their internal regime." It consists of 31 states and one Federal District (Mexico City) with a current population of over 100 million.

The constitution granted the federal government, and especially the President, substantial discretionary powers. The distribution of powers heavily favours the federal government. Although the residual power technically resides in the states, until reforms in the 1990s the federal government's exclusive jurisdiction even included the major areas of education, health and labour. In these areas the state governments now have responsibility, relying on conditional grants from the federal government to deliver these "social rights" guaranteed by the constitution. In terms of fiscal powers, the federal government collects all the major sources of revenue, with the states and local governments receiving a share of the proceeds, but the criteria for this distribution have been a source of controversy, since the allocation has been largely discretionary.

The Mexican Congress is bicameral, with a Chamber of Deputies and a Senate. One interesting feature intended to prevent corruption is a constitutional provision that prevents re-election of all elected officials.

From 1989 on, as opposition parties gained power in some states, federalism has become more of a reality in Mexico. With the election of President Vicente Fox of the Partido Acción Nacional (PAN) in 2000, state governments began to play a more meaningful role in the federation. This regime change in Mexican politics and the renewal of Mexico as a federation has led a significant number of politicians, academics and journalists to advocate the need for a new constitution that reflects these changes.

THE FEDERATION OF MALAYSIA (1963)

The Malaysian federation now comprises 13 states with a population of over 24 million. It was established in 1963 when Singapore and the Borneo states of Sabah and Sarawak joined the already existing Federation of Malaya that had achieved independence in 1957. Singapore was expelled from the Federation of Malaysia just two years later, and since that time the federation has consisted of the 11 states of the Malay peninsula and the two more autonomous states on the island of Borneo.

A significant political feature of Malaysia is the diversity of its population in terms of race, ethnicity, language, religion and social customs. The population is approximately 65 percent Malay and other indigenous peoples, 26 percent Chinese and 7 percent Indian. Malays are a majority in most of the peninsular states, but there are strong concentrations of Chinese in the west coast states, and other indigenous peoples, composed of a variety of linguistic groups, form the vast majority in the two Borneo states. The federal system has been an important factor therefore in maintaining the delicate communal balance within the federation.

As in India, the Malaysian federation was initially characterized by a high degree of centralization, which in the latter case was derived from the preceding Malayan constitution, itself modelled on the *Government of India Act, 1935* and hence indirectly on the *British North America Act, 1867*. Like India, there are three exhaustive lists of powers (exclusive federal, exclusive state and concurrent), but the residual powers are assigned to the state governments. One distinguishing feature of the Malaysian distribution of powers is the asymmetry in the legislative, executive and financial autonomy ascribed to some constituent units. The 11 states of the Malay peninsula — the original states of the Federation of Malaya — stand in a symmetrical relationship to the federal government, but the two Borneo states have been allocated greater autonomy as a means of safeguarding their special "non-Malayan" interests. Unlike India, the Malaysian federation has, however, continued to maintain its relatively centralized character, as a result of the dominant political party situation. Nevertheless, citizens' loyalty to their states and political leaders, and the dependence of the federal government on the states for the administration of many of its programs have maintained the political viability of the states.[4]

---

[4] William Case, "Semi-democracy and minimalist federalism in Malaysia," in Baogang He, Brian Galligan, Takashi Inoguchi, eds., *Federalism in Asia* (Cheltenham, UK: Edward Elgan, 2007), pp. 124-143, esp. pp. 127-131.

Malaysia has incorporated the institutions of cabinets responsible to the legislature within both levels of government, but it has a unique form of rotating monarchy to provide the formal head of state of the federation. The *Yang di-Pertuan Agong* is selected for a five-year term from among the heredity rulers of nine of the Malay states.

The Malaysian Federation is of interest because it is a complex delicate balance of diverse communities within a relatively centralized parliamentary federation that has experienced rapid economic development, and because it incorporates asymmetry in the powers of constituent states in order to safeguard the particular interests of the Borneo states.

THE ISLAMIC REPUBLIC OF PAKISTAN (1973)

Following the partition of India in 1947, Pakistan, with a total population then of about 90 million, was a country of two large fragments severed from the structure of old India. Each of these parts was very different in every way except one – religion – and separated by a thousand miles of hostile territory. The result was a federation of two basic units, West Pakistan, largely Urdu-speaking, Middle-Eastern in character, and the wealthier unit, and East Pakistan, Bengali-speaking, South-East Asian in outlook, and the more populous with 55 percent of the population. The 1956 federal constitution established a federation of two provinces, each with parity in representation in a unicameral federal legislature. However, bipolar tensions between the two units resulted in the secession of East Pakistan (later Bangladesh) in 1971. The former province of West Pakistan then became a federation of four provinces in 1973. It now has a population of about 145 million. Of the four provinces, Punjab alone has 55.6 percent of the total federal population and, therefore, is in a politically dominant position.

The 1973 constitution, despite repeated suspension and numerous arbitrary amendments by the military, most notably in 1985 and 2002, remains in force. While the constitution is federal in form, its operation is that of a centralized devolved unitary state. The federal government wields extensive powers through 67 enumerated exclusive federal powers and 47 concurrent powers. Although the provinces are assigned the residual authority outside these enumerated areas, the federal government has the ability to intervene in matters of provincial concern. The federal government has the power to appoint provincial governors, approve the dissolution of a provincial assembly, confer on a province functions that fall under the executive authority of the central government, and give directions to the provinces. When coupled with the provinces' relative dependence on the federal government for fiscal transfers, the autonomy of the provinces is severely limited.

The constitution establishes a bicameral federal legislature. The 342 seats in the National Assembly are allocated among the 4 provinces, 6 Federally Administered Tribal Areas and the Federal Capital on the basis of population elected from single-member constituencies by plurality. The Senate is intended to represent the constituent units, each provincial assembly electing 22 members (14 general members, 4 women and 4 technocrats). The Federal Capital elects 4 members (two general members, one woman and one technocrat) and the Federally Administered Tribal Areas elect 8 senators through direct ballot.

In 1999 President General Pervez Musharraf took power in a military coup and his presidency was confirmed in a referendum in 2002. President Musharraf chairs the National Security Council, which is where most of the decision-making authority is currently vested. This council is composed of military chiefs, the prime minister and cabinet members. In 2002 and since, a series of legal and constitutional changes have been manipulated to entrench military rule and restrict the operation of some political parties.

Thus, while nominally a federation, Pakistan has in practice become a predominantly centralized military regime. By the end of 2007, after eight years of the latest period of a Punjabi-dominated military regime, not only had the federal parliament been reduced to a rubber-stamp and the smaller provinces deprived of a significant voice, but the stability of the country had come into question.

THE KINGDOM OF SPAIN (1978)

Spain has been going through a dual process of federalization relating to internal devolution and external integration within the European Union. In 1978, after some forty years of totalitarian centralization under the dictatorship of General Franco, Spain adopted a new constitution establishing a system of parliamentary democracy. As part of post-Franco democratization and as a means of balancing powerful regional interests fostered by revived Basque and Catalonian nationalism, Spain pursued a process of regionalization. It has provided for units called "Autonomous Communities," of which there are internally 17 in a country of over 44 million.

Although traditionally a strongly centralized unitary state, Spain has in fact contained considerable diversity. While the political culture of the Castilians has tended to be hierarchical and centralistic, the Aragonese, Basques, Catalonians, Galicians, Navarrese and Valencians have each had a strong interest in preserving their way of life and securing the power to maintain their cultural identity.

The Spanish response to this situation after the adoption of the 1978 constitution was to grant progressively to each region its own statute of autonomy tailored to its particular situation or based upon a particular set of compromises negotiated between the regional leadership and the central government. Subsequent actions of the Madrid government have, however, leaned to a more uniform distribution of jurisdiction. Although the different regions have been proceeding to autonomy at different speeds, the intention has been that ultimately the situation of the Autonomous Communities will be less asymmetrical. While the Spanish constitution does not define itself as explicitly federal, it does provide for lists of powers that are exclusive to either the general or regional governments, while leaving the residual power to the central government. Thus, Spain is a federation in all but name, with the 17 Autonomous Communities possessing constitutional authority for a considerable degree of self-rule. Spain is now one of the most decentralized countries in Europe, but the political regionalization has been derived less from constitutional mandate than from party strategies, competition and bargaining within a loose institutional framework.[5]

The central government is a parliamentary monarchy with the Council of Ministers responsible to the lower house of the Cortés, Spain's bicameral legislature. The Senate, the second chamber of the Cortés, consists mainly of directly elected members, but 51 of the 259 senators are appointed by the autonomous parliaments.

The asymmetry among the Autonomous Communities extends to the intergovernmental fiscal arrangements where there are two regimes in place, a "common" one for most Autonomous Communities and a special *"foral"* one derived from long-standing traditional rights for Navarre and the Basque Country. Under the latter, Navarre and the Basque Country levy all national taxes, but in return pay a subsidy for the services provided by the central government.

For a period, the central government rejected virtually all calls for further increased autonomy, basing its position on a conservative interpretation of the constitution, which holds that it is untouchable because it reflects and upholds civic consensus. The Spanish Socialist Workers' Party, elected in 2004, however, has been more amenable to further decentralization. In June 2006 a referendum in Catalonia, already one of the most advanced in terms of self-government, was passed to expand its autonomy further, and leaders in a number of other autonomous communities have been pressing for an increased devolution of powers. Meanwhile, the Basque Country has continued to be the source of a secessionist movement.

As a unitary state engaged in devolutionary federalization within its own borders by a process characterized by considerable asymmetry, Spain is an interesting example of an effort to accommodate variations in the strengths of regional pressures for autonomy.

THE FEDERATIVE REPUBLIC OF BRAZIL (1988)

The Brazilian federation as it now exists was established in 1988, but before that Brazil had periodically operated as a federation during the years following the military coup that ended monarchical rule in 1889. With a substantial population of about 180 million, the constitution recognizes 26 states and one federal district,

---

[5] Josep M. Colomer, "The Spanish 'State of Autonomies': Non-Institutional Federalism," in P. Heywood, ed., *West European Politics*, 21:4 (1998), special issue on "Politics and Party Democracy in Spain: No Longer Different?" pp. 40–52.

as well as some 5,500 municipalities. Brazil is one of few federal countries that have explicit provisions in the constitution regarding municipalities.

The operation of this federation has been strongly influenced by the pressure of state interests in the national government. This predominance of the sub-national governments has been principally due to political rather than constitutional provisions; although the 1988 constitution allocates the residual power to the state governments, it includes an exhaustive list of exclusive federal powers that limit the scope of this residual clause. On an informal level, however, state governors play an important role in the federal legislative process, because of the nature of the presidential system and the necessity of securing agreement of three-fifths of all state legislatures for any significant constitutional reforms.

Federal-state relations focus particularly on financial relations. The 1988 constitution strengthened the already significant tax base of the states and municipalities, and subsequent amendments to the tax system in 2003 have reinforced the trend to fiscal decentralization. A notable feature has been the effort to terminate the "fiscal war" between the states.

The regionally concentrated social and economic disparities in this large country have been a major source of political conflict. The affluent southern states have pushed for greater fiscal decentralization. The less affluent northern and central states have benefited from peculiarities that overrepresent these regions in the federal institutions. A constitutional provision guarantees each state at least eight and no more than 70, seats in the Chamber of Deputies. The biggest loser in this situation is Sao Paulo, the most populous and most affluent state, which would be entitled to 111 seats if there were no upper limit. The configuration of the federal Senate accentuates this by giving the northern, northeastern and centre-western states (which have 43 percent of the population) 74 percent of the membership.

Recent reforms by President Lula da Silva have included constitutional amendments to address the unsustainable social security system and the reassignment of some taxes to the state governments. Also, attempts have been made to reform intergovernmental relations so that they operate in a more cooperative manner. However, reforms have been made difficult by the problems of the separation of presidential and legislative branches and the lack of legislative support for presidential initiatives.

Brazil is a useful example of the pressures created by regional disparities and fiscal decentralization.

THE KINGDOM OF BELGIUM (1993)

Belgium was founded in 1830 as a unitary constitutional monarchy, but four stages of devolution in 1970, 1980, 1988 and 1993 culminated in a formal federation with a population of just over 10 million people. It is composed of six constituent units. Three are regions territorially defined (the Flemish, Walloon and Brussels Regions) with councils responsible largely for regional economic matters.

Overlapping these are three "Communities" (the Dutch-speaking, French-speaking and German-speaking Communities) with their own councils responsible mainly for cultural and educational matters. The former represent a *territorial* jurisdiction and the latter a *personal* jurisdiction. The Flemish Region and Community, however, have merged their institutions thereby further accentuating the asymmetry within the Belgian federation.

The primary motivating force for the process of devolutionary federalization has been the political polarization of the two main linguistic groups, the Dutch-speaking (58 percent) and French-speaking (41 percent) Belgians. The German-speaking minority constitutes less than one percent of the population. The bipolar character of Belgian politics has been accentuated by the greater prosperity of the Flemish Region (reversing the nineteenth-century situation) and by the resentment of the Dutch-speaking majority at the political dominance that had traditionally been exercised by the French-speaking Belgians within the unitary Belgian state.

The distribution of powers, because of the devolutionary character of the federalization process, has generally taken the form of specifying the increased powers of the regional and community councils, leaving the unspecified residual jurisdiction with the central government. Nevertheless, in 1993 it was agreed that the distribution of powers should be redrafted to enumerate federal powers and leave residual jurisdiction to the constituent units. Three features distinguish the Belgian distribution of powers: (1) the progressive devolution has in fact produced a high degree of decentralization; (2) the powers allocated to each order of government have been mostly in the form of exclusive powers; and (3) the considerable measure of asymmetry among the constituent units illustrated by the difference between Regions and Communities as two distinctly different types of constituent units with different responsibilities, the differing interrelationships between Regional and Community councils in the Dutch-speaking and French-speaking areas, and the particular situation of Brussels as the capital located in the Flemish Region but with a French-speaking majority.

The federal institutions of the Belgian federation are those of a constitutional monarchy with a cabinet responsible to the Chamber of Deputies in a bicameral parliament.

Despite the extensive decentralization, social services and taxation remain major areas of federal government responsibility. In 2001 the francophone parties agreed to the decentralization of agriculture, foreign trade, parts of foreign aid and local/provincial law in exchange for increased funding for the Communities, but they have resisted the devolution of social security. This agreement has been accompanied by determined calls in Flanders, however, for greater federalization of social policy and even threats of secession. The political parties have all divided along linguistic lines, and consequently federal governments have depended on tenuous coalitions across the linguistic divide in order to survive. Following the 2007 federal elections, disagreements between the Flemish and French-speaking parties over whether to devolve social security to the regions led to a stalemate preventing the formation of a coalition federal government for a protracted period of crisis.

Although the emergent Belgian federation is too recent to allow firm conclusions to be drawn about its operation, the devolutionary federalization process is of particular interest because of its intense linguistically bipolar character. It also serves as an example of a country responding to simultaneous pressures for federalization in two directions: through internal devolution, which has converted it from a unitary state into a federation, and through external integration arising from its membership in the European Union.

THE RUSSIAN FEDERATION (1993)

The Russian Federation, with an area of 17, 075, 000 km^2, is territorially the world's largest federation, spanning two continents and eleven times zones. Its population is approximately 145 million.

The Russian Federation evolved out of the Russian Soviet Federated Socialist Republic (RSFSR), the largest member state in the Soviet Union. After 75 years of communist rule, with the disintegration of the Union of Soviet Socialist Republics in 1991, the Russian Federation became independent with Boris Yeltsin as its first president.

During Boris Yeltsin's presidency (1991–99), in an attempt to construct a stable and integrated federal state, Yeltsin offered decentralizing concessions to the regions. The volume and diversity of Russia's sub-national units was a testament to this process, with as many as 89 constituent units of various types existing in 1991. Although the 89 sub-national units were considered equal members of the federation, under the constitution, only the 21 republics were entitled to their own constitutions and law; other types of constituent units only had access to ordinary statutes and laws.

The constitution contained both symmetric and asymmetric federal features. While the constitution stated that all 89 constituent units were equal in their relations with federal bodies, the constitution not only differentiated categories of constituent units but also provided for the negotiation of individual treaties and agreements for the relationship of these with the federal government. During Yeltsin's presidency, in fact, more than half of the constituent units signed special bilateral treaties defining their powers. The process of continued decentralization of power during the Yeltsin regime weakened the federal government and undermined its ability to coordinate a national reform program.

Under President Vladimir Putin since 1999, the process has been reversed, with a series of centralizing reforms aimed at concentrating and stabilizing federal power. Putin spearheaded a major reorganization of Russia's political structures which has strengthened the presidency at the expense of regional powers. The individual bilateral treaties with constituent units have almost all been virtually terminated. The federation has been divided into seven federal districts, each with a federal representative to oversee the activities of the constituent units. Voluntary regional consolidation has been encouraged to reduce the number of constituent units, to date reduced from 89 to 86 (21 republics, 48 oblasts, 7 autonomous okrugs, 7 krais, 2 federal cities and one autonomous oblast), and further consolidations are planned. The president and federal bodies have been given the right to nominate regional governors for approval by regional legislatures in place of direct election of regional governors and to dismiss regional governors and legislatures in the event that they violate federal legislation. There has also been an emphasis on harmonizing federal and regional legislation, a major concern in fields of concurrent jurisdiction. This centralizing trend has also coincided with increasing federal control over the mass media. Buoyed by world resource prices, especially oil, the system of fiscal federalism has been reformed to place the federal government in a financially dominant position. Two-thirds of Russians have considered the concentration of power in President Putin's hands favourably because the oil-price boom has brought economic growth and a new sense of stability.

Under the constitution, the hybrid presidential-parliamentary system has a directly elected president, who appoints the prime minister and cabinet, who in turn are responsible to the Federal Assembly. The bicameral Federal Assembly consists of a 178-seat Federation Council and the 450-seat State Duma. Originally the Federation Council was composed of two representatives from each constituent unit: the heads of the regional legislative and executive bodies. But as the result of a reform initiated by President Putin, the executive of each state authority now appoints one representative to the Federation Council, while the other is elected by the legislature, thus effectively weakening the council's political influence. Half of the members of the State Duma are elected for a four-year term by party list proportional representation, while the other half are determined by single-member constituency elections.

The federal constitution introduced in 1993 gave sweeping potential powers to the President. The President has the authority to issue decrees that have the force of law, as long as they do not violate existing laws; however, laws passed by the Federal Assembly can supersede these decrees. Under specific conditions, the presidential power also extends to the dissolution of Parliament. The weakness of Russia's civil society and the lack of effective opposition political parties has left the Putin presidency in a predominant position. President Putin's second and final term as president runs out in March 2008, however, and there are indications that his continued predominance may be maintained by his taking the post of prime minister under his successor as president. If that occurs it will change the balance in the roles of the president and the prime minister.

Although more than 80 percent of the population identifies as Russian, there are more than 100 distinct nationalities and ethnic groups. Some of these groups are territorially concentrated, with special rights to preserve and promote their respective cultures and identities. Despite the reassertion of central authority, elements of federal dynamics remain because of the challenge of ensuring national unity within a geographically vast and ethnically diverse country.

THE ARGENTINE REPUBLIC (1994)

The Argentine Federation was first established in 1853. During the succeeding 140 years, however, it was marked by periods of oligarchic or military rule that generally resulted in a centralized state. In 1983 the Argentinean military handed over power to civilian authorities, and the 1994 constitutional reforms were built on the constitution of 1853 plus changes made in 1860, 1866, 1880, 1898 and 1957. The reform of 1994 attempted to reverse the previous "defederalization" by strengthening the federal aspects. As such, the federation consists of 23 provinces and one federal district, with a total population of over 38 million.

All provinces have their own constitutions and full autonomy to deal with local matters, but they must respect the representative and republican principle embodied in the national constitution. Furthermore, provinces are bound by federal legislation, and under certain conditions the federal government can intervene in the provinces, including the removal and replacement of provincial authorities. Although the residual clause favours the provincial governments, the federal government can exercise authority in areas where provincial provisions could interfere with matters assigned to the federal government. Together, these peculiarities provide some quasi-federal features. In the realm of financial arrangements, despite provisions for sharing of resources between the federal and provincial governments, there has been a tendency for the federal government to use intergovernmental transfers to secure provincial support for national policies.

Argentina's constitution provides for a clear division between the executive, legislative and judicial branches of government. The bicameral federal legislature has been characterized by an overrepresentation of less populated provinces in both the 257-seat Chamber of National Deputies and the 72-member Senate, composed of 3 senators elected from each province and from the federal district of Buenos Aires.

The resurgence of civilian government since 1983 did not coincided with political stability. The relationship between the federal government and the provinces remained a major area of tension. For a period, economic decline also contributed to dislocation and a widespread distrust of politicians but more recently the economy has been booming. Among the issues affecting the operation of federalism in Argentina have been the impact of overrepresentation of the smaller provinces in the National Congress, the power of provincial governors and local party bosses over the drafting of party lists leading to their influence over national legislators, and the discretionary use of fiscal transfers by the national executive to build alliances with provincial units to achieve their objectives. Despite the hopes embodied in the reforms of 1994, the Argentine federation still seeks long-term economic and political stability.

THE FEDERAL DEMOCRATIC REPUBLIC OF ETHIOPIA (1995)

Following the military success of the Ethiopian Peoples' Revolutionary Democratic Front (EPRDF) and the approval by referendum of the Constituent Assembly proposals, the new constitution of the Federal Democratic Republic of Ethiopia, with a population of some 67 million, came into force in 1995. This embodied a radical form of federal devolution to nine new regional states along predominantly ethnic lines.

The Ethiopian federation was designed with the goal of accommodating a high degree of ethnic and religious diversity. Many powers are devolved to the region states to accommodate the many ethnicities and significant Muslim and Christian populations. Although the country's official language is Amharic, all the regions are able to determine their own languages, to accommodate the more than 80 languages and 200 dialects spoken by Ethiopia's citizens. Indeed with the aim of accommodating its ethnic diversity, Ethiopia has one of the few federal constitutions that outlines a right of sub-national units to secede from the federation, in addition to outlining a process for ethnic groups within existing states to form new regions.

The Ethiopian federation is a parliamentary democracy with a president elected by a two-thirds vote of a joint session of Parliament and a prime minister responsible to the House of People's Representatives. The Parliament is bicameral with a second chamber, the House of Federation. The election of its members can be direct or indirect according to the decision of the state councils, and each nation or nationality receives one additional member for each one million of its population. The House of Federation plays a unique role as the sole custodian of the constitution, having the exclusive right and ultimate authority to interpret the constitution. It also reviews and approves the annual budget in terms of the allocation of resources to the states. As well, it deals with inter-state disputes, such as borders and cross-boundary issues.

The differing fiscal capacity, development and population of the regional states has affected the degree to which these constituent units have been able to take advantage of the high degree of self-determination. The operation of the federation is also affected by the fact that the federal policy process has been mainly channelled by the EPRDF as the dominant political party, thus in practice making the political processes much more centralized than its constitutional form.[6]

---

[6] Assefa Fiseha, *Federalism and Accommodation of Diversity in Ethiopia: A Comparative Study*, revised edition (Nijmegen: Wolf Legal Publishers, 2007), p. 450.

Ethiopia's experiment with "ethnic federalism" offers some insights for other federations with significant ethnic, religious and linguistic diversity. The Ethiopian experience, however, is faced with serious challenges from one of the highest levels of poverty in the world and its reliance on a rainfall-based economy.

THE REPUBLIC OF SOUTH AFRICA (1996)

In 1910 the Union of South Africa became a self-governing dominion within the British Commonwealth, with a decentralized unitary system. The apartheid system developed in the 1950s involved a massive attempt at social engineering which collapsed in the 1990s. Following Nelson Mandela's release from prison, negotiations led to an interparty agreement on an interim quasi-federal constitution in 1993. After the holding of democratic elections and the formation of a coalition government, a Constitutional Assembly drafted a new constitution, which came into effect in 1996. In this constitution the label "federal" is avoided and South Africa is formally a devolved union, but its features have a strong federal character, drawing especially on the German model of integrated federalism.

The 1996 constitution established a republic of nine provinces for a country of over 43 million people, of whom 75.2 percent were black, 13.6 percent white, 8.6 percent coloured and 2.6 percent Indian. The nine provinces deliberately do not coincide with racial or tribal boundaries in an effort to avoid difficulties that might arise from units coinciding with geographically concentrated ethnic populations.

The constitution recognized three "spheres" of government (the term "levels" was specifically avoided), giving formal constitutional recognition to the central, provincial and local governments, and it was designed to promote cooperative federalism rather than competitive federalism. The legislative powers of all three spheres are set out, but the central government is favoured, since concurrent powers are extensive and the central government may set national standards and norms and may override provincial standards that threaten national unity or national standards.

The hybrid presidential-parliamentary form of government has a bicameral legislature. The National Assembly, to which the Cabinet is responsible, consists of 400 representatives elected by proportional representation on a party list system. The second chamber, the National Council of Provinces (NCOP), was modelled somewhat on the German Bundesrat but attempted to improve on it by including representatives of both the provincial executives and the legislatures. Its 90 members consist of 10 from each province, 6 representing the legislature and 4 representing the executive. The veto power of the NCOP varies according to whether central legislation affects the jurisdiction of the provinces and is designed to ensure that provincial interests are not seriously undermined. Taxing powers are highly centralized, but a Finance and Fiscal Commission was established by the constitution to make recommendations on the distribution of revenues. The Constitutional Court is responsible for resolving constitutional conflicts, but the constitution in section 41(3) includes a unique provision requiring all spheres of government to exhaust every reasonable effort to resolve any dispute through intergovernmental negotiation before approaching the courts to resolve the matter.

A major factor affecting the operation of South Africa since 1996 has been the dominance of the African National Congress (ANC) within virtually all spheres of government. This has meant that despite the many federal features of the constitution, the predominance of the ANC has led in practice to a high degree of centralization in policy making,

THE FEDERAL REPUBLIC OF NIGERIA (1999)

The Nigerian federation as it now exists is relatively new. In 1999 a new constitution established a federation consisting of 36 states and a federal capital territory, encompassing an estimated 132 million people and therefore the most populous country in Africa.

The Nigerian experience with federalism, however, goes back to the colonial period when after several stages of devolution an orthodox federal constitution was adopted for the federation composed of three large regions. At the time of independence in 1960, Nigeria's three regions — one of which, the Northern Region, had three-quarters of the country's area and 54 percent of its population — were distinguished in every conceivable way: by language, religion, social institutions, geography, history and even political parties. The early years of independence were marked by the politics of aggressive ethnoregionalism and persistent minority insecurity within each region. In 1963 a republican constitution was adopted, and in response to minority pressures a new fourth region, the Mid-Western Region, was created. This marked the beginning of a process that over subsequent years has increased the number of constituent units in the federation from 3 to 36.

Beginning with a military coup in 1966, followed by a civil war until 1970, Nigeria experienced a series of military regimes, 1970–75, 1975–76, 1976–79, but in 1979 a new federal constitution came into force. This did not last long as further military regimes took over power 1983–85, 1985–93, 1993–98, 1998–99. Thus, for most of the time since independence Nigeria has been under various military regimes, which maintained the formal trappings of a federation but in reality imposed a high degree of centralization.

The 1999 constitution retained many of the provisions of the 1979 constitution but with a number of amendments. The new constitution makes specific provision for 36 states and the Federal Capital Territory, recognizes local governments as a third order of government, and establishes a presidential system of government. The bicameral National Assembly is made up of a 360-seat House of Representatives and a Senate that has three representatives from each state.

The division of powers includes an extensive list of 68 exclusive powers, 12 major concurrent powers, and assigns the residual authority to the states. Although the "federal character" of Nigeria is entrenched in the constitution, the legacy of the long periods of military rule is displayed in the high degree of centralization that remains.

Two features of the Nigerian federal financial arrangements are of interest. First, although virtually all revenues are levied and collected by the federal government, the constitution provides for a "Federation Account" (derived from the concept of a "Distributable Pool" introduced by the Raisman commission in 1958) into which most of those revenues are paid with allocations from this account being made to federal, state and local governments. Allocations are based on the advice of a National Revenue Mobilization Allocation and Fiscal Commission (NRMAFC) employing such criteria as population, equality of states, internal revenue generation and land mass.

Second, particularly contentious has been the allocation of revenues generated by natural resources and oil, particularly since they constitute nearly all the revenues levied by the federal government but are generated in one region of the country, the south-eastern states. Nigeria is the most oil dependent of all established federations and, therefore, oil resources dominate both its public finance and its politics. The constitution provides that at least 13 percent of the revenue generated from natural resources should be distributed on the principle of derivation. Consequently, the producing states receive more per capita than other states, but the overbearing way the federal government has managed the resource and the corrupt and poor management by the states receiving these funds has left the population in the oil-rich Niger Delta, strongly aggrieved at not experiencing the benefits of these resources. This has been the source of serious unrest and even violence.

An election in 2007 produced a new president, but he faced some pressing problems: challenges to the validity of the election, massive endemic corruption, insurgency and gangsterism in the oil-producing Niger Delta region, and a dismally erratic supply of electricity.

Nigeria's current attempts to overcome a history of centralizing military regimes and to assure national unity in a highly diverse society through a civilian federal regime, its attempts to deal with the allocation of natural resource revenues, and the efforts to reduce pervasive corruption illustrate issues that are of importance in a number of emergent federations.

THE BOLIVARIAN REPUBLIC OF VENEZUELA (1999)

The Venezuelan federation has struggled with anti-democratic elements and excessive centralization since its earliest incarnation in 1811. Although the country maintained its federal form, repeated military and autocratic regimes during the nineteenth and twentieth centuries meant that the territorial distribution of power and the autonomy of the states virtually disappeared. Significant reforms were introduced in 1989, giving Venezuela's 23 states increased autonomy. This positive step was reinforced by electoral reforms that mandated the democratic election of state governors. These 1989 reforms served to counter to some degree the previously high degree of centralization.

This marginal process was undone by the new constitution introduced by President Hugo Chavez in 1999. This document further centralized Venezuela's already centralized federal system by drastically limiting the role, responsibilities and powers of state governments. The formerly bicameral legislature was reduced to the unicameral National Assembly, its 165 members being elected by proportional representation. The abolition of an upper legislative house greatly diminished state representation in the institutions of central government. Nominal recognition of state interests is accommodated through constitutional provisions that require the federal government to consult with state bodies before passing any legislation that concerns the states. However, this has not been the case in practice.

The responsibilities of state governments were greatly diminished by the division of constitutional powers in the 1999 constitution, which enumerated a significant number of solely federal powers and a few matters of concurrent jurisdiction. While the residual power had previously been with state governments, the new constitution introduced a parallel residual power at the federal level.

This centralization is further entrenched by a system of fiscal federalism that devotes no sources of revenue to the state governments. The federal government retains all significant sources of taxation revenue, with municipal governments given responsibility for local taxes. In contrast, the state governments must rely entirely on transfers from the federal government to finance their responsibilities.

Non-democratic processes have reinforced the centralizing tendencies of the current Chavez government. The blend of centralization, presidentialism and militarism has given the Venezuelan federation a distinctly authoritarian inclination. The highly centralized nature of federalism in Venezuela and the tenuous grasp of democratic institutions remain the twin challenges to this country in the present day.

2.3 MICRO-FEDERATIONS[7]

THE FEDERATED STATES OF MICRONESIA (1978)

The Federated States of Micronesia (FSM), created in 1978, comprises four island groups (Yap, Pohnpei, Chuuk and Kosrae) and 108,000 people. The constitution recognizes three levels of government: national, state and local. The

---

[7] See especially Dag Anckar, "Lilliput Federalism: Profiles and Varieties," *Regional and Federal Studies*, 13:3 (2003): 107–124.

Micronesian experience with federalism has been influenced greatly by the United States, which was assigned administration of all island groups in the Micronesian archipelago in 1947 under a United Nations Trusteeship Agreement. The FSM became formally independent in 1991, but the United States retains a significant degree of involvement. Although the division of powers enumerates many areas of responsibility of the federal government, in practice the United States has delivered these services (including postal services, currency and defence) as part of the free association agreement last negotiated in 2003. The system of fiscal federalism takes into account each state's right to 50 percent of taxes collected within its territory, but also to a certain percentage of development aid.

The Congress, the federation's unicameral legislature, has 14 seats. Each state elects one member "at large" to represent the territory, while the remaining 10 are elected on the basis of representation by population. The President and Vice-President are elected by Congress and serve four-year terms with the possibility of one re-election. An ongoing challenge for the FSM is the lack of attachment to the institutions and offices of central government since some citizens regard the federal government as another colonial administration. Additionally, the islands making up the FSM are geographically dispersed with only a small land mass.

Given the dispersal of the islands within Micronesia and the islands' wish for autonomy, and the wish of the United States to deal with the Trust Territory as a single entity, a federal solution emerged as the only solution for holding together this entity.

THE REPUBLIC OF BELAU (1981)

Belau, like Micronesia, was a United Nations Trust Territory administered by the United States, but its electorate rejected inclusion in the projected Federated States of Micronesia in 1978. Belau opted to maintain the principle of federalism, however, by establishing a federation of 16 states. Given the diminutive size of the federation with a total population of 17,000, these states operate at the level of local governments elsewhere, some of them having in fact fewer than 200 people.

The constitution is modelled on the U.S. constitution. Of the four microfederations, Belau is the only one to have a bicameral rather than unicameral federal legislature. The constitution prescribes the powers of the local states but leaves the residual authority with the federal government, which may delegate powers to the states. The powers delegated to the states are, however, few. Given the small size and local nature of the states, it is not surprising that their powers are relatively limited.

The adoption of a federal structure when there was such a small population has provided a means of accommodating the historical traditions of the previous 16 loosely tied village clusters. Belau became independent in 1994.

THE FEDERATION OF ST. KITTS AND NEVIS (1985)

The islands of St. Kitts and Nevis are located in the Lesser Antilles chain of islands in the eastern Caribbean, separated by just over 3 kilometres. With a total population of 46,000, 76 percent reside in St. Kitts and 24 percent in Nevis. Together with Anguilla these islands formed a single territory within the short-lived Federation of the West Indies (1958–62). The three islands became a state in voluntary association with Britain in 1967, but Anguilla, resentful of the domination of St. Kitts, left the arrangement in the early 1970s. In 1983, St. Kitts and Nevis obtained independence as a federation.

The new constitution adopted the Westminster form of government. As such, a Governor General acts as a representative of the monarch as the head of state, while the Prime Minister is the head of a parliamentary government vested in the unicameral National Assembly. The National Assembly currently has 11 seats elected by a first-past-the-post electoral system, 8 of which are allocated to St. Kitts and the remaining 3 to Nevis. In addition, the Governor General appoints three senators on advice of the Prime Minister and the Leader of the Opposition; these senators also sit in the National Assembly, giving this body 14 seats in total.

The St. Kitts and Nevis constitution differs from most federations in two respects. First, the federation is unbalanced in that Nevis has its own government and assembly as a constituent unit while St. Kitts does not. Second, the constitution provides explicitly for the process of Nevis's secession requiring a two-thirds majority in a referendum. The Nevis Island Assembly is allocated a considerable measure of jurisdiction, but this power is limited by the constitutional requirement that it cannot take action in many matters without the concurrence of the federal prime minister. This imbalance has created a political dynamic where the drive for Nevis's secession was virtually inevitable, and indeed in 1998 a referendum fell just short of the required two-thirds, with 62 percent.

Political life within the federation continues to be contentious and unstable, illustrating the problems inherent in a binary and asymmetric federal structure.

THE UNION OF THE COMOROS (2001)

The largest of the micro-federations with a total population of 630,000, Comoros has had three federal constitutions since independence in 1975. Successive federal constitutions in 1978, 1992 and 2001 have attempted to unite the islands of Grande Comore, Anjouan and Mohéli (a fourth island, Mayotte, opted to remain a French dependency). Despite the aim of these constitutions to achieve unity with a measure of autonomy for each island, the federation has been marked by secession movements, several violent military coups and general instability.

The 2001 constitution attempted to solve these problems by giving more autonomy to the islands. Although the constitution adopts the title "union," it has many federal features. The Assembly of the Union is unicameral, but island assemblies elect half of the 30 members (5 per island), the other 15 seats (5 per island) being filled by popular vote. There is a small list of enumerated federal powers (external affairs, defence, currency, nationality and religion), with the islands being granted increased autonomy over their own affairs. The Union President and the Federal Assembly, however, have continued to retain considerable control in practice over defence, posts and telecommunications, transit, civil, penal and industrial law, and external trade.

There is a significant asymmetry in the island governments. Grande Comore, which constitutes 51 percent of the federal population, has its own president (as the executive heads of each island are known), but unlike the other islands does not have its own sub-national assembly. The result has been clashes between the President of the Union and the President of Grande Comore over which ministries each controls, particularly relating to the revenue-generating departments such as finance and customs.

To date, the operation of the Comoros federation has been turbulent as a result of concerns about the adequacy of devolution.

2.4 CONFEDERAL-FEDERAL HYBRIDS

UNITED ARAB EMIRATES (1971)

The United Arab Emirates, situated on the eastern tip of the Arabian Peninsula, has a population of just over three million people and comprises seven emirates. The 1971 provisional constitution, which was made permanent in 1996, proclaims the United Arab Emirates to be a "federal state," but in form it is largely confederal in character.

The Supreme Council of Rulers, consisting of the seven non-elected traditional emirate rulers, is the highest federal authority and has both the legislative and executive authority. Since the emirs derive their status from their position within the emirates, this gives the Supreme Council a confederal character. There is a Council of Ministers with a prime minister appointed by the President of the Supreme Council to serve executive functions, but the Supreme Council formulates the general policy of the federation. There is a unicameral federal legislature, the Federal National Council, to which representatives for each emirate are appointed by the ruler, but it is a consultative body only, with legislative authority residing with the Supreme Council and the Council of Ministers. Federations are normally characterized by democratic processes, but other than the election of the president and vice-president of the Supreme Council by the rulers of the emirates, there are no elections. Late in 2007, the President of the Supreme Council announced, however, plans to institute elections for half the members of the Federal National Council by an electoral college of 2000 leading UAE figures, a very modest step towards representative government.

Since Abu Dhabi and Dubai constitute 41 and 26 percent respectively of the federal population, these two possess a veto within the Supreme Council. All decisions on substantive matters require the consent of five of the seven rulers, and this majority must include Abu Dhabi and Dubai. The procedure for amending the constitution is similar: the Council of Ministers proposes an amendment and after passage by the National Council (in this case, by a two-thirds majority), the Supreme Council can ratify it, accepting or rejecting any of the recommendations, but it must have the consent of Abu Dhabi and Dubai.

The constitution assigns an apparently broad array of federal powers, but in practice the contrasting centralist and autonomist views of Abu Dhabi and Dubai have produced a loose federation. The financial resources of the federal government are dependent upon funds provided by the individual emirates, most of which historically have been contributed by Abu Dhabi.

The oil wealth of the county has contributed to the stability of the UAE and to its development of a modern welfare state while retaining the predominance of its traditional rulers.

THE EUROPEAN UNION (1993)

The origins of the European Union were fundamentally confederal but during the course of its development is has become a unique hybrid of some features typical of confederations and some features typical of federations. The process of European integration began after World War II when the political leadership in France, Germany and the Low Countries saw economic integration as necessary to provide a durable peace and an ability to compete economically with the then two superpowers: the United States and the Soviet Union. Its beginnings lay in the Treaty of Paris (1951), which established the European Coal and Steel Community (ECSC), and the Treaties of Rome (1957), which set up the European Economic Community (EEC) and the European Atomic Energy Community (Euratom). After a period of relative economic stagnation, the process of integration was intensified by the development of the common market into a single market for the free movement of people, goods, services and capital under the *Single European Act 1987*, and by the Maastricht Treaty on European Union, 1993.

The European Union (EU), established in 1993, was based on three pillars: one completing the supranational project of an economic and monetary union, a second establishing intergovernmental cooperation on foreign and security policy, and a third involving cooperation on matters of justice and home affairs. The first of these pillars is the core of the EU with its hybrid confederal-federal character while the other two pillars are less developed and more confederal. With relation to the first pillar the intergovernmental Council of Ministers remained the primary legislative body, but in 1993 the previously limited powers of the European Parliament were strengthened by a co-decision authority in a number of important policy areas. The further Treaties of Amsterdam (1997) and Nice (2003) strengthened the processes of majority rule within the Council of Ministers and the co-decision authority of the European Parliament. By 2007 the process of widening the EU had embraced 27 member countries encompassing a population of over 490 million.

In institutional terms there are four key bodies within the first pillar of the EU, two of which are legislative bodies. The Council of Ministers is the main decision-making institution. It is composed of 27 member state ministers, the number of votes held by each being roughly proportional to the member state's population. There is also the European parliament with 785 seats as of 1 January 2007; the seats are allocated among states in proportion to population, and members are elected by direct universal suffrage for a five-year term. A third institution is the European Commission, with one commissioner for each of the 27 member states. Its function is to prepare proposals for the Council of Ministers and the European Parliament to consider. The President of the Commission is designated by the member governments and is confirmed by the European Parliament; working from member state recommendations, the President then assembles a "college" of Commission members, who as an entire commission are confirmed by the European Parliament for a five-year term. The fourth is the European Court of Justice whose judgments not only regulate the conduct and relationship of the member states but also apply directly to individual citizens and business corporations.

The distribution of authority within the EU differs from that in most federations which define the distribution in terms of "jurisdiction." In the EU the distribution is defined primarily in terms of "objectives," thus leaving considerable scope for interpretation. The "subsidiary principle" is stipulated as a basic yardstick. According to this, the EU would adopt new powers only where individual member states by their own action are not able to achieve the policy goals. Since this standard is defined by collective agreement, in practice its restraint on EU policy making has mainly been rhetorical.

The institutions and distribution of powers have made the EU a unique hybrid of features found in both confederations and federations.[8] Derived from its confederal roots are the prominence of the intergovernmental Council of Ministers, the Commission composed of one commissioner from each member state, its fiscal minimalism and reliance largely on financial transfers from the member states, the retention by member states of most traditional powers over domestic and foreign policy, and its legal basis in a series of treaties that require the unanimous consent of all the member states. On the other hand, there are a number of features not normally found in confederations and more akin to those found in federations. These include the roles of the European Commission, which in many

---

[8] See David McKay, *Designing Europe: Comparative Lessons from the Federal Experience* (Oxford: Oxford University Press, 2001).

respects is similar to that of an executive body, of the directly elected European Parliament with its co-decision powers, and of the European Court as a judicial body enforcing the supremacy of EU law. Furthermore, voting in the Council of Ministers on a wide range of issues has increasingly been based on the qualified majority principle rather than unanimity. In terms of functions, there has been a distribution of responsibilities, with trade and commerce heavily in the hands of the EU and social policy in the hands of the member states.

The European Union displays some aspects of formal asymmetry among its member states. Most significant was the creation in 1999 of a monetary union with a new currency, the euro applying to all the EU states except the United Kingdom, Sweden and Denmark.

From 2000 on, there developed a strong move to draft a European constitution that would transform the EU into a federation of European nation-states. In 2002 the European Constitutional Convention was established, and this culminated in a draft Constitutional Treaty signed in 2004 in Rome, giving member states two years to ratify it by parliamentary vote or national referendum. Its defeat in French and Dutch referendums in May–June 2005 dealt a severe setback to the ratification process, but in June 2007 agreement was reached to proceed to a treaty, rather than a constitution, that would retain virtually all of the substance of the proposed constitution less some of the grandiose language and reference to symbols. Among the main institutional changes would be an end to the rotating Council presidency in favour of a single person for a conventional term of office, an enhanced role for the foreign policy High Representative, a slimmed down number of commissioners, and a reform of the Council voting weights with a double majority system (by population and number of member states). In December 2007, the Treaty of Lisbon implementing these provisions was duly signed at a summit of the European leaders. Thus, this unique hybrid combining elements of a confederation and a federation continues to evolve.

2.5 POST-CONFLICT FEDERAL EXPERIMENTS

THE REPUBLIC OF BOSNIA AND HERZEGOVINA (1995)

Bosnia-Herzegovina was one of the six republics that composed the Federal Socialist Republic of Yugoslavia created at the end of World War II. With the secession of Slovenia, Macedonia and Croatia from the federation in the early 1990s, Bosnia too declared its independence in 1992. The resulting war led to international pressure and the Dayton Peace Agreement in 1995 for the creation of a new federation of Bosnia and Herzegovina consisting of two "entities": the Bosniac-Croat Federation (itself a federation of eight cantons with its own strong central government but serving as one entity within the broader federation); and the unitary Serbian Republika Srpska.

The Bosniac-Croat Federation and the Republika Srpska share a central bicameral legislature (the House of Representatives and the House of Peoples) and a three-member presidency composed of Bosnian, Croat and Serb representatives. In both legislative houses seats are allocated with one-third to each of the three ethnic groups. Among the procedures for resolving constitutional conflicts are a Constitutional Court and a special parliamentary procedure enabling each ethnic group to block legislation vital to its interests.

Bosnia and Herzegovina is a relatively decentralized federation, with the residual powers assigned to the constituent units. Jurisdiction over taxation is not explicitly mentioned in the division of powers, and thus this important power falls to the entities. The Bosniac-Croat Federation provides two-thirds and the Republika Srpska one-third of the revenues required by the federal budget. The decentralized division of powers also allows the constituent units to act in areas that may appear to overlap the central government's jurisdiction over foreign policy and trade, such as establishing relationships with neighbouring states and entering agreements with foreign states and international organizations (with the consent of the federal Parliamentary Assembly). This reflects the imperative of accommodating diverse and regionally concentrated populations. However, the Dayton Peace Agreement allows for some powers that were temporarily entrusted to the entities to be eventually transferred back to the central government, and it empowers the central government to create additional institutions to preserve the sovereignty, territorial integrity, political independence and international personality of the country.

The complex institutions created to accommodate diversity have at times threatened Bosnia and Herzegovina with paralysis. As such, recent reform efforts have attempted to reinforce the institutions of the central government. Whether the international community's continued interventionist role exercised by the United Nations up to 2002 and by the European Union and NATO after that can succeed in establishing a prosperous and stable Bosnia and Herzegovina remains to be seen.

REPUBLIC OF SUDAN (2005)

Military regimes favouring Islamic-oriented governments have dominated national politics in Sudan since independence from the United Kingdom in 1956. Sudan was embroiled in two prolonged civil wars during most of the remainder of the twentieth century. These conflicts were rooted in northern economic, political and social domination of the southern Sudanese, largely non-Muslim, non-Arab. The first civil war ended in 1972 but broke out again in 1983. The second war and famine-related effects resulted in more than 4 million people displaced and more than 2 million deaths over a period of two decades. Peace talks gained momentum in 2002–04 with the signing of several accords. The final North/South Comprehensive Peace Agreement, signed in 2005, granted the southern rebels autonomy for six years, after which a referendum on whether the South should be independent is scheduled to be held. The Interim National Constitution of 2005 established a federation of 25 states, with a bicameral federal legislature and a president who is both head of state and head of government from the north and a vice-president from the south. A distribution of powers listing federal, state and concurrent powers was set out.

Meanwhile, a separate conflict, which broke out in the western region of Darfur in 2003, has displaced nearly 2 million people and caused an estimated 200,000 to 400,000 deaths. As of 2007, peacekeeping troops were struggling to stabilize the situation, which has become increasingly regional in scope and has brought instability to eastern Chad as well as Sudanese incursions into the Central African Republic. Sudan also has faced large refugee influxes from neighbouring countries, primarily Ethiopia and Chad. Armed conflict, poor transport infrastructure, and lack of government support have chronically obstructed the provision of humanitarian assistance to affected populations.

While there has been some progress on the autonomy promised to the south, there have been accusations that Khartoum has been dragging its heels on the sharing of oil revenues and the recognition of a border between the north and south. As a result, during October 2007, the party representing the black mostly Christian south pulled out of the predominantly Arab and Muslim coalition that runs the federal government. While talks followed to redress the southern grievances, the tendency to northern intransigence may have a significant impact on the referendum on independence for the south scheduled for 2011.

REPUBLIC OF IRAQ (2005)

Following the invasion of Iraq and the replacement of the Saddam Hussein regime in 2003 by a coalition led by the United States, a Transitional National Assembly was elected, which proceeded to draft a constitution that was approved by a referendum in October 2005.[9] This constitution was intended to be federal in form although a number of features were either ambiguous or incomplete. The central institutions included the interim Presidency Council with a president and two vice-presidents representing the Shia, Sunni and Kurdish communities, a prime minister and cabinet, and a bicameral federal legislature but with the membership and authority of the second chamber, the Federation Council, left undefined. Two categories of constituent units were specified: 18 governorates, which were basically administrative units; and regions with greater powers, combining governorates

---

[9] For an assessment see Markus E. Bouillon, David M. Malone and Ben Rowswell, *Iraq: Preventing a New Generation of Conflict* (Boulder, CO.: Lynne Rienner Publishers, 2007).

where they choose to join together and including a Kurdish region from the beginning. The distribution of powers set out federal and concurrent powers but contained a number of ambiguities, especially relating to control of natural resources such as oil and gas ownership. In the area of concurrent jurisdiction paramountcy was assigned to regional law over federal law. An election under the constitution was held in December 2005, but many of the ambiguities remained unresolved, and despite the continued presence of coalition forces a virtual state of civil war has continued to persist. In the meantime a constitutional review committee has made proposals which, if accepted, would clarify and strengthen the role of the central government and establish a number of key central institutions. These proposals have not yet been approved, however.

THE DEMOCRATIC REPUBLIC OF CONGO (2006)

After a prolonged period of ethnic strife and civil war beginning in 1994, the Pretoria Accord in late 2002 was signed by the warring parties to end the fighting and establish a government of national unity for this country of 68 million people with some 250 ethnic groups. The transitional government held a successful constitutional referendum in December 2005 and the new constitution came into effect in February 2006. The National Assembly was established in September 2006, a president was chosen in December 2006, and provincial assemblies governors and national senators came into office early in 2007. The federation consists of 25 provinces plus Kinshasa as the capital. The head of state is elected for a five-year term and the Prime Minister as head of government is appointed by the President. The federal Parliament is bicameral, the Senate members being elected by the provincial assemblies. The distribution of powers is strongly weighted to the federal government, but the residual authority lies with the provinces. There is a Constitutional Council to ensure the constitutionality of laws. Constitutional amendments require passage by the two houses convened in Congress by a two-thirds majority followed by approval in a referendum.

To date, the constitution has been in operation for insufficient time to judge its effectiveness in resolving the previous conflicts that afflicted this country. With continued violence in eastern Congo's North Kivu province during 2007, the dangers of the Congo and Rwanda and of the Hutus and Tutsis returning to war have remained a concern.

Chapter 3

The Formation of Federations

3.1 THE VARIETY OF FACTORS AND PROCESSES

What factors and processes have led to the adoption or creation of federations? Some analysts have tried to identify a single common factor. For instance, W.H Riker attributed a significant external or internal threat as the factor common to the creation of all federations.[1] But while this factor has been important in a number of cases, notably Switzerland, Canada and Mexico, there are a number of other instances, such as Australia, where it was clearly not the major factor. Indeed, in most federations it has been a combination of factors that was responsible for the choice by political leaders of federation as a form of government, and the particular combination of factors and the process of formation has varied from federation to federation.

3.2 THE BALANCE OF PRESSURES

While the particular factors encouraging unity and regional autonomy have varied in the formation of federations, what is common to all the successful instances is the existence of a relative balance in the pressures for political integration and for regional autonomy. It should be noted that it is possible for a strong integrative consciousness in a wider community to coexist with an equally strong regional consciousness, as has been the case in India for instance, or for both forces to be

---

[1] W.H. Riker, "Federalism," in Fred I. Greenstein and Nelson W. Polsby. eds., *Handbook of Political Science: Government Institutions and Processes*, vol.5 (Reading, MA: Addison Wesley, 1975).

relatively weak, as was the case in the founding of the Australian federation; but what both these cases had in common was the relative balance in the forces for unity and for regional autonomy.

Where one of the these pressures is strong and the other weak, the result is likely to be either unitary political integration, on the one hand, or the independence of the regional units or at least a confederal solution, on the other. Where both motivations exist in something approaching an equal balance, federation as a solution is likely to appeal by enabling both an effective federal government and genuine regional autonomy to coexist. This latter situation arises because people may be members of and feel loyalty to several groups and communities at the same time (e.g., family, work group, professional association, church, ethnic or linguistic community, political movement, village or city, regional community, nation, supranational association or global community) rather than being focused on only one of them to the exclusion of the others. Because people's attachments to these different groups or communities vary in intensity and over time, these loyalties are not necessarily mutually exclusive; hence, the possibility of the coexistence of both uniting and regionalizing pressures at the same time.

It needs to be emphasized that while this relative balance of motivations is common to federations, the particular factors contributing to the balance has in each case been the unique result of differing historical and social forces and the choices made by political leaders. As a result, each federation has in a sense been a unique experiment, combining in its own distinctive way a particular regional structure, distribution of powers, arrangements for intergovernmental cooperation, organization of central government, and protection for the supremacy of the constitution — all to fit its own particular circumstances.

It should be noted that the balance of factors encouraging unity and regional autonomy is important not only in leading to the creation of federations but also in their subsequent operation. Over time, the importance of particular factors may change, shifting the balance of pressures. For instance, typically in colonial federations, movements for independence have provided a strong uniting force, but once independence has been achieved the strength of that unifying motivation has dissipated. In a number of cases this led to the subsequent difficulties or even disintegration of newly independent federations in the 1960s and 1970s. This indicates that in assessing the effectiveness of a federal political system, it is necessary to consider not only whether initially the particular form of its institutions appropriately exposed and reconciled the conflicting demands of the society on which it was based, but whether subsequently it continues to reflect changes and shifts in the factors affecting aspirations for both unity and regional autonomy. The splitting of overcentralized Pakistan in 1970 and the disintegration of the ineffectual Federation of the West Indies in 1962 illustrate cases where the particular form of the federation failed to reflect accurately the balance in the aspirations for united action and for regional autonomy.

3.3 DIFFERING PROCESSES IN THE CREATION OF FEDERATIONS

A number of analysts have noted that federations have been created in different ways. Carl Friedrich in 1968 drew attention to the importance of the process by which federations were created and to the fact that while some were established by bringing separate units together, others involved devolving power to regional units.[2] More recently, Alfred Stepan has emphasized the distinction between federations created by the "coming together" of formerly separate units and those resulting from "holding together" regions in a formerly united polity.[3]

Federations have, in fact, been created in three different ways. One is the aggregation of formerly separate units. The United States, Switzerland, and Australia provide classic examples. In these the process of aggregation led in the early stages to an emphasis on retaining a large element of autonomy for the federating units. A second pattern has been through devolution from a previous unitary regime. Examples of this pattern are provided by Belgium, Germany (after the Third Reich), Nigeria and Spain. This pattern, at least initially, has usually resulted in a greater relative emphasis on federal powers. A third pattern has been the combination of these two processes, Canada and India providing major examples. The creation of the Canadian federation involved a devolution to two new provinces (Ontario and Quebec) from what had previously been a single unitary Province of Canada, and also the addition of two previously separate colonies (New Brunswick and Nova Scotia) as provinces of the new federation. The Union of India established by the 1950 constitution included a devolution to states that had previously been provinces and the incorporation of the previously separate princely states into the new federation.

These examples illustrate the variety of processes by which federations have been created. The different paths have often affected the character of the resulting federation, although common to them all has been the eventual establishment, as a result of political negotiation, of a compound polity in which each of the different orders of government derives its authority from a supreme constitution rather than from another level of government.

---

[2] Carl J. Friedrich, *Trends of Federalism in Theory and Practice* (New York: Praeger, 1968).

[3] Alfred Stepan, "Toward a New Comparative Politics of Federalism, Multinationalism and Democracy: Beyond Rikerian Federalism," in E.L. Gibson, ed., *Federalism and Democracy in Latin America* (Balitimore & London: Johns Hopkins University Press, 2004), pp. 33–7.

3.4 CATALYSTS OF POLITICAL INTEGRATION

One set of factors found in the formation of federations has been those contributing to political integration. While the specific factors contributing to the motivation for distinct regional groups to come together or when devolution occurs to maintain common institutions of shared-rule has varied from federation to federation, the existence of some desire for shared-rule has been common to all of them.

The pressure for united action in at least some areas has depended on the following factors. The first is the influence of the background conditions, including (a) the degree of spillover from pre-existing national, economic and social links or integration anong the constituent units, (b) the geographical proximity of the constituent units, (c) the relative size and bargaining power of the constituent units, and (d) the affinities between their elites. Second is the strength of the integrative motives present, including (a) the desire for security from external or internal threats, (b) the desire for economic benefits from the larger market or complementary products, (c) the desire for greater international influence, and (d) the desire for a common identity. Third is the character of the integration process itself in terms of (a) the character of the bargaining process, (b) the role of political leaders, (c) the role of external governments or, in the case of colonial federations, the imperial government, and (d) the timing and sequence of steps in the process of negotiation and unification.

3.5 CATALYSTS OF CONSTITUENT UNIT AUTONOMY

The strongest catalyst for political union into larger federations since the middle of the twentieth century has been increasing worldwide interdependence in an era when advances in technology and communications have made it difficult for even nation-states to be self-sufficient economically or to defend their own security. Paradoxically, it has been the awareness of this trend that has also frequently encouraged a stronger regional consciousness within political systems. The growth of larger and remote political structures, coupled with the increasing pervasiveness of vast governmental structures and bureaucracies impinging upon the life of citizens, has often provoked a counter-reaction.

The heightened resistance to political integration and the vigorous demand for self-expression, dignity and self-rule have been particularly strong where regional groups have been marked by differences of language, race, religion, social structure, and cultural tradition. In such cases as Switzerland, Canada, India, Pakistan, Malaysia, Nigeria, Ethiopia, Belgium and Spain, linguistic, religious or racial minorities, fearing discrimination at the hands of political majorities, have insisted on regional autonomy as a way to preserve their distinct identities. Where the threat to this distinctiveness has been perceived as particularly serious, such regional groups have sometimes turned to outright secession as the only sure defence against assimilation, even when that means forgoing the benefits of the wider federation.

Linguistic identity has been a particularly potent force for regionalism. This is not surprising, since language differences often serve as barriers to communication. Moreover, a shared language provides a means of expression and communion, which is a most important ingredient in one's awareness of a social identity and a treasured heritage of a common past. Not surprisingly, any community governed through a language other than its own has usually felt disenfranchised. Significantly, linguistic regionalism has been a greater problem in societies that are industrial or are in the process of modernization compared with primitive agrarian societies, because in the former, official recognition of a language substantially affects career opportunities and employment. Where different linguistic groups exist within a country, it would appear that conflict is particularly severe where members of different language groups are under unequal pressures to learn the language of others.

Other cultural factors can also be divisive. In Switzerland, for example, political divisions have as often followed confessional as linguistic lines. Elsewhere, as on the Indian sub-continent, ostensibly religious differences have been explosive. Generally, regional consciousness has been strongest where differences of language, race, religion and social institutions have reinforced rather than cut across each other, as in Switzerland, or where they have been associated with economic subordination, as in Belgium and Malaysia.

Among other factors contributing to the intensity of regional consciousness are differences in the degree of modernization. Where some regions have lagged behind, this has been a source not only of resentment but also of fears of exploitation or domination by the more advanced regions.

Differences of economic interest have also been an important factor. While economic differences have often contributed to integration through opening the possibility of exchange of different products across regional boundaries, they may also foster regional consciousness because of differences in problems of production, types of exports, sources of foreign capital and appropriate policies for the promotion of economic development. Furthermore, although political union may bring economic gains to the union as a whole, economic integration may not only have "trade-creation" effects but may also have "trade-diversion" effects that impose hardship and inequality on some regions. It is noteworthy that many ostensibly linguistic, racial or cultural movements for regional autonomy or separateness in countries such as Canada, India, Malaysia and Nigeria have had strong economic undercurrents related to the struggle for jobs and economic opportunities.

In federations such as the United States, Australia, Brazil and Argentina, where linguistic or cultural divisions have been more moderate, economic and also historical differences among the federating units have been sufficiently strong to fuel the pressure for regional autonomy.

Not to be overlooked is the impact in some cases of direct or indirect external influences upon regional consciousness. Quebec in Canada, Biafra in Nigeria and the Jura in Switzerland provide powerful examples of the impact of direct encouragement of a regional separatist movement by a foreign government.

This discussion suggests that to understand regionalism it must be examined not simply in terms of the absence of factors encouraging political union, but also in terms of factors that encourage a regional consciousness. These factors parallel the factors for united action identified in section 3.2 above, but encourage regional consciousness. First, there are the background conditions, including (a) the degree to which each particular region is internally homogenous in language, religion, race and culture, (b) differences in the level of modernization, economic development and political ideology or outlook, (c) the degree of disparity in relative wealth and potential influence among constituent units within the proposed federation, and (d) the competitiveness of the elites in the different regimes. Second, the strength of the immediate motives for regional autonomy is significant, including (a) the desire to secure the distinctive features of the regional society against potential threats of assimilation, (b) the desire to enhance the economic benefits for the specific regional group, and (c) the strength of the desire for a sense of regional identity or even nationhood. Third, also important is the character of the process for negotiating a federal solution involving regional autonomy in terms of (a) the character of the negotiating process (e.g., use of referendums, elections, or guerrilla campaigns), (b) the role of leading regional elites, (c) the responses of neighbouring regions, (d) the impact of direct and indirect external influences, and (e) the timing and sequence of steps in the negotiations.

3.6 THE CAPACITY FOR FEDERAL GOVERNMENT

K.C. Wheare, in examining factors leading to the creation of federations, drew attention to an important difference between the factors that contributed to the desire for federation and those that contributed to the capacity to create and operate a federal form of government. The desire for federation is itself an important element in the capacity to operate a federal system. There must be a strong enough sense of joint identity and interest to achieve loyalty to a common federal government for certain purposes and to make the necessary accommodations to achieve this. There must also be a strong enough sense of distinct identities to maintain real autonomy at the regional level.

A number of other factors are also important for the capacity to operate a federal system. Among these are the availability of sufficient trained human and financial resources to support the operation of two or more orders of government. Another crucial element is the existence of a supportive political culture. Since federations are distinguished by each order of government receiving its authority from the constitution, a respect for constitutionalism and the rule of law is a crucial prerequisite for effective operation. Since federations involve accommodating and reconciling territorial diversity, a political culture emphasizing tolerance and compromise is an equally important prerequisite. These prerequisites mean that the existence of reasonably functioning democratic processes are an important factor. The failure of such nominal federations as the former Soviet Union, Yugoslavia and Czechoslovakia and the ineffective operation of the new constitutions of Sudan and Iraq point to the importance of these prerequisites.

3.7 THE INFLUENCE OF MODELS

Earlier federations have often served as models providing institutional precedents and examples that have been of influence to political leaders establishing subsequent federations. This influence has taken both positive and negative forms where particular institutional arrangements have been followed or avoided in the light of previous experience.

The United States of America as the first modern federation, established in 1789, not only influenced a number of features adopted by the Swiss in 1848, such as the bicameral legislature (but the avoidance of a non-collegial presidency), and the Australian federation in terms of the form of the distribution of powers, but it also was the predominant model followed by the Latin American federations, which all adopted the presidential-congressional form of institutions. On the other hand, in the 1860s during the period of the civil war in the United States, Canadians deliberately chose a more centralized form of federation to avoid the apparent weakness of the U.S. federal government.

Switzerland has perhaps had a less pervasive influence than warranted, but the use of referendums with a double majority (federation-wide majority and majorities in a majority of constituent units) for constitutional amendments has served as a model not only for Australia but for a number of other more recent federations.

Canada, founded as a federation in 1867, was the first federation to incorporate Westminster parliamentary institutions, and this pattern was followed in most of the former British colonies that subsequently became federations. Australian political leaders, despite expressly preferring the more decentralized U.S. form of the division of powers, followed the Canadian precedent of incorporating parliamentary institutions on the Westminster pattern. India and Malaysia, in part through the influence of the *Government of India Act, 1935*, itself modelled on the *British North America Act, 1867*, were heavily influenced by the Canadian model, even to including some quasi-federal elements. It is noteworthy too that most of the subsequent European federations have incorporated parliamentary rather than presidential-congressional institutions.

Australia, with bodies such as the Loan Council, the Commonwealth Grants Commission, and the Council of Australian Governments (COAG), has been a pioneer in the establishment of intergovernmental councils, especially in relation to issues of federal finances, but also more broadly. This example has influenced the establishment of such bodies in India, Pakistan, Nigeria, Malaysia and South Africa, among others.

The German federation, with its emphasis on administrative rather than legislative decentralization and concomitant interlocking federal-state relationships, has influenced not only a number of European federations but particularly the cooperative character of the South Africa federation. The South African federal second chamber, the National Council of Provinces, was an attempt to improve on the German Bundesrat by incorporating both executive and legislative representation from the provinces.

Whether in terms of imitations, variations or express avoidance of features of earlier federations, later federations have clearly exhibited an awareness of and have taken account of the earlier examples.

Chapter 4

The Constituent Units

4.1 THE BUILDING BLOCKS OF FEDERATIONS

The constituent units representing one of the orders of government constitute the building blocks on which a federation is based. In different federations the basic constituent units have gone by different names: "states" in Australia, Belau, Brazil, Ethiopia, India, Malaysia, Mexico, Micronesia, Nigeria, the United States and Venezuela; "provinces" in Argentina, Canada, Pakistan and South Africa; "Länder" in Austria and Germany; "cantons" in Switzerland; "Autonomous Communities" in Spain; "Regions" and "Communities" in Belgium; "subjects" in Russia; "islands" in Comoros and St. Kitts and Nevis; "emirates" in the United Arab Emirates; and "entities" in Bosnia and Herzegovina. All of these, however, represent the basic governmental components in these federations.

4.2 THE NUMBER OF CONSTITUENT UNITS

The number of constituent units plays an important role in shaping the dynamics of political relationships within federations. In this respect there has been a great variety among federations (see table 8). In nine federations there are 20 or more basic constituent units, the largest number being originally 89 (in 1993) but now 86 (in 2007) subjects in Russia, and 50 states in the United States. The others are Argentina with 23, Brazil with 26, India with 28, Mexico with 31, Nigeria with 36, Switzerland with 26 and Venezuela with 23. Having such a large number of constituent units has usually meant that none of them is in a position to dominate politics within the federation or to individually counterbalance the federal government.

At the other extreme are federations with 2 to 4 constituent units. Examples are found in three of the micro-federations: Comoros with 3; Micronesia with 4; and St. Kitts and Nevis with 2. Other examples are Pakistan since 1973 with 4 provinces; Bosnia and Herzegovina with 2 entities; and in its early years as a federation until 1963, Nigeria with 3 regions. Also notable are the bicommunal characters of Pakistan 1956–71 before the separation of Bangladash, Czechoslovakia prior to segregation in 1992, and Serbia and Montenegro 1992–2006. In all these federations the small number of regional units, often with one dominant region, has made it possible for individual units to challenge the federal government, typically producing quite unstable political relationships.

The remainder of the federations fall between these two extremes: Australia with 6 states, Austria with 9 Länder, Belgium with nominally 3 Communities and 3 Regions, Canada with 10 provinces, Ethiopia with 9 states, Germany with 16 Länder, Malaysia with 13 states, South Africa with 9 provinces, Spain with 17 Autonomous Communities, and the United Arab Emirates with 7 emirates. In these instances, individual constituent units have been able to exert more political influence than in the federations that have a larger number of units, especially where one or two regional units have themselves been significantly large or wealthy, but they have not experienced the degree of instability displayed by the federations with only two to four constituent units.

4.3 THE SIZE AND WEALTH OF CONSTITUENT UNITS

There are also enormous variations in the size of the constituent units among the contemporary functioning federations listed in table 8. The largest units – Uttar Pradesh in India with 166 million, Punjab in Pakistan with 80 million and California in the United States with 34 million – are each larger than the total population of many federations. At the other extreme, some constituent units in Belau have barely more than 200 inhabitants, while Kosrae in Micronesia has a population of only 8,000, Nevis in St. Kitts and Nevis 10,000, and Appenzell–Inner Rhodes in Switzerland 15,000.

The absolute size of constituent units is significant because this may affect the range of functions that they have the capacity to perform. On the other hand, where constituent units are of the immense size of Uttar Pradesh in India, Punjab in Pakistan or California in the United States, questions arise about how responsive they can be to the interests of individual citizens or to distinct local communities.

Another important aspect relating to the size of constituent units is the relative variation among the regional units within a given federation. Many federations are marked by enormous variations, as table 8 indicates. This means that within a federation there may be a wide difference among constituent units in terms of their capacity to perform functions and in their influence on federal policy making.

TABLE 8: Population of Full-Fledged Constituent Units

Federal System	No. of Units	Total Population	Largest Unit	Population of Largest Unit	Population % of Federation	Smallest Unit	Population of Smallest Unit	Population % of Federation	Population of Largest to Smallest
India	28	1028.6 m	Uttar Pradesh	166.2 m	16.2%	Sikkim	0.5 m	0.5%	307.2
European Union	27	461.4 m	Germany	82.5 m	17.0%	Malta	0.4 m	0.1%	205.2
Ethiopia	9	67.3 m	Oromia	23.7 m	35.2%	Harar	0.2 m	0.3%	117.3
Belgium	6	10.5 m	Flemish Community	6.2 m	59.7%	German Community	0.07 m	0.68%	87.3
Switzerland	26	7.4 m	Zurich	1.3 m	17.0%	Appenzell-Inner Rhodes	0.015 m	0.2%	86.7
Canada	10	30.0 m	Ontario	11.4 m	38.0%	Prince Edward Island	0.1 m	0.5%	84.5
Micronesia	4	0.1 m	Chuuk	0.05 m	50.1%	Kosrae	0.008 m	7.2%	71.4
Argentina	23	36.3 m	Buenos Aires	13.8 m	38.1%	Santa Cruz Province	0.2 m	0.5%	70.2
United States	50	281.4 m	California	33.9 m	12.0%	Wyoming	0.5 m	0.1%	68.7
Venezuela	23	22.8 m	Zulia	2.9 m	12.9%	Amazonas	0.07 m	0.3%	43.9
Germany	16	82.4 m	Nordrhein-Westfalen	18.1 m	21.6%	Bremen	0.6 m	0.8%	28.5
Mexico	31	103.3 m	Mexico	14.0 m	13.6%	Baja California Sur	0.5 m	0.5%	27.4
Spain	17	44.1 m	Andalucia	7.8 m	17.8%	La Rioja	0.3 m	0.7%	26.1
Malaysia	13	23.3 m	Selangor	4.2 m	18.0%	Perlis	0.02 m	0.9%	21.0
Australia	6	18.8 m	New South Wales	6.3 m	33.6%	Tasmania	0.5 m	2.4%	13.9
Pakistan (1973–)	4	144.9 m	Punjab	80.6 m	55.6%	Islamabad	0.9 m	0.6%	11.7
Serbia and Montenegro (1992–2006)	2	8.2 m	Serbia	7.5 m	91.8%	Montenegro	0.7 m	8.2%	11.2
South Africa	9	45.6 m	KwaZulu-Natal	9.6 m	21.0%	Northern Cape	0.8 m	1.8%	10.5
Comoros	3	0.6 m	Grande Comore	0.3 m	51.3%	Moheli	0.03 m	5.6%	9.1
Russia	86	144.0 m	Moscow (city)	10.2 m	7.1%	Evenki	1.4 m	0.01%	7.1
Austria	9	8.3 m	Vienna	1.7 m	20.0%	Burgenland	0.3 m	3.3%	5.9
Nigeria	36	132.8 m	Lagos	8.6 m	6.5%	Ebonyi	1.5 m	1.1%	5.9
St. Kitts-Nevis	2	0.04 m	St. Kitts	0.04 m	75.8%	Nevis	0.01 m	24.2%	3.2
Czechoslovakia (1920–1992)	2	15.6 m	Czech Republic	10.4 m	66.4%	Slovak Republic	5.2 m	33.7%	2.0
Bosnia-Herzegovina	2	4.1 m	Bosniac-Croat Federation	2.5 m	61.0%	Republika Srpska	1.6 m	39.0%	1.6
Pakistan (1956–1971)	2	95.6 m	East Pakistan	51.6 m	54.0%	West Pakistan	42.2 m	44.2%	1.2
Belau	16	0.02 m							

Sources: Country statistics bureaus and Forum of Federations, *Handbook of Federal Countries, 2005* (Montreal & Kingston: McGill-Queen's University Press, 2005).

Particularly significant in this latter respect are federations where one or two constituents may constitute a majority or nearly a majority of the federal population. Notable examples where a single constituent unit contains a majority of the federal population are the Flemish Region in Belgium (59.7 percent), the Bosniac-Croat Federation as an entity in Bosnia and Herzegovina (61 percent), Grande Comore within Comoros (51.3 percent), Chuuk within Micronesia (50.1 percent), Punjab within Pakistan (55.6 percent), and St. Kitts within St. Kitts and Nevis (75.8 percent). The tensions such a situation may give rise to are illustrated by the disintegration of such federations as the Federation of the West Indies (1958–62) where Jamaica, one of ten territories, had 52 percent of the federal population; Pakistan 1956–71 where one unit, East Pakistan, had 54 percent of the federal population; Czechoslovakia 1920–92 where the Czech Republic had 66.4 percent of the population; and Serbia and Montenegro from 1992 until its demise in 2006, where Serbia had 91.8 percent of the population. Also a considerable source of tensions are cases where two constituent units together have constituted a majority of the federal population or close to it. Examples are Abu Dhabi (41 percent) and Dubai (26 percent), totalling 67 percent of the UAE population; Ontario (38 percent) and Quebec (24 percent), totalling 62 percent in Canada; Oromia (35 percent) and Amhara (26 percent), totalling 61 percent in Ethiopia; New South Wales (34 percent) and Victoria (25 percent), totalling 59 percent in Australia; and Buenos Aires (38 percent) and Cordoba (9 percent), totalling 47 percent in Argentina. These units have tended to play a predominant role in the federal politics of their federations, to the resentment of the more numerous smaller constituent units. It is of interest to note that despite the large absolute size of their populations, Uttar Pradesh in India and California in the United States represent only 16 and 12 percent of their total federal populations, thus moderating their influence in federal politics.

In most federations there is also a considerable variation in the wealth of their constituent units, especially in relation to natural resources. As in the case of population, this is significant in terms of their capacity to perform the functions constitutionally assigned to them. Also, variations within each federation in terms of their relative wealth have been a factor affecting the influence of particular constituent units in the dynamics of federal politics.

4.4 CATEGORIES OF CONSTITUENT UNITS

In most federations there is just one category of full-fledged constitutional units although, as noted in section 4.1, their labels may vary. In a few cases, however, these full-fledged constituent units may be placed into several categories.

Most notable in this respect is Belgium where two kinds of constituent units were established in 1970 with different jurisdictions assigned to them. Three of the constituent units (Flanders, Wallonia and Brussels) are Regions territorially demarcated and responsible mainly for regional economic development, public works, transportation, international trade and agricultural policy. Three constituent units are culturally defined Communities (Flemish, French and German) overlapping the Regions and with powers over language, culture, education and social services such as health care. The situation is further complicated by the fact that since 1980 the Flemish Region and Community have merged their institutions.

The Russian Federation as created in 1993 comprised 89 constituent units in several categories inherited from the previous Soviet Union. These were 21 republics, 49 oblasts (regions), 6 krais (territories), 10 autonomous okrugs (districts), one autonomous oblast, and 2 federal cities (Moscow and St. Petersburg). According to the constitution all have equal legislative and executive powers, but the republics are distinguished by the fact that they contain significant non-Russian ethnic populations (e.g., Tartars in Tartarstan, Bashkirs in Bashkortostan, and so on). Oblasts and krais are non-ethnically based regions. Autonomous okrugs are ethnically based districts that are homelands to indigenous Aboriginal populations. They are considered both separate members of the federation and parts of the oblasts or krais in which they are located, a situation that has led frequently to jurisdictional disputes.[1]

Spain, in addition to its 17 Autonomous Communities, has 2 non-indigenous Autonomous Communities, Ceuta and Melilla (located on the north coast of Morocco), which were granted eligibility to become Autonomous Communities in 1995.

In a number of federations there are secondary classes of constituent units with less autonomy than the full-fledged constituent units and with special funding arrangements. These less autonomous units, most commonly called "territories," usually are remote and thinly populated regions lacking the resources to sustain full self-government, or they are special tribal areas, overseas possessions or federal capital districts. The arrangements of federal capital districts is dealt with below in section 4.7. Examples of non-capital territories are found in Australia (the Northern Territory plus 7 administrative territories), Canada (Northwest Territories, Nunavut and Yukon), India (7 Union Territories), Pakistan (6 Federally Administered Tribal Areas), Spain (3 directly administered sovereign areas off the coast of Morocco), and Venezuela (one federally controlled dependency consisting of 11 federally controlled island groups with a total of 72 individual islands). In some cases, notably the United States, Brazil, Canada and India, historically new full-fledged states have been created out of former territories when their populations and development provided the basis to sustain self-government at the level of the primary constituent units.

---

[1] A.L. Griffiths, ed., *Handbook of Federal Countries, 2005* (Montreal and Kingston: McGill-Queen's University Press, 2005), pp. 266–67.

Some federations have also had a looser federacy or associate state relationship with certain units. Examples of federacies are the Northern Mariana Islands and Puerto Rico in relation to the United States. Examples of associated states are Bhutan in relation to India and Liechtenstein in relation to Switzerland. In the case of Spain, until 1993, Andorra functioned under the joint rule of Spain and France as a condominium.

4.5 THE REGIONAL DISTINCTIVENESS OF CONSTITUENT UNITS

In some federations, such as Argentina, Austria, Australia, Brazil, Germany, Mexico, the United Arab Emirates, the United States, and Venezuela, where there is clearly a dominant language and relatively low levels of religious or ethnic divisions within the federation, the constituent units have not represented distinct ethnic, linguistic or religious cleavages. In these cases there have often been historical and economic regional differences among the constituent units, but not the depth of distinctiveness engendered by ethnicity, language or religion.

Other federations, such as Belgium, Canada, Ethiopia, India, Nigeria, Russia, Spain and Switzerland, contain constituent units marked by different linguistic, ethnic or religious majorities. In these, the consciousness of regional distinctiveness tends to be particularly sharp. The first such federation was Switzerland, which was established in its current form in 1848, and the second was Canada, established in 1867, but the number of such federations proliferated in the latter half of the twentieth century.

Two strategies have been advocated for dealing with such deep regional cleavages. One is that of weakening potentially divisive ethno-nationalism by designing the constituent units to prevent ethnic, linguistic or religious minorities from becoming majorities within constituent units. Among advocates of this view are Donald Horowitz and Daniel Elazar, building on earlier work by S.M. Lipset and an earlier American tradition going back to James Madison.[2] This strategy grows out of a concern at the sharp divisions and secessionism that strong ethno-

---

[2] D. Horowitz, *Ethnic Groups in Conflict* (Berkeley: University of California Press, 1985), pp. 601–52; D. Elazar, *Federalism and the Way to Peace* (Kingston: Institute of Intergovernmental Relations, Queen's University, 1994), p. 168; S.M. Lipset, *Political Man: The Social Bases of Politics* (Garden City, New York: Doubleday, 1960), pp. 91–2; J. McGarry and B. O'Leary, "Federation as a Method of Ethnic Conflict Resolution," in M. Burgess, ed., *Multinational Federations* (London & New York: Routledge, 2007): 180–211.

nationalism can engender. The objective is to proliferate when possible the multiple points of power away from a focus on ethno-nationalism. Among federations with ethnic, linguistic and religious differences, this specific strategy in the design of constituent units was attempted in India originally in 1950 (although abandoned in 1956) and in South Africa when establishing the boundaries of its nine new provinces.

An alternative strategy has been to accommodate ethnic, linguistic and regional groups by establishing regional units within which they may form a majority with the power to protect and promote their distinctiveness through a measure of self-government.[3] Those advocating this approach see it as reducing interethnic tension by giving each group a sense of security in protecting its distinctiveness. Among federations clearly following this path have been Switzerland, Canada, Belgium, Spain, Russia and Ethiopia. In Switzerland, as noted in chapter 2, most of the cantons are predominantly unilingual and have either a Roman Catholic or Protestant majority. In Canada, the French-speaking population is heavily concentrated in Quebec, where it constitutes about 80 percent of the population; New Brunswick is officially bilingual and the other eight provinces have overwhelming English-speaking majorities. In Belgium, the three constituent units labelled "Communities" clearly represent the Flemish-, French- and German-speaking peoples. The Spanish constituent units, labelled "Autonomous Communities" have permitted the re-emergence of historic nationalities as political entities. While the predominant ethnicity and language in the Russian Federation is Russian, the republics and the autonomous okrugs specifically represent non-Russian ethnic populations. Ethiopia as a federation was explicitly established to recognize its diverse ethnic groups although it was not possible to give every ethnic group its own state and one of the largest states is very multi-ethnic.

It is also significant that over time both India and Nigeria have found it necessary to follow this approach. Originally, the Constituent Assembly of India, fearing it would sharpen divisions, resisted defining the states on the basis of language, but beginning with the *States Reorganization Act in* 1956 and during the following decade, state boundaries were redrawn largely on linguistic lines and in the case of Punjab taking religious differences into consideration; subsequently, the process was continued further to recognize some smaller new states in the northeast. Nigeria, too, which at the time of independence in 1960 consisted of 3 large regional units, has since 1963 progressively increased the number of states to a total of 36, largely defined to reflect distinct linguistic, ethnic and religious groups.

---

[3] W. Kymlicka, *Multicultural Citizenship* (Oxford: Oxford University Press, 1995).

4.6 REFORMING CONSTITUENT UNIT BOUNDARIES

Most federations have a special constitutional amending procedure for altering the boundaries of constituent units and for creating new constituent units. Revising constituent unit boundaries usually requires the consent of the constituent units directly affected. For the creation of new constituent units, this usually requires the consent of any constituent units directly affected or a special majority of all existing constituent units. The reason for these procedures is to assure constituent units that their interests as distinct units will not be vulnerable to federal action. Thus, as a rule, in most federations the redrawing of internal boundaries, once they have been established, is a difficult process.

There are exceptions to this pattern, however. In the United States, Canada, Brazil and Argentina, federal action has created new states or provinces out of former "territories," or provinces have been enlarged by adding former territorial lands to them. In India, the Constituent Assembly, anticipating a need to redraw state boundaries after the immediate crises of independence, partition and the integration of the princely states had been surmounted, provided a particularly flexible constitutional amendment process specifically for this purpose — namely, passage by the Union Parliament by ordinary law.[4] This facilitated the subsequent systematic redrawing of state boundaries from 1956 on. In the case of Nigeria, most of the evolution from the 3 regions of 1960 to the 36 states of today was facilitated by the action of the military regimes when democracy was suspended. The process adopted by Switzerland to define the boundaries of the new canton of Jura out of the canton of Bern is of interest: a series of cascading referendums was used to determine its creation and boundaries.

In the current efforts to merge some constituent units in Russia, referendums have also been used. Under the amendments to the Russian constitution in 2001 and 2005, the territorial integrity of the subjects of the federation is guaranteed: their borders cannot be changed without their consent as well as that of the Federation Council. On the other hand, the subjects of the federation have the right to merge with another subject of the federation to form a new constituent unit. The procedure for such mergers is established by federal law. As of 1 January 2007, referendums had passed approving two mergers involving 5 constituent units reducing the total number of subjects in the federation to 86, and 3 further mergers involving 6 subjects, which would reduce the total to 83, were projected.

---

[4] Such bills can be introduced only by the government, however, and only after the views of the legislatures in the affected states have been obtained.

4.7 FEDERAL CAPITALS

Every federation faces the difficult task of deciding how its federal capital should be governed. The problem is a difficult one because usually it involves a conflict of interests. The federal government usually wishes to control and develop the capital and the seat of federal government in the interests of the federation as a whole. If the capital is itself a member state or comes under the jurisdiction of one of the members states, then that state is in a position to dominate the federal capital, and the control of the federal government over its own seat of government is restricted. On the other hand, the citizens of the capital city usually wish to govern themselves to the greatest extent possible, rather than being controlled by the federal government. These issues are compounded by the fact that federal capitals are often characteristically large and rapidly growing cities with populations spilling beyond the legal boundaries of the central city into the neighbouring territory. The objectives usually sought in the organization of federal capitals include generating a pride throughout the federation in its capital; meeting the needs of the federal legislature, ministries, security and foreign diplomatic representatives; and avoiding the appearance of favouring one particular state or province.

Broadly speaking, there are three main types of constitutional organization for the government of federal capitals: a federal district, a city-state, and government under the jurisdiction of one of the states. Each has its own advantages and peculiar problems.

Many but by no means all federations have established a federal district or territory under the exclusive jurisdiction of the federal government as the way of governing the federal capital. Eight significant examples are Washington, DC (USA), Canberra, the Australian Capital Territory (Australia), the Federal District of Mexico City (Mexico), the Federal District of Caracas (Venezuela), the Union Territory of Delhi (India), the Capital Territory of Islamabad (Pakistan), Abuja Federal Capital Territory (Nigeria) and the Federal Capital City of Addis Ababa (Ethiopia).

Among the advantages of this type of arrangement is that it gives the central government sufficient control over the planning and development of its own capital. Furthermore, it avoids having the laws of any one member state dominating the capital of the whole federation, interfering with the organs of the central government, or imposing its legal and cultural dominance on the federal capital.

Among the disadvantages typical of the federal district type of arrangement is the tendency for there to be too much central control over local residents. In many of these cases (although not all), there is no locally elected government, and in a number of them their residents also do not elect representatives to the federal congress or parliament. There are a few cases, however, such as Caracas, Mexico City and Delhi, where a considerable degree of local self-government is in fact provided. Generally this has worked well, but it can create problems where different political parties dominate the federal government and the elected local council. A further disadvantage with the federal district arrangements is that if they are not made large enough to begin with, problems arise when the urban population spreads beyond their boundaries (e.g., Buenos Aires, Caracas, Mexico City, Washington) especially since boundary changes requiring constitutional amendments are usually difficult to implement.

In terms of the appropriateness of this form of federal capital organization, it exists in both centralized and decentralized federations and for large and small capital cities. It has been a particularly popular arrangement when new capitals have been established where there was previously no significant local population. While this form of capital organization has also been created around existing old cities, general experience suggests that in this type of federal capital organization the predominant legal, financial and political power of the federal governments tips the balance between central control and local interests strongly in favour of the former. It may be worth noting that in a few cases non-capital cities have been given a similar special status in the form of federally chartered cities, an example being Dire Dawa in Ethiopia.

In some cases, the federal capital is given the status of a full-fledged state within the federation. There are four notable examples: Vienna (Austria), Moscow (Russia), Berlin (Germany since reunification 1990), and Brussels (Belgium). The Brussels Capital Region is one of the three regions in Belgium. It should be noted that Brussels also serves as the capital of the EU. There are other cases of federations containing non-capital city-states as full-fledged member states that have worked quite effectively (e.g., Bremen and Hamburg in Germany, and St. Petersburg in Russia). As an arrangement for a federal capital, in contrast to the federal district form of organization, status as a full-fledged member state ensures local self-government while at the same time avoiding subservience to one of the other member states.

The disadvantage of this arrangement is that because of the autonomy intrinsic with full statehood, the federal government is left with minimal control over its own seat of government. Furthermore, because of the usual rigidity of state boundaries, if the area is not big enough at the time of creation, a subsequent spillover of population may create problems with neighbouring states or regions. This is exemplified by the spillover of population from Brussels into the Flemish Region and by the as yet unsuccessful efforts to merge Berlin and Brandenburg in Germany.

Where the capital is very large and has many industrial and other substantial interests not directly related to its functions as a capital, there is a case for this arrangement. To some extent its appropriateness depends significantly on the degree of decentralization in the powers assigned generally to the states. Where the federation is relatively centralized, as in Austria, Germany and Russia, the federal government may have sufficient powers to influence the operation of the capital even though it is a city-state. Where, however, the federation is significantly decentralized, this arrangement may severely limit the scope of the federal government to control and develop its capital.

In some federations there is a third kind of arrangement. The capital city comes under the jurisdiction of the member state within which it is located, in a manner broadly similar to other cities within that state.

Eight examples are Bern (Bern, Switzerland), Ottawa (Ontario, Canada), Kuala Lumpur (Selangor, Malaysia), Bonn (North Rhine Westphalia, Germany, during 1949–90), Madrid (Madrid Autonomous Community, Spain), Basseterre (St. Kitts, St. Kitts and Nevis), Pretoria (Gauteng, South Africa)[5] and Abu Dhabi (Abu Dhabi, United Arab Emirates). In many of these cases, the federal capital is situated in the largest member state, and sometimes, as with Bern, Basseterre and Abu Dhabi, it is also the capital of that state.

Two advantages of this arrangement are that the management of the boundaries of the federal capital with the neighbouring areas is open to flexibility, and that it has usually provided for the general operation of local self-government in the federal capital in the same way as elsewhere in the state of which it is a part.

This arrangement, however, clearly limits the degree to which the federal government can manage the development and control of its own capital city. This has been the case particularly in more decentralized federations such as Switzerland (Bern) and Canada (Ottawa). In the case of Canada, federal government influence over the capital district has been mainly through spending on the National Capital Commission and public works. In such cases, it has required a high degree of voluntary intergovernmental cooperation between the federal government and the canton or province within whose jurisdiction the federal capital falls.

Generally speaking, state-governed federal capitals (especially in decentralized federations) have enjoyed a high degree of self-government, but they have suffered from problems of divided jurisdiction, financial insufficiency, cultural domination by the governing state, and limitations upon the ability of the federal government to control its capital city in the interests of the federation as a whole. In more centralized federations where the scope of the state government jurisdiction is more limited, this has to some extent been less of a problem. One compromise approach is that applied in Malaysia, a relatively centralized federation, where the federal government has used powers assigned to it under the general distribution of powers to legislate a *Federal Capital Act* (1960) for Kuala Lumpur without establishing a federal district or territory and while leaving it otherwise under the jurisdiction of the state of Selangor.

---

[5] Pretoria is the administrative capital, Cape Town is the seat of Parliament, and Bloemfontein is the seat of the Constitutional Court.

To summarize, each of the arrangements for the organization of federal capitals has its peculiar advantages and disadvantages. They also vary according to the general distribution of powers between the federal and member state governments affecting the degree of centralization or decentralization within the federation. The federal district form of organization avoids the situation of placing the federal capital under the dominance of the state in which it is located. But generally, the federal district form of organization has resulted in limited local self-government, although Caracas and Delhi provide examples that this is not inevitable. Because of the tendency for local self-government to be restricted in federal capital territories, where such a form of organization is adopted there has been a need to include specific provisions for local political rights and self-government.

On the other hand, there are numerous examples where federal capitals have operated either as city-states or under the jurisdiction of the state in which they are located. These have generally been marked by greater degrees of local self-government and in the case of federal capitals in a state by greater flexibility of boundaries. But these advantages come at the expense of limited scope for the federal government to control and develop its own capital. The example of Kuala Lumpur, however, indicates that even without creating a federal district, there can be arrangements for giving the central government some exclusive or concurrent jurisdiction over some aspects of the organization of the federal capital in order to allow its needs to be met.

Chapter 5

The Distribution of Authority in Federations

5.1 A FUNDAMENTAL FEATURE OF FEDERATIONS

In all federations, a common feature has been the existence at one and the same time of powerful motives to be united for certain purposes and of deep-rooted motives for autonomous regional governments for other purposes. This has expressed itself in the design of federations by the distribution of powers between those assigned to the federal government for the purposes shared in common and those assigned to the regional units of government for the purposes related to the expression of regional identity. Thus the fundamental defining institutional characteristic of federations has been the constitutional distribution of powers between the federal and regional governments. Furthermore, what distinguishes federations from other forms of federal systems such as decentralized unions or confederations is the constitutional guarantee of autonomy over a certain range of assigned functions for each order of government.

The specific form and allocation of the distribution of powers has varied, however, relating to the underlying degrees and kinds of common interests and diversity within the particular society in question.[1] Different geographical, historical, economic, ecological, security, linguistic, cultural, intellectual, demographic and international factors and the interrelation of these have been significant in

---

[1] See, for instance, Akhtar Majeed, Ronald L. Watts and Douglas M. Brown, eds., *Distribution of Powers and Responsibilities in Federal Countries*, Forum of Federations and International Association of Centres for Federal Studies, *A Global Dialogue on Federalism*, Volume 2 (Montreal & Kingston: McGill-Queen's University Press, 2006) for a recent detailed analysis of the distribution of powers in eleven federations.

contributing to the strength of the motives for union and for regional identity, and therefore have affected the particular distribution of powers in different federations. Generally the more the degree of homogeneity within a society the greater the powers that have been allocated to the federal government, and the more the degree of diversity the greater the powers that have been assigned to the constituent units of government. Even in the latter case it has often been considered desirable, however, that the federal government should have sufficient powers to resist tendencies to balkanization.

In addition to expressing a balance between unity and diversity, the design of federations has also required a balance between the independence and interdependence of the federal and regional governments in relation to each other. The classic view of federation, as enunciated by K.C. Wheare and often quoted in the United States, Switzerland, Canada and Australia, considered the ideal distribution of powers between governments in a federation to be one in which each government was able to act independently within its own watertight sphere of responsibility.[2] In practice federations have found it impossible to avoid overlaps in the responsibilities of governments, and a measure of interdependence is typical of all federations. An example of this in its most extreme form is the interlocking relationship between governments in the German federation which has developed because there most of the federal legislation is administered by the states. Such a strong emphasis upon coordination through joint decision making may carry its own price in terms of reduction in opportunities for flexibility and variety of policy through autonomous decision making by different governments. Indeed, in both Germany and Austria, which represent in extreme form interlocking relationships, there have been recent efforts to disentangle some of these in order to encourage more autonomous initiatives in each level of government. There is therefore a need to find a balance between the independence and interdependence of governments within a federation.

The process by which federations are established may affect the character of the distribution of powers. Where the process of establishment has involved the aggregation of previously distinct units giving up some of their sovereignty to establish a new federal government, the emphasis has usually been upon specifying a limited set of exclusive and concurrent federal powers with the residual (usually unspecified) powers remaining with the constituent units. The United States, Switzerland and Australia provide classic examples. Austria and Germany followed this traditional pattern although their reconstruction during the post-war period did involve some devolution by comparison with the preceding autocratic regimes. Where the creation of a federation has involved a process of devolution

---

[2] See, for instance, K.C. Wheare, *Federal Government*, 4th edn (London: Oxford University Press, 1963), p.14.

from a formerly unitary state, the reverse has usually been the case: the powers of regional units have been specified and the residual authority has remained with the federal government. Belgium and Spain provide examples. Some federations, such as Canada, India and Malaysia, have involved a combination of these processes of aggregation and devolution, and they have listed specifically exclusive federal, exclusive provincial, and concurrent powers with the residual authority, in Canada and India (and the earlier Malayan Federation) but not in the Malaysian Federation, assigned to the federal government.

Note should also be taken of three other sets of factors affecting the distribution of powers in federations. One is the period in which the constitutional distribution of powers was drafted. The eighteenth- and nineteenth-century constitutions of the United States, Switzerland and Canada distributed powers in fairly general terms, while the newer federal constitutions of the latter half of the twentieth or early twenty-first centuries have often included minutely detailed lists of powers and extensive provisions for intergovernmental institutions and processes. Examples are the three lists (exclusively federal, concurrent and exclusively state) of powers in the Seventh Schedule of the Indian constitution containing 97, 47 and 66 entries, respectively, or the very finely detailed distribution scheme in the Swiss constitution of 1999.

Second, the prevalence of a common law tradition (as in the United States, Australia, India, Malaysia and Nigeria), a mixed common law and civil law legal system (as in Canada, South Africa and Nigeria), or a civil law tradition (as in European and Latin American federations such as Switzerland, Germany, Austria, Belgium, Spain, Brazil and Mexico) has had a strong bearing on how the constitutional law is applied and interpreted. In federations where the civil law tradition has prevailed the result has usually been a much more explicit delineation of jurisdiction and a more limited scope for judicial review.[3]

Finally, a factor that has had some impact upon the form and operation of the distribution of powers is the character of the federal legislative and executive institutions (dealt with more fully in chapter 10 below). Whether these institutions are presidential-congressional in form (as in the United States, the Latin American federations and some others) or essentially parliamentary in form (as in most of the other federations) affects the diffused or fused way in which the assigned legislative powers are handled within each level of government and therefore the character of interactions between governments.

---

[3] Majeed, Watts and Brown, op. cit., p. 325; Katy Le Roy and Cheryl Saunders, eds., *A Global Dialogue on Federalism*, vol. 3: *Legislative, Executive and Judicial Governance in Federal Countries* (Montreal and Kingston: McGill-Queen's University Press, 2006), p. 348.

5.2 RELATIONSHIP BETWEEN LEGISLATIVE AND EXECUTIVE AUTHORITY

In some federations, particularly those in the Anglo-Saxon tradition, each order of government has generally been assigned executive responsibilities in the same fields for which it has legislative powers. Classical examples are the USA, Canada and Australia. There are several reasons for favouring such an arrangement. First, it reinforces the autonomy of the legislative bodies. Second, it assures to each government the authority to implement its own legislation which might otherwise prove meaningless. Third, in such cases as Canada and Australia where the principle of parliamentary executives responsible to their legislatures has been adopted, it is only if legislative and executive jurisdiction coincides that the legislature can exercise control over the body executing its laws. Nevertheless, the European parliamentary federal regimes and the Indian parliamentary regime in relation to areas of concurrent jurisdiction and Canada in relation to criminal law, have, however, managed to live with an arrangement where significant areas of legislative and executive jurisdiction have not coincided.

In European federations, particularly Switzerland, Austria and Germany, more commonly administrative responsibility has not coincided with legislative authority, administration for many areas of federal legislative authority being assigned by the constitution to the governments of the constituent units. This enables the federal legislature to lay down considerable uniform legislation while leaving this to be applied by constituent unit governments in ways that take account of varying regional circumstances. Such an arrangement does in practice require more extensive collaboration and coordination between the levels of government, however. In its extreme form as exhibited by Germany and Austria it has created an interlocking relationship between governments at different levels.

In practice the contrast between these two approaches is not quite so sharp. Even in the Anglo-Saxon federations federal governments have delegated considerable responsibilities for federal programs to constituent governments, often by providing financial assistance through grant-in-aid programs. Furthermore, in Canada the constitution itself provides an exception to the general pattern by providing for federal legislation and provincial administration in the sphere of criminal law. Newer federations in former British colonial areas such as India and Malaysia have also provided more broadly in their constitutions for state administration of federal laws made in areas of shared concurrent jurisdiction. The current Russian constitution even stipulates that the federal and unit executive bodies constitute a single system of executive authority within the federation. On the other hand, Belgium contrasts with the other European federations, since the allocation of executive powers is closely tied to the allocation of legislative powers.

The advantage of assigning a responsibility exclusively to one government or another is twofold. It reinforces the autonomy of that government and it makes clear which government is accountable for policy in that area. In practice, however, even where most powers have been assigned exclusively to one level of government or the other, experience, such as that of Switzerland, Canada and Belgium, has indicated that overlaps of jurisdiction are unavoidable because it is virtually impossible to define absolutely, watertight compartments of exclusive jurisdiction. This has, in practice, softened the exclusivity of the allocated powers even where they have been emphasized.

5.3 VARIATIONS IN THE FORM OF THE DISTRIBUTION OF LEGISLATIVE AUTHORITY

EXCLUSIVE LEGISLATIVE AUTHORITY

In most federations some legislative powers are assigned exclusively to the federal government, but the extent of these varies. The allocation of exclusive federal jurisdiction is relatively limited in the United States and Australia, with most federal powers being identified as shared or concurrent powers. In Austria, Germany, India, Malaysia, Argentina, Brazil, Mexico, Nigeria, Russia and Ethiopia, the exclusive jurisdiction assigned to the federal legislature is more extensive, but the distribution of powers in these federations also includes large areas of concurrent jurisdiction.

In some federations, notably Switzerland, Canada, Belgium, India, Malaysia, South Africa and the United Arab Emirates, fields of exclusive jurisdiction of the constituent units are constitutionally defined, but in most other federations the exclusive legislative powers of the constituent units are left undefined as residual powers. The form of the Spanish distribution of powers is distinctive. The constitution lists the exclusive powers of the central government but transfers the determination of the powers of the Autonomous Communities to separate Statutes of Autonomy. Under these, despite an emphasis upon exclusivity in the assignment of the powers of the Autonomous Communities, many areas have required joint governmental intervention.

A notable feature of the constitutions of South Africa, Brazil, Venezuela, and India (as a result of the Seventy-Third and Seventy-Fourth Constitutional Amendments 1992) is the additional constitutional specification of the jurisdiction also of local governments.

CONCURRENT LEGISLATIVE AUTHORITY

The recognition of the inevitability of overlaps in many areas has led to extensive areas of concurrent legislative jurisdiction being allocated in the constitutions of the USA, Australia, Germany, India, Malaysia, Pakistan, Brazil, Mexico, Nigeria, Russia, Ethiopia and Venezuela. This contrasts with Canada, where the only constitutionally specified areas of concurrent jurisdiction are agriculture, immigration, old age pensions and benefits, and export of non-renewable natural resources, forest products and electrical energy.

Concurrency has a number of advantages in federations. It has provided an element of flexibility in the distribution of powers, enabling the federal government to postpone the exercise of potential authority in a particular field until it becomes a matter of federal importance. The constituent governments can thus be left in the meantime to pursue their own initiatives. The federal legislature may use concurrent jurisdiction to legislate federation-wide standards while giving regional governments room to legislate the details and to deliver the services in a manner sensitive to local circumstances. Indeed, in Austria and Germany (and in some respects in Spain, Mexico and Brazil) there is a special constitutional category of jurisdiction specifying a federal power to enact "framework legislation" in certain fields, leaving the Länder to fill out these areas with more detailed laws. In addition, in Germany a constitutional amendment in 1969 added a category of "joint tasks" in relation to higher education, improvement of regional economic structures, and agrarian improvement and coastal preservation in which the federal government would participate in the discharge of Länder responsibilities.

Concurrent lists of legislative power avoid the necessity of enumerating complicated minute subdivisions of individual functions to be assigned exclusively to one area of government or the other, and reduce the likelihood that such minute subdivisions will over time become obsolete in changing circumstances.

Normally where concurrent jurisdiction is specified, the constitution has specified that in cases of conflict between federal law and unit law the federal law prevails. Consequently, areas of concurrent jurisdiction are potentially areas where federal legislation may predominate. One notable exception occurs in Canada where old-age pensions are an area of concurrent jurisdiction but in cases of conflict provincial law prevails over federal law. This has enabled Quebec to preserve its own pension system and other provinces to accept federal pension jurisdiction. The proposed constitution of Iraq, affirmed by the referendum of October 2005, is unique in extending the area of concurrent jurisdiction in which regional law prevails to virtually all areas of concurrent jurisdiction. A problem with the Sudanese constitution is that although it provides for areas of concurrent jurisdiction, no paramountcy or clear criteria are specified for the courts to establish which law should prevail in cases of conflict.

SHARED AUTHORITY

There is a category of powers akin to concurrent authority but distinct from it. "Shared powers" occur where both orders of government have related powers. This is distinct from concurrency over a specific common head of power. An example is the nature of power over environmental matters in many federations. For example in Canada both orders of government have exclusive powers with environmental significance that permit them to regulate large projects, but to proceed with such projects requires the consent of both orders because neither has paramountcy. Similar issues can arise in certain other areas of regulation and lawmaking. It is only when the laws of different orders of government are in direct conflict that the courts may rule on their validity in terms of essence or colouration.

RESIDUAL AUTHORITY

The residual authority represents assignment by the constitution of jurisdiction over those matters not otherwise listed in the constitution. In most federations, especially those created by a process of aggregating previously separate units (although also in some others), the residual power has been retained by the unit governments. Examples are the USA, Switzerland, Australia, Germany, Malaysia, Argentina, Brazil, Mexico, Nigeria, Russia, Pakistan and the United Arab Emirates. In some federations, however, usually where devolution from a more centralized unitary regime characterized the process of federal formation, the residual powers have been left with the federal government. Examples are Canada, India, the Federation of Malaya before it was expanded into Malaysia, South Africa and Belgium, although in the case of Belgium it has been agreed (but yet to be implemented) to reformulate the constitutional distribution of powers so that the residual power lies with the unit governments. In Spain under the 1978 constitution, 5 of the 17 Autonomous Communities were assigned the residual authority, but for the others it remains with the central government. The residual authority in Venezuela is retained by the states, but the 1999 constitution limited this power by granting the federal government a parallel residual competency in taxation.

The significance of the residual powers is related to the number and comprehensiveness of the enumerated lists of legislative power in the constitution. The greater the enumeration of powers, the less the scope of the residual power. Thus in federations such as India, Malaysia, South Africa and to a lesser extent Canada, where the constitutions set out three exhaustive and comprehensive lists of exclusive federal, exclusive provincial and concurrent legislative powers, the residual power has been relatively less significant. By contrast, in federations such as the USA, Australia, Germany, Brazil, Mexico, Nigeria, Russia and Pakistan, where the state powers were not enumerated but simply covered by a substantial unspecified residual power, the scope of the residual authority can be highly significant, although in some cases like Nigeria, Russia, Pakistan, Brazil and Mexico the extensiveness of the federal exclusive and concurrent lists of authority has actually left little room for exclusive constituent unit legislation. The assignment of residual power to the states was intended to underline their autonomy and the limited nature of powers assigned to the federal government. It is important to note, however, that in practice there has been a tendency in these federations for the courts to read the maximum "implied powers" into the specified

federal authority at the expense of the scope of the undefined residual state powers, thus producing a tendency over time towards the progressive centralization of
government powers. Paradoxically, in such federations as Canada, India and Malaysia, where the centralist founders enumerated what were intended to be limited
specific provincial powers, there has been a tendency for the courts to read those
powers broadly, thus tempering the expansion of federal authority.

EMERGENCY OR OVERRIDE POWERS

In a few federations the constitution provides the federal government with specific override or emergency powers to invade or curtail in certain conditions
otherwise normally provincial constitutional powers. These have been the result
of the fears of their founders about the prospect of potential balkanization or
disintegration. The most extensive examples of such quasi-unitary powers are
found in the Indian, Pakistani, Malaysian and Argentine constitutions. During the
Putin presidency, some quasi-unitary powers have also been introduced. The Canadian constitution continues to include the powers of reservation and disallowance
of provincial legislation; the declaratory power relating to public works in the
national interest; and the peace, order and good government clause, but in practice, over the past half-century, almost all of these federal unilateral powers have
fallen into disuse. On the other hand, the extensive emergency powers embodied
in the Indian constitution of 1950 have been frequently used, although the Supreme Court has ruled that the use of this power may be subject to judicial review
and there is now growing political pressure to limit their use. In South Africa the
central government may within certain constraints override provincial legislation
that threatens national unity or national standards.

5.4 THE SCOPE OF LEGISLATIVE AUTHORITY ALLOCATED

In addition to variations in the form that the constitutional distribution of powers
has taken, the particular powers assigned to each order of government have also
varied from federation to federation according to the particular circumstances
and balance of interests within each federation.

Broadly speaking, in most federations international relations, defence, the functioning of the economic and monetary union including currency, customs and
excise, international trade and interstate trade, major taxing powers (although
corporate and income taxes are sometimes shared), interregional transportation,
major physical infrastructure, and pensions have been placed under exclusive federal jurisdiction, or occasionally under concurrent jurisdiction. Social policy
(including primary and secondary education, health services, social welfare and
labour relations), maintenance of law and security and local governments have
usually been assigned exclusively to the constituent unit governments. Parts of

these areas, however, especially those relating to social services and income security, are often shared. Among areas for which the assignment has varied are agriculture, natural resources, postsecondary education, environment, criminal law, civil law, courts and police. In a number of cases these have represented shared responsibilities. While this represents a general pattern, there is considerable variation in the specific allocations within different federations, depending on the degree of emphasis placed upon common action or upon non-centralization as well as the impact of particular circumstances.

Some subject matters have proved particularly troublesome. Foreign affairs is an example.[4] In many federations a sweeping federal jurisdiction over foreign affairs and treaties has sometimes been used to override jurisdiction that would otherwise belong to the governments of the constituent units. In a few federations, however, the federal treaty power has been limited by the requirement that where treaties affect the jurisdiction of regional governments consultation must occur or their consent must be obtained. In the case of Canada, as a result of judicial interpretation of the constitution, implementing provincial legislation is required where treaties relate to fields in the exclusive jurisdiction of the provinces. In Germany such treaties have required the endorsement of a majority in the Bundesrat composed of delegates of the Land governments, and since 1993 the German Basic Law has required extensive consultation or agreement of the Länder with regard to European Union matters. Two of the most recent constitutions, that of Belgium (1993) and Switzerland (1999), assign to their respective constituent units a significant role in the conduct of foreign relations or require their extensive consultation regarding foreign policy decisions.

Coordinating public debt has also sometimes been a problem because a constituent unit government may by its external borrowing affect the credit-worthiness of other governments within the federation. This led in Australia to provision for the coordination of public borrowing by an intergovernmental Loan Council with power to make decisions binding on both levels of government. In some other federations such concerns have led to federal control of public borrowing, particularly foreign borrowing, by constituent unit governments.

Two areas where in practice there has tended to be extensive activity by both levels of government are economic policy and social affairs. In the former, regional units of government have been concerned to ensure the economic welfare

---

[4] See H.J. Michelmann, ed., *Foreign Relations in Federal Countries*, Forum of Federations and International Association of Centres of Federal Studies, *A Global Dialogue on Federalism*, vol. 5 (Montreal & Kingston: McGill-Queen's University Press, forthcoming 2008); J. Kincaid, "Comparative Observations," in J. Kincaid and G.A. Tarr, eds., *Constitutional Origins, Structure and Change in Federal Countries*, Forum of Federations and International Association of Centres of Federal Studies, *A Global Dialogue on Federalism*, vol. 1 (Montreal & Kingston: McGill-Queen's University Press, 2005), pp. 434–5.

of their citizens and to develop policies related to their own particular economic interests. This has sometimes extended to the establishing of trade offices in foreign countries to encourage both trade and investment, a pattern found in such federations as the United States, Canada, Australia and Germany. In the area of social affairs, including health, primary and secondary education and social services, regional governments have usually had primary constitutional responsibility. But, commonly, extensive federal financial assistance has often been necessary because of program costs and because of the pressures for federation-wide standards of service to citizens. Where constituent units have welcomed such federal financial assistance, it has frequently proved to be a Trojan horse for federal dominance.

The increased interrelation of economic and cultural policy in the contemporary world has made the resolution of multi-ethnic issues within federations more complex than in the past. The original simple Canadian solution of 1867, which consisted of centralizing control of economic policy but assigning responsibility for cultural distinctiveness and related social programs to the provinces, has been complicated by two developments. One is the greatly increased cost of social policies requiring federal financial assistance, and the other is the realization by regionally concentrated ethnic groups that their distinctiveness depends not just upon cultural policy but also upon being able to shape economic policies regarding their own welfare. A further complication is that different ethnic groups are never completely demarcated in territorial terms. Consequently, any distribution of powers has to take account of the need to protect minorities within minorities by placing constitutional limits upon state or provincial governments regarding their policies towards internal minorities.

In the distribution of responsibilities within the European Union the principle of *subsidiarity* has been adopted as the basis. This is the principle that only subjects that cannot be adequately dealt with by a lower order of government should be performed by the higher order of government. As a principle, it has had considerable appeal. By itself as a principle, however, it leaves open the issue of who decides on its application to a particular subject matter. This is not merely a technical issue but in many ways may have to do with fundamental values and issues of identity. If the decision is made by the higher order of government, that leaves the lower order vulnerable; while if it is made by the governments of the lower order, they may — despite difficulties — resist transferring responsibility.

5.5 DISTRIBUTION OF ADMINISTRATIVE RESPONSIBILITIES

As noted in section 5.2, in a number of federations, especially those in the Anglo-Saxon tradition (e.g., the USA, Canada and Australia), the distribution of administrative responsibilities in most matters corresponds with the distribution of legislative authority. However, in some federations, as also noted in section 5.2, there are constitutionally mandated and entrenched provisions for splitting legislative and administrative jurisdiction in an area between different orders of government. These permanent and constitutionalized arrangements are to be distinguished from temporary delegations of legislative and executive authority that also occur in many federations. Examples of extensive constitutionalized allocation of executive and administrative responsibilities differing from the allocation of legislative jurisdiction occur in Switzerland, Austria, Germany, India and Malaysia. In all five, autonomous canton and state governments are constitutionally responsible for the implementation and administration of a wide range of federal legislation. In India and Malaysia all federal legislation enacted in the area of concurrent jurisdiction is specified by the constitution as resting with the states for its administration. Thus, while these federations are relatively centralized legislatively, they are much more decentralized administratively. These federations have shown that benefits can flow from the administrative decentralization of federal legislation particularly in adapting it to the different circumstances and sensitivities of the various regions.

5.6 EVOLUTION OF THE DISTRIBUTIONS OF POWERS

Federations are not static organizations, and over time the distribution of powers in each has had to adapt and evolve to respond to changing needs and circumstances and the development of new issues and policy areas. For instance, federations established during the eighteenth or nineteenth centuries have had to work out which governments should be responsible for environmental and energy issues. This adaptation has required a balance between flexibility and rigidity; too much flexibility may undermine the sense of security of regional and minority groups, while too much rigidity may make effective response to changing circumstances difficult.

In seeking the balance, federations have relied on a number of processes with varying emphasis in different federations, as will be discussed in subsequent chapters: formal constitutional amendments (chapter 11), judicial interpretation of the constitution (chapter 11), intergovernmental financial adjustments (chapter 6) and intergovernmental collaboration and agreements (chapter 7).

Some other factors affecting the distributions of powers also considered in subsequent chapters are the extent of symmetry or asymmetry in the allocations of authority (chapter 8), participation in supra-federation federal organizations (chapter 9), and the operation of the federative institutions of federal governments (chapter 10). The cumulative effect of these provides the basis for assessing the overall degree of non-centralization in each federation (chapter 12).

Chapter 6

The Distribution of Finances

6.1 IMPORTANCE OF THE ALLOCATION OF FINANCIAL RESOURCES

The allocation of financial resources to each order of government within a federation is important for two main reasons: first, these resources enable or constrain governments in achieving their policy objectives within their constitutionally assigned legislative and executive responsibilities; second, taxing powers and expenditure are themselves important instruments for affecting and regulating the economy.[1]

6.2 THE DISTRIBUTION OF REVENUE POWERS

A number of sometimes conflicting principles are involved in the effective assignment of revenue-raising powers among governments in federations. Some principles point to the desirability of federal assignment and some to assignment to the constituent units. Among the former are the *administrative* advantages of centralizing certain kinds of revenue levying and collection. Another is *avoiding tax competition* among constituent units that would influence mobile companies and individuals to locate in a particular region. This problem is illustrated by the "tax wars" that occurred in Brazil following the devolution of revenue powers, making necessary a reversal of fiscal decentralization and a "fiscal discipline"

---

[1] For a recent analysis of financial arrangements in twelve federations, see Anwar Shah, ed., *The Practice of Fiscal Federalism*, Forum of Federations and International Association of Centres for Federal Studies, *A Global Dialogue on Federalism*, vol.4 (Montreal & Kingston: McGill-Queen's University Press, 2007).

law enacted in 2000. Another consideration is *equity*. This may require a concentration of revenues in the federal government in order that it may play a redistributive role to avoid sharply different tax levels among constituent units with varied wealth.

On the other side, to enhance *accountability* of governments to their electors, it is often argued that governments should be responsible for raising most of the revenues they spend. Furthermore, some economists favour a measure of *tax competition* as a positive encouragement to better policies among governments. Ultimately there is also the desirability of constituent unit *autonomy* rather than dependency upon federal transfers.

ALLOCATION OF TAX POWERS

Most federations specify in their constitutions (or in the case of Belgium in special legislation) the revenue-raising powers of the two orders of government. These powers may be exclusive, concurrent or shared. Where they are concurrent the paramountcy rules determine the ultimate authority in cases of conflict. Where both orders share a tax field, they can both levy taxes with no constitutional limit, the only constraints being political in the form of the taxpayers' tolerance and the politicians' reluctance to bear the blame.

The major taxing powers usually identified are customs and excise, corporate taxes, personal income taxes and various sales and consumption taxes. Customs and excise taxes have almost always been placed under federal jurisdiction in the interests of ensuring an effective internal customs and economic union. Corporate income taxes have also most often come under federal jurisdiction because corporations in earning their income tend to cross the boundaries of the internal regional units, and the location of their headquarters does not necessarily reflect the geographical sources of their income. Nevertheless, in some federations this taxation may be shared and if so usually comes under concurrent jurisdiction. Personal income taxes may be more directly attributed to location of residence and therefore is often an area shared by federal and regional governments, although in some federations it has been exclusively federal (e.g., Austria and India). Sales and consumption taxes are areas which in most federations both federal and regional governments share, although there are some exceptions to this pattern.

A common characteristic of the allocation of fiscal powers in nearly all federations is that the majority of major revenue sources have been assigned to the federal governments. Even where some tax fields are shared or placed under concurrent jurisdiction, the federal governments tend to predominate because of the federal power to pre-empt a field of concurrent jurisdiction and because of provisions limiting the range of tax sources, both direct and indirect, that regional governments have been assigned. Two factors have been particularly influential in creating this general pattern. One is the concentration of resources in the federal government necessary if it is to perform the redistributive role usually expected of it. The other is the influence of Keynesian theories concerning policies for economic stability and development prevalent at the time when many of the current federal fiscal arrangements were developed in these federations.

Table 9 gives an indication of the degree to which the levying of revenues has been generally concentrated in federal governments and the range of variation. Two points are worthy of note. First, generally in the allocation of revenue powers, federal governments have been favoured over states and local governments. Second, quite clearly, control of revenues has been much more concentrated in the federal governments of more recent emergent federations than in the mature federations. In the mature federations the contemporary range of federally levied revenues as a percentage of total federal, state and local revenues generally ranges from 40 percent in Switzerland to 65 percent in Germany with Australia as the outlier at 75 percent. Historically, however, this has varied with in some cases a much higher federal percentage during the two World Wars. Among emergent federations the contemporary range is from Brazil with 69 percent to Nigeria at 98 percent.

NATURAL RESOURCE REVENUES

One controversial area in a number of federations where natural resources are concentrated in some regions and not in others has been whether the taxing powers and royalties relating to these should lie with the federal or regional governments.[2] Federations had a significant share of global oil (48 percent) and gas (59 percent) in 2006, and therefore the issue of allocation of natural resource revenues has been important in a number of them. Because the concentration of resources in some regions can lead to enormous disparities in the wealth of the constituent units, this has been an extremely contentious issue in such federations as Canada, Nigeria, Russia, Argentina, Mexico, Venezuela and Sudan and has been a source of major contention in the constitutional negotiations in Iraq. In Nigeria and Iraq, petroleum resources account for well over 90 percent of government revenues; in Sudan and Venezuela for well over half and in Russia for about thirty percent.

Natural resource revenues come principally from royalties, license fees, export taxes and corporate taxes. In those federations which are rich in natural resources such as oil, gas, diamonds, and some metals, these are typically extremely unevenly distributed among the constituent units. In some federations the federal

---

[2] The Forum of Federations, Ottawa, is currently conducting under the leadership of George Anderson a study on non-renewable natural resources in federations which is likely to lead to publications commencing in 2008.

government owns these resources and in others the governments of the constituent units. Inevitably there have been sharp debates about who should collect the revenues from these resources and whether they should benefit the federation as a whole or the constituent unit in which they are located, and in the latter case whether they should be taken into account in efforts to equalize the revenues of the constituent units. In Canada, the provinces own their resources, and this has meant that Alberta with its oil resources has vastly more revenue per capita than other provinces. The Canadian equalization systems brings poorer provinces up to the national standard, but does not bring the richer provinces down and it could not afford to bring all provinces to anything close to Alberta's fiscal capacity. Furthermore, the federal government has lost its powers to apply export taxes to energy exports. Consequently, Canada has had a major debate over how to treat natural resource revenues for the purposes of equalization, with poorer resource producing provinces arguing that their equalization entitlements should not be reduced on this account.

When Argentina transferred natural resources to the provinces the result was that some small but resource rich provinces came to enjoy a substantial fiscal advantage. In the United States, most resources are owned by the states or private individuals, but there are also extensive "federal lands" in the western states and Alaska. Alaska's resource revenues have permitted annual payments to citizens.

In most federations with twentieth century constitutions, the federal government largely controls resource development and revenues. In Nigeria where natural resources are the overwhelming source of revenues, the federal government collects these and makes transfers to the states on a variety of criteria of which "derivation" is one. This has meant significant more per capita revenue for the producing states, but because they are underdeveloped and poor they have complained that this share is inadequate. They also want a special share of offshore revenues, though the offshore lies outside state boundaries. In addition, the producing states want a greater say in the actual management of the resources, which has often been done in an environmentally damaging fashion and with little regard for the local population. The seriousness of this issue, complicated by considerable corruption and lack of transparency regarding what happens to resources revenues, has fed a continuing insurgency in the oil-producing region.

In Russia, after a period when it was highly decentralized the federal government has reasserted control of the levying and collection of royalties and export taxes on natural resources. Producing subjects of the federation now get only about 5 percent of the oil revenues and none of the gas revenues. Russia has taken advantage of its very high petroleum revenues to pay off much of its debt and to create a lont-term revenue stabilization fund.

In both Sudan and Iraq the issue of whether resource revenues belong to the country as a whole or to the producing regions has been a highly contentious issue. In Sudan interim, but not fully implemented, revenue sharing arrangements give a per capita larger share to South Sudan, the main source of production. In Iraq, where oil is the main source of revenue, the constitution has left ambiguous the issues of where control of oil revenues should lie, thus prolonging controversy over the issue.

Mexico has a highly centralized regime based upon a state oil company and in 2006 committed one half of surplus revenues (those exceeding the five-year mean price) to be shared between the states and municipalities.

A particular issue in many federations is control over offshore resources. Typically, courts have found that state boundaries do not extend beyond the highwater mark or, at most, the three mile territorial limit. However, the economic zone extends to two hundred miles and even beyond in some cases. In most federations the federal government has retained control of offshore management and resources, though Canada has effectively given both to the adjacent provinces. In the United States, some states, using their control of the shoreline, have been able to impose moratoriums on offshore development for environmental reasons. There is a major debate over oil and gas development on federal lands, notably in Alaska.

OTHER REVENUE RAISING ISSUES

In some federations, notably Spain and Belgium, different financial arrangements apply to different sets of constituent units. In Spain the "common" system applies to 15 of the 17 Autonomous Communities, but for the two *foral* Autonomous Communities of Basque and Navarre there is a "special" scheme based on longstanding ancient rights. For the former, the major taxing powers remain with the federal government and although some taxes have been devolved, the major sources of revenue for the Autonomous Communities lie in revenue sharing and equalizing grant transfers from the federal government. The functioning of the financial system for the *foral* Autonomous Communities is radically different, entailing maximum tax autonomy for these constituent units and transfers to the federal government for the services it provides. Belgium also has two financial systems, one for the Regions and one for the Communities. That for the Regions involves some measure of regional taxes (28 percent of regional revenues), while the Communities are almost totally dependent on federal transfers (see table 11).

In addition to taxation there are two other important sources for governmental raising of funds. The first is public borrowing, a source open to both levels of government in most federations, although foreign borrowing in some cases (most notably Austria, India and Malaysia) is placed under exclusive federal jurisdiction. In the case of Australia, all major public borrowing by both levels is coordinated through the operation of the intergovernmental Loan Council. The second source is the operation of public corporations and enterprises, the profits of which may serve as a source of governmental income. In most federations this latter is a revenue source for both levels of government.

6.3 THE ALLOCATION OF EXPENDITURE POWERS

Broadly speaking, the distribution of expenditure powers in each federation corresponds to the combined scope of the legislative and administrative responsibilities assigned to each government within the federation. But several points should be noted.

First, where the administration of a substantial portion of federal legislation is constitutionally assigned to the governments of the constituent units as in Switzerland, Austria, Germany, India and Malaysia, the constitutional expenditure responsibilities of the regional governments are significantly broader than would be indicated by the distribution of legislative powers taken alone.

Second, the expenditure requirements of different areas of responsibility may vary. For instance, in relative terms health, education and social services are higher-cost functions by comparison with functions relating more to regulation than the provision of services.

Third, in most federations the *spending power* of each order of government has not been limited strictly to the enumerated legislative and administrative jurisdiction. Governments have usually been taken to possess a *general* spending power.[3] Thus, federal governments have used their general spending power to pursue certain objectives in areas of state jurisdiction by providing grants to regional governments that otherwise could not afford to provide the services being demanded of them. For their part, constituent unit governments in a number of federations have used their general spending power to establish trade promotion offices outside the federation even where there was no constitutional jurisdiction in external affairs specified.

The use of the federal spending power in areas of exclusive provincial jurisdiction has been politically contentious in Canadian intergovernmental relations but has not been successfully challenged in the courts. The courts have ruled that federal spending is not limited solely to areas of legislative jurisdiction assigned by the constitution. Consequently, federal governments in Canada have frequently used their spending power to make grants in support of provincial programs in order to encourage provinces to implement federal priorities and to undertake direct spending in such areas as culture, research and student aid. Provincial governments have complained that this unilateral use of the federal spending power undermines their autonomy in areas assigned by the constitution exclusively to

---

[3] For a fuller comparative analysis of the spending power in federal systems, see Ronald L. Watts, *The Spending Power in Federal Systems: A Comparative Study* (Kingston: Institute of Intergovernmental Relations, Queen's University, 1999).

them. The practice is not unique to the Canadian federation, however. It has occurred extensively in the USA and Australia since the economic depression of the 1930s. Regional governments in federations have frequently accepted the federal assistance, but where it has taken the form of grants with conditions attached they have resented this as an invasion of their areas of exclusive jurisdiction. This has particularly been the case where federal spending on matters within regional authority is commenced uninvited or is withdrawn without notice. In both Canada and the United States such unilateral withdrawals of assistance have lead to charges of "off loading" and of "fend-for-yourself federalism."

It should be noted that in some older federations such as the United States and Canada, where the use of the federal general spending power has been widespread, the constitution does not explicitly identify a general spending power. Nonetheless, their courts in varying degrees have recognized that the taxing and appropriating powers of the federal governments can be used to affect a field of activity beyond the strict confines of their normal legislative powers. Some federal constitutions, such as Australia, India and Malaysia, designed in the light of practice in older federations, have made explicit recognition in their constitutions of the authority of their federal governments to provide grants to state governments for *any* purpose, whether that purpose is under federal government jurisdiction or not. In other federations, however, there are limits upon the exercise of a general spending power. In Spain, for example, the Constitutional Court in 1992 (judgment no. 13) permitted a federal spending power in areas of exclusive jurisdiction of the Autonomous Communities, but only within certain limits. In Switzerland the constitution generally does not permit federal spending in areas of exclusive cantonal jurisdiction, although the only check on such spending would be by referendums (rather than court rulings) and these have not occurred. In Germany federal decisions on spending affecting the Länder require a weighted majority of Länder votes in the Bundesrat, the second chamber composed of delegates of the Länder. Belgium explicitly limits spending of governments to areas of legislative competence.

In those federations where the constitution assigns to the state governments administrative responsibility for a considerable portion of federal legislation, substantial federal transfers, either as portions of federal tax proceeds or in the form of unconditional and conditional grants, are a typical feature.

Table 10 shows the cumulative level of federal expenditures as a percentage of total federal, state and local expenditures after intergovernmental transfers in a large number of federations. By comparison with the distribution of revenues (in table 9) the range of variation is considerably less, although generally the federal proportion of expenditures has been higher in the emergent federations than in the mature federations. In most federations the federal portion of expenditures falls between 45 and 60 percent, with Malaysia above that and Belgium, Germany, Canada and Switzerland below it.

TABLE 9: Federal Government Revenues before Intergovernmental Transfers
as a Percentage of Total (Federal-State-Local) Government
Revenues

	2000–04
Nigeria	98.0
Mexico	91.3
Russia	91.0
Malaysia	86.9
South Africa	82.0
Australia	74.8
Belgium	71.0
Spain	69.2
Brazil	69.2
Germany	65.0
Austria	61.8
India	61.1
United States	54.2
Canada	47.2
Switzerland	40.0

Note: Revenue shares are before intergovernmental transfers and represent "own-source" revenues. In cases of revenue sharing, revenue sources have been allocated according to the government that has the power to levy and set rates (usually the federal government). Figures are rounded to one decimal point. Countries are listed broadly in descending order of centralization. Depending on source, these figures are the latest available between 2000 and 2004.

Sources for Tables 9–13: Various country statistics from Department of Finance websites and statistics bureaus adjusted for comparability. Also OECD Centre for Tax Policy and Administration, *Fiscal Federalism Network*, 2002; IMF Government Finance Statistics, various years; Anwar Shah, *A Global Dialogue on Federalism*, vol.4: *The Practice of Fiscal Federalism: Comparative Perspectives* (Montreal & Kingston: McGill-Queen's University Press, 2007); M.M. Guijale and S.B. Webb, *Achievement and Challenges of Fiscal Decentralization: Lessons from Mexico* (World Bank, 2000); A. Jimoh, "Fiscal Federalism: The Nigerian Experience," in Economic Commission for Africa, *Fiscal Policy and Growth in Africa: Fiscal Federalism, Decentralization and Incidence of Taxation* (Addis Ababa, 7–9 October 2003); M. Nicolas, "Financial Arrangements between the Australian Government and the Australian States," *Regional and Federal Studies*, 13:4 (2003): 153–82; E.L. Gibson, ed., *Federalism and Democracy in Latin America* (Baltimore & London: John Hopkins University Press, 2004); R.L. Watts, *Dencentralization and Recentralization: Recent Developments in Russian Federalism* (Kingston: Institute of Intergovernmental Relations, Queen's University, Working Paper 2007(2)).

TABLE 10: Federal Government Expenditures after Intergovernmental Transfers as a Percentage of Total (Federal-State-Local) Government Expenditures

	2000–04
Malaysia	84.3
Brazil	59.5
Nigeria	59.7
Australia	59.3
Mexico	58.7
Austria	55.0
Spain	51.0
South Africa	50.0
Russia	46.0
United States	45.9
India	44.6
Belgium	38.1
Germany	37.0
Canada	37.0
Switzerland	32.0

Note: Expenditures are after transfers of shares of federal taxes and grants to state and local governments. Figures are rounded to one decimal point. Countries are listed broadly in descending order of centralization. Depending on the source, these figures are the latest available between 2000 and 2004.

Sources: See table 9.

6.4 THE ISSUE OF VERTICAL AND HORIZONTAL IMBALANCES

Virtually every federation has found the need to correct two kinds of financial imbalances. The vertical imbalances occur when constitutionally assigned federal and unit government revenues do not match their constitutionally assigned expenditure responsibilities. These imbalances occur generally for two reasons. First, it has usually been found desirable to allocate the major taxing powers to the federal government because they are closely related to the development of the customs union and more broadly to an effective economic union, while some of the most expensive expenditure responsibilities such as health, education and social services have usually been considered best administered on a regional basis where particular regional circumstances can be taken into account. Tables 9 and 10 read together illustrate the differences in the proportions of total (federal-state-local combined) revenues and of total (federal-state-local combined) expenditure responsibilities of federal governments in the different federations. A second reason for vertical imbalances is that no matter how carefully the original designers of the federation may attempt to match the revenue resources and expenditure responsibilities of each order of government, over time the significance of different taxes change (such as income taxes and consumption taxes) and the costs of expenditures vary in unforeseen ways. Consequently, there is a need to build in processes whereby these imbalances can be adjusted from time to time.

Horizontal imbalances represent a second form that requires correction. Horizontal imbalances occur when the revenue capacities of different constituent units vary so that they are not able to provide their citizens with services at the same level on the basis of comparable tax levels. In addition to horizontal revenue imbalances, there can also be interprovincial imbalances on the expenditure side due to differences in the "expenditure needs" of different constituent units because of variations in sociodemographic characteristics of their populations, such as population dispersion, urbanization, social composition and age structure, and the cost of providing services affected by such factors as the scale of public administration and the physical and economic environment.

6.5 THE ROLE OF FINANCIAL TRANSFERS

In order to correct these imbalances most federations have arrangements for financial transfers from one level of government to another. Because federal governments generally have controlled the major tax sources, adjustments have usually taken the form of transfers from the federal to the regional units of government. Their purpose has been both to remove vertical imbalances by transfers in the form of tax-shares, unconditional block grants or specific-purpose conditional grants, and to remove horizontal imbalances through assistance to poorer units. Table 11 gives an indication of the significance of these transfers as a portion of total provincial or state revenues and the degree of resulting provincial or state dependence on transfers. As the table indicates, there is an enormous variation among federations in terms of their reliance and dependence upon intergovernmental transfers.

It should be noted that in tables 9 and 11, revenue sharing of the proceeds of federal taxes, even when constitutionally required, has been classified as an "intergovernmental transfer" rather than as "own-source" revenues of the states. Many analyses adopt the latter interpretation, but that is misleading because the states do not control the size of these proceeds when the federal government levies these taxes and sets the rates. In a few cases, notably the "ceded" taxes in Spain, some freedom to adjust tax levels and exemptions in relation to the federal taxes has been given to the Autonomous Communities, but such arrangements are relatively unusual.[4]

Revenue sharing of particular federal taxes as a form of unconditional transfers to the constituent units has often been favoured over simple unconditional grants, because in the former the proceeds normally grow in proportion to the growth in the federal tax, whereas in the case of unconditional grants growth requires a deliberate decision by the federal government. In some federations revenue sharing for the states is drawn from a pool of federal taxes, the most

TABLE 11: Intergovernmental Transfers as a Percentage of Provincial or State Revenues

	2000–04
South Africa	96.1
Nigeria	89.0
Mexico	87.9
Spain	72.8
Belgium – Communities 96.5	68.0
Regions 57.4	
Austria	47.4
India	46.0
Australia	45.6
Germany	43.8
Malaysia	30.4
Brazil	30.0
United States	25.6
Mexico	25.4
Russia	25.0
Switzerland	24.8
Canada	12.9

Note: Figures are the latest available between 2000 and 2004, and are rounded to one decimal point. Countries are listed in descending order of dependence on federal transfers.

Sources: See table 9. Also M. Verdonck and K. Deschouwer, "Patterns and Principles of Fiscal Federalism in Belgium," *Regional and Federal Studies*, 13:4, (2003): 91–110.

---

[4] V.R. Almendral, "Fiscal Rights for Communities in the Spanish Constitution," *Federations*, 6:1 (2007): 16–20

complete form of this being the Federation Account in Nigeria from which federal, state and local allocations are drawn. In practice, the Indian Finance Commissions have also come to treat most central revenues as a pool for sharing, but where in Nigeria the transfers from this pool represent nearly the totality of state revenues (89 percent), in India the states still raise about 54 percent of their own revenues (table 11).

6.6 CONDITIONAL OR UNCONDITIONAL TRANSFERS

The degree of provincial or state dependence is affected not only by the proportion that federal transfers represent in their revenues but even more by whether these transfers are conditional or unconditional in character. Federal transfers to regional units of government may have conditions attached to them in order to influence how they are spent. This "golden lead," as it is referred to in Germany, may however undermine the autonomy of the regional units of government, especially if conditional transfers constitute a high proportion of the transfers and hence a significant portion of total state or provincial revenues. To avoid this, transfers may take the form of unconditional transfers (either through revenue sharing by set percentages of certain federal tax proceeds, as occurs in many of the newer federations, or unconditional block grants). Although strictly comparable statistics are difficult to obtain, there is clearly a considerable variation among federations in the extent to which federal transfers have been conditional or unconditional. Table 12 setting out conditional transfers as a percentage of federal transfers indicates an enormous range here too in the proportion of conditional transfers, ranging from 100 percent in the United States to around 6 percent in Belgium. This variation reflects differences in the emphasis upon accountability in the expenditure of federal funds or upon the importance of constituent unit autonomy. There are also differences in the specificity of the conditions set for conditional grants. While those in the United States and Australia tend to be highly specific, those in Canada have been so general as to be virtually unconditional. The figure for Canada in table 12 depends on whether the Canadian Health and Social Transfers (CHT/CST), which are at most semi-conditional in character, are regarded as conditional or unconditional. If these transfers are classified as conditional, the comparable Canadian figure for the proportion of transfers that are conditional is 65 percent, as shown in the table; but if they are classified as unconditional, the proportion would be 27 percent.

The proportion of total state or provincial revenue made up by federal conditional transfers provides one significant measure of the constraints upon state or provincial autonomy. As table 13 indicates, in most federations conditional transfers constitute between 10 and 26 percent of total state or provincial revenues, with Mexico, Spain and Austria as higher outliers and Brazil, Belgium and Russia as lower outliers.

TABLE 12: Conditional Transfers as a Percentage of Federal Transfers

	2004
United States	100.0
Austria	78.9
Switzerland	73.1
Spain	66.1
Canada	64.9[‡]
Germany	64.5
Mexico	55.5
Australia	40.9
India	40.7
Malaysia	39.3
Brazil	25.0
South Africa	11.5
Russia	9.0
Belgium – Communities 5.0	5.7
Regions 6.1	

Note: Depending on source, figures are the latest available between 2000 and 2004, in descending order conditionality.

[‡] The CHT/CST transfer is included here as conditional; if treated as unconditional because of the very general nature of the conditions, the figure for Canada would be 26.8 percent.

Sources: See tables 9 and 11.

Arguments have been advanced in support of both forms of transfer. In support of conditional grants has been an argument which has particularly tended to dominate discussion of the subject in the United States. This is based on the principle of financial responsibility and accountability, i.e., that the federal government, which has the nasty task of raising the funds by taxation, should in the interests of accountability to the tax-payer, control and set the conditions for the use of these funds by the state governments. Consequently, in recent decades, conditional grants have predominated in the federal transfers in the United States.

Countering this, however, is the concern to which more attention has been paid in some other federations that conditional grants are likely to undermine the autonomy of the regional units of government by inducing them to undertake expenditures not necessarily in tune with their own priorities. Furthermore, in those federations where the regional units of government have parliamentary executives responsible to their own legislatures, it has been argued that these

Comparing Federal Systems

TABLE 13: Federal Conditional Transfers as a Percentage of Total
Provincial/State Government Revenues

	2000–04
Mexico	48.8
Spain	41.9
Austria	37.4
United States	25.6
India	18.7
Australia	18.6
Switzerland	17.0
Canada	14.1[‡]
Malaysia	12.0
South Africa	11.0
Germany	9.8
Brazil	7.5
Belgium – Communities 4.8	4.0
Regions 3.5	
Russia	2.5

Note: Depending on source, figures are the latest available between 2000 and 2004.
‡ CHT/CST transfer is included here as conditional; if treated as unconditional because
of the very general nature of the conditions, the figure for Canada would be 3.7 percent.
Sources: See tables 9 and 11.

governments can be held responsible for the use of unconditional transfers through
their accountability to their own legislatures and hence electorates. These arguments have led in the case of most parliamentary federations to a significantly
lower reliance upon conditional transfers and a higher proportion of unconditional transfers than in the United States where members of the Congress have
focused on securing identified benefits for their states or districts rather than leaving
discretion to the state administrations.

6.7 EQUALIZATION TRANSFERS

The importance of "equalization" transfers lies in the view that all citizens within
a federation should be entitled to comparable services without having to be subject to excessively different tax rates. The need for such transfers has arisen in

most federations from a recognition that disparities in wealth among regions within a federation are likely to have a corrosive effect on cohesion within a federation. Indeed, it is for this reason that in most European federations equalization transfers have been labelled "solidarity" transfers.

The arrangements for equalization transfers have varied from federation to federation and these are set out in summary form in table 14. Several points are especially noteworthy. First, the extent of the equalization transfers varies considerably. Most federations, with the exception of the United States and Mexico, have some formal equalization scheme, but the scope of such transfers has been greater in some (such as Germany, Canada and Australia) than in others (such as Switzerland).

Second, in all but the German case and in the proposed Swiss reforms, equalization is achieved totally by redistribution effected by federal transfers to the poorer regional units of government. Germany has been unique in providing constitutionally for interstate transfers to cover a substantial portion for adjusting horizontal imbalances. Initially this was the sole method of equalization in Germany, but later, federal transfers in the form of supplementary per capita payments derived from the Value Added Tax (VAT) have provided a substantial further equalizing redistribution. Similarly, the proposed reforms for Switzerland include an element of intercantonal payments.

Third, in Canada the effort to correct horizontal imbalances through federal equalization payments has focused primarily on adjusting for differences in the revenue capacities of the provinces. While this approach is typical of many federations, in some and most notably in Australia, there has been considerable effort to account as well for equalizing expenditure imbalances.

Fourth, the form of equalization transfers to regional units of government varies. There are those that are based on an agreed formula, e.g., Switzerland, Canada, Germany, Austria, Malaysia, Belgium and Spain (although in some of these cases the federal government dominates the process of arriving at an agreement). In others, notably Australia, India, South Africa and Nigeria, the allocations have been based largely on the recommendation of standing or periodic independent commissions (which may themselves use a variety of formulae to arrive at their recommendations).

Fifth, in some circumstances there may be a relationship between the degree of decentralization in a federation and the need for equalization arrangements. The more fiscally decentralized a federation is and the greater the interstate disparities in revenue capacity and expenditure need, the greater is likely to be the need for equalizing mechanisms to promote horizontal balance.

Sixth, the size of regional fiscal disparities varies greatly among federations, and where these are large it is harder for the federal government to afford to apply full equalization. Furthermore, the ability of the federal government to afford full equalization is affected by the extent to which revenue sources are centralized.

TABLE 14: Equalization Arrangements

United States	No coherent generalized equalization scheme; some equalization occurs from the cumulative effect of provisions in specific federal grant-in-aid schemes as approved by Congress.
Switzerland	Federal transfers: based on formulae involving a range of criteria ranking cantons by financial capacity and need as the basis for tax-sharing and conditional grants, but the equalizing transfer system is smaller than in Germany, Canada and Australia. Reform of fiscal equalization as of 2008: grants will cover burdens of urban areas, mountain regions, and poorer cantons (lifting to within 85% of the national average) and will include an element of intercantonal transfers.
Canada	Federal transfers: equalization scheme based on formula (adjusted from time to time) assessing provincial revenue capacity in terms of a representative set of provincial taxes and non-tax revenue sources against a middle-range five-province standard and providing unconditional grants representing 42% of all transfers. Reform of equalization as of 2007: move towards equal per capita cash payments for federal block funding transfers to all provinces and some restoration of formula-based equalization to correct recent non-formula modifications.
Australia	Federal transfers: based between 1933 and 1981–82 on recommendations derived from determination of needs of claimant states by a standing independent Commonwealth Grants Commission; from 1981/2 to 2000, transfers took the form of adjustments to the general Adjustment Grant based on calculation of relativities of revenue capacities and of expenditure needs among states; since 2000, the federal government has collected a goods and services tax (GST) that funds General Purpose Payments to the states. Allocation is based on calculation of revenue capacity and expenditure needs from comparisons of 18 revenue categories and 41 expenditure categories.
Germany	Primarily interstate transfers (62%): equalization through an interstate revenue pool to which rich Länder pay and from which poor Länder draw according to a formula; plus federal transfers (38%): Federal Supplementary Payments of 1.5% of value-added tax (VAT). The primary per capita distribution of the shares of the Länder of a portion of the VAT also has an equalizing effect. Forthcoming reforms under negotiation will address the prevention and management of budget crises and realigning revenue-raising capabilities with expenditure responsibilities.
Austria	Federal transfers: Länder receive a per capita federal grant sufficient to bring their average per capita tax revenue up to the national average (a little more than half the Länder qualify). The primary distribution of Land shares of federal taxes also has an equalization effect.
India	Federal transfers: based on recommendations of quinquennial independent Finance Commissions recommending share of federal taxes and distribution of unconditional and conditional grants to fill gaps in state revenues, taking account of differences among states in population, per capita income, area, economic and rural infrastructure needs, and tax effort. However, Planning Commission transfers for specific projects tend to counter equalization effects.

... continued

TABLE 14 (*continued*)

Malaysia	Federal transfers: determined by federal government following consultation with intergovernmental National Finance Council and based on a combination of unconditional shares of certain federal taxes and unconditional and conditional per capita grants.
Belgium	Before 2000: federal transfers: a "national solidarity" unconditional grant was paid to Regions where personal income tax revenue per capita is below the national average (to adjust for the receipt by Regions of a percentage of personal income taxes on the basis of derivation). Since 2000: allocation of the shared portion of personal income tax is based on the regional yield of the tax and the increase in the amount at the same pace as inflation and growth in GNP.
Spain	Federal transfers: since 1987 criteria including population, size, personal income, fiscal effort, number of internal provinces within Autonomous Community, and distance to state capital; applied by federal government to shares of federal tax revenue transferred to Autonomous Communities.
Brazil	A Revenue Sharing Fund of the States and a Revenue Sharing Fund of the Municipalities are derived from revenue sharing of three main federal taxes: personal income taxes, corporate income taxes, and the selective VAT. The distribution of these among the states and municipalities is mainly based on redistributive criteria, but horizontal inequalities in the distribution of fiscal resources remain highly significant.
Mexico	Multiple programs of revenue sharing and unconditional and conditional grants with various criteria and no coherent equalization objective. However, the net effect of more than 20 unrelated individual transfer programs plus own-source revenues reveals considerable horizontal balance.
Nigeria	Federal transfers assigned by the National Assembly with distribution among states based on criteria specified in the constitution: population (and population density), equality of states, internal revenue effort, land mass, terrain, rural road/inland waterway, potable water, education, health, and at least 13 percent based on derivation (to reflect resource revenues). The appropriate allocation of revenues from natural resources remains highly contentious. The emphasis upon equality of states (40 percent of transfers) has meant that because of large differences in the size of the states per capita revenues have in fact varied sharply.
Russia	Federal transfers: formula-driven equalization transfers from the Fund for Financial Support of Regions. Changes to regional fiscal capacity equalization methods and whether support to extremely weak constituent units should be under strict federal control remain a much-discussed topic in Russia today. In practice equalization is up to about 60 percent of the wealthiest constituent units.
South Africa	Federal transfers: based on the recommendation of the independent Finance and Fiscal Commission to meet the constitutional requirement of "equitable" division among provinces and municipalities. The Commission has developed a formula taking account of specific factors of demography and economic activity.

Seventh, it would appear that the different federations vary in terms of the tolerance of their citizens for horizontal imbalances and their emphasis upon "derivation" as the basis of distribution of transfers. For example, egalitarian Australia, which is blessed with relatively modest interstate disparities in revenue capacity, goes to great lengths to equalize fully on both the revenue and expenditure aspects. Germany also provides nearly full equalization, at least on the revenue side. The United States, with relatively large interstate disparities but no formal equalization system at all, appears to have a much greater tolerance for horizontal imbalances. Canada lies somewhere between these two extremes. It has a substantial equalization program that, because of the particularly large revenue disparities among the provinces, only delivers partial equalization. One factor affecting variations in the tolerance for horizontal imbalances in different federations is the relative value placed upon equity as opposed to provincial autonomy and non-centralization. Another factor is the extent of the opportunities for interjurisdictional mobility within the federation and the value placed on mobility, a feature lessening the pressure for equalization arrangements in the United States.

Eighth, because they involve a redistribution of resources among constituent units, the operation or modification of equalization arrangements is often controversial involving conflicting positions among the wealthy and poorer constituent units within a federation.

It should be noted that in addition to equalization transfers to poorer states, some redistribution within federations may be effected through the regional location of direct federal government spending. Examples are direct federal spending on major infrastructure projects, military expenditure or transfers to individuals for social welfare. In such cases the location of federal spending is usually determined by political consideration rather than constitutional requirements.

6.8 PROCESSES AND INSTITUTIONS FOR ADJUSTING FINANCIAL ARRANGEMENTS

Because, as already noted, the values of revenue resources and expenditure responsibilities change over time, federations have found it necessary to establish processes and institutions to facilitate dealing regularly with vertical and horizontal imbalances. Table 15 summaries the arenas in which these issues have been fought out in different federations. It is noteworthy that in those federations characterized by a separation of executive and legislative powers within each order of government, such as the United States, the primary arena is the federal legislature. In the other federations characterized by fused parliamentary executives, the primary arena has been that of executive federalism, i.e., negotiations between the executives representing the federal and regional units of government.

TABLE 15: Arenas for Resolving Issues of Federal Finance

United States	Congress: negotiations among representatives of different states in Congress over allocation of grant-in-aid programs; representatives of state administrations act as lobbyists.
Switzerland	Federal Parliament: negotiations within Federal Council (i.e., federal executive) and Parliament (containing cantonal representatives) but with extensive consultation of the Conference of Cantonal Governments, and assisted from time to time by commissions.
Canada	Processes of executive federalism predominate. Ultimate decision lies with federal government and federal legislation, but in practice for each five-year period renewal is preceded by extensive federal-provincial negotiations through officials and federal and provincial finance ministers to arrive at an agreed program. Recently, disputes over previous equalization modifications led to an independent commission (2006 Expert Panel on Equalization and Territorial Finance).
Australia	Processes of executive federalism predominate. Ultimate decision lies with federal government and federal legislation, but equalization transfers from the GST pool are based on recommendations of an independent expert Commonwealth Grants Commission (CGC), whose recommendations are usually implemented, the recommendations being made within a context established by an intergovernmental ministerial council.
Austria	Executive federalism: intergovernmental negotiation with dominant federal government role, but federal second chamber is composed of representatives of state legislatures.
Germany	Executive federalism: ultimately fiscal arrangements require endorsement by a majority in the Bundesrat, which is composed of delegates of governments of Länder.
India	Ultimate decision lies with Union government, but constitutionally mandated quinquennial independent Finance Commissions make recommendations for the total state share of shared central taxes and for unconditional grants to states, and for distributions of both among states. Recommendations have in practice usually been implemented. These transfers are supplemented by substantial conditional grants allocated on the recommendation of the Planning Commission.
Malaysia	Executive federalism: dominant role of federal government, but it is constitutionally required to consult National Finance Council which includes a representative of each state.
Belgium	Interparty coalition bargaining within the federal government and intergovernmental negotiation.

... continued

TABLE 15 (*continued*)

Spain	Executive federalism: regional financial arrangements are negotiated every five years in the Fiscal and Financial Policy Council, an intergovernmental ministerial body with the decisions made by a qualified majority vote in which the vote of the two central government ministers is equal to that of all the regional councillors. Legally an advisory body but in practice decisive.
Brazil	General lack of institutional structures for financial arrangements except for the National Council for Fiscal Policy (CONFAZ) for coordinating the fiscal and tax policies of the states, but in practice this performs purely formal functions. Ultimate approval is by Congress where the smaller states have disproportionate influence.
Mexico	Lack of institutional structures. In response to dissatisfaction with fiscal federalism at the sub-national level, the federal government introduced a "New Federalism" program that sought to transfer resources to states and municipalities, to reduce the discretionary power of the federal government in the allocation of funds, and to simplify and clarify the process of resource distribution to states and municipalities.
Nigeria	Allocations from the Federation Account to the federal, state and local governments are based on recommendations of the National Revenue Mobilization, Allocation and Fiscal Commission (NRMAFC), but ultimately must be approved by the National Assembly.
Russia	Intergovernmental negotiation determines revenue flows, leading to an ineffective dispute-resolution process dominated by the federal government.
South Africa	Ultimate decisions lie with the national government, but an independent Financial and Fiscal Commission (FFC) of 22 members, of whom 9 are appointed by provinces and 2 by local governments, is mandated by the constitution to make recommendations on the "equitable shares" for state and for local governments and on the formula for distribution. These are reviewed by the Budget Council and the Budget Forum (both intergovernmental councils). In practice, the FFC has been treated by the Finance Ministry of the national government largely as an advisory body.
Ethiopia	A joint session of Parliament has to vote by a two-thirds majority on tax powers not specifically assigned by the constitution separately or jointly to one or both orders of government. The House of Federation determines the formula for subsidies states are entitled to receive from the federal government. Revenues from joint federal and state tax sources and subsides provided by the federal government to the states are also determined by the House of Federation based on recommendations made by the Committee of Revenue Sharing.

In terms of the processes for adjusting issues of federal finance, four distinct patterns can be identified.[5] In Australia and India, although in different form, expert commissions established by the federal government have been entrusted with the primary task of determining distributive formulae. That in Australia is a standing commission, while that in India is quinquennial and established by constitutional requirement. These commissions hear representations from the state governments and report to the federal government which normally follows their recommendations. South Africa with its Financial and Fiscal Commission follows this general pattern, but in practice the central Finance Ministry has more often departed from the Commission's recommendations, thus weakening its value as an independent authority. Nigeria has had a long history of finance commissions dating back to the Phillipson Commission of 1946, and up to the National Revenue Mobilization, Allocation and Fiscal Commission since 1989. A feature of the current Nigerian financial arrangements, derived from the original concept of a "Distributive Pool" introduced by the Raisman Commission in 1958, is that nearly all of the revenues are levied by the federal government, though most of them go into a Federation Account. Allocations are made from this Federation Account to the federal, state and local governments on the recommendation of the National Revenue Mobilization, Allocation and Fiscal Commission although these allocations must ultimately be approved by the National Assembly.[6]

A second pattern is the constitutional provision for an intergovernmental council composed of federal and state representatives, the Malaysian National Finance Council and the Pakistan quinquennial National Finance Commission being examples.

A third pattern is exemplified by Germany, Austria, Switzerland, Belgium, the United States, Brazil and Argentina, where grants to the states are determined by the federal legislature, but since there are formal representatives of the states in the federal legislature, state representatives are involved in the approval process (although arrangements vary in these federations).

A fourth pattern is found in Canada, where the determination of equalization formula, other tax transfer programs and tax agreements, are under the control of the federal government whose legislature contains no provision for formal representation of regional governments. Nevertheless, because of the importance of

---

[5] Richard M. Bird, "A Comparative Perspective on Federal Finance," in Keith G. Banting, Douglas M. Brown, and Thomas J. Courchene, eds., *The Future of Fiscal Federalism* (Kingston: School of Policy Studies, Institute of Intergovernmental Relations, John Deutsch Institute for the Study of Economic Policy, Queen's University, 1994), pp. 304–5.

[6] J. Isawa Elaigwu, *The Politics of Federalism in Nigeria* (Jos: Aha Publishing House, 2005), pp. 243–316; J. Isawa Elaigwu, ed., *Fiscal Federalism in Nigeria: Facing the Challenges of the Future* (Jos: Aha Publishing House, 2007).

these issues, federal-provincial financial relations have been a matter for extended discussion in innumerable committees of federal and provincial officials, and are the source of much public polemics between federal and provincial governments.[7] From time to time a key role has been played by commissions such as the Rowell-Sirois Commission and much more recently by an advisory panel on equalization.

In virtually all federations, but most notably Australia, India, Malaysia, Nigeria, South Africa, Germany and Canada, a variety of intergovernmental councils, commissions and committees have been developed to facilitate adaptation of the financial arrangements. Australia has gone furthest in developing such institutions with three intergovernmental institutions worth noting here. The Premiers Council plays a key role in deliberations on the transfers but is not a body established by the constitution. The Loan Council, which coordinates federal and state borrowing, was established by a constitutional amendment in 1927 and can make decisions binding both levels of government. The Commonwealth Grants Commission is a standing body that since 1933 has advised the Australian federal government on equalization transfers. In India, too, intergovernmental institutions have played an important role, both the Finance Commissions primarily concerned with correcting vertical and horizontal imbalances and the Planning Commission concerned with development projects having set the pattern of transfers to the states. In Germany, the Bundesrat and its committees, because of the unique character of this federal second legislative chamber composed of the delegates of the Land executives, has played a key role in intergovernmental deliberations relating to the adjustment of the financial arrangements. In other federations, including Switzerland and Belgium, periodic commissions have from time to time advised governments on the adjustment of intergovernmental financial arrangements.

---

[7] Bird, "A Comparative Perspective," 305.

Chapter 7

Intergovernmental Relations

7.1 IMPORTANCE OF PROCESSES FOR INTERGOVERNMENTAL COLLABORATION

The inevitability within federations of overlaps and interdependence in the exercise by governments of the powers distributed to them has generally required the different orders of government to treat each other as partners. This has necessitated extensive consultation, cooperation and coordination between governments.[1]

The institutions and processes for intergovernmental collaboration serve two important functions: conflict resolution and a means of adapting to changing circumstances.

Furthermore, intergovernmental relations have two important dimensions. One is that of relations between the federal and unit governments. The other is that of inter-unit relations. Typically in federations both kinds of intergovernmental relations have played an important role.

---

[1] See, for instance, R. Agranoff, "Autonomy, Devolution and Intergovernmental Relations," *Regional and Federal Studies*, 14:1 (2004): 25–65; Forum of Federations, *Intergovernmental Relations in Federal Countries* (Ottawa: Forum of Federations, 2001); R.L. Watts, *Executive Federalism: A Comparative Analysis* (Kingston: Institute of Intergovernmental Relations, Queen's University, 1989); J. Kincaid and G.A. Tarr, eds., *Constitutional Origins, Structure, and Change in Federal Countries* Forum of Federations and International Association of Centres for Federal Studies, *A Global Dialogue on Federalism*, vol. 1 (Montreal & Kingston: McGill-Queen's University Press, 2005), pp. 438–9; K. Le Roy and C. Saunders, eds., *Legislative, Executive and Judicial Governance in Federal Countries* Forum of Federations and International Association of Centres for Federal Studies, *A Global Dialogue on Federalism*, vol. 3 (Montreal & Kingston: McGill-Queen's University Press, 2006), pp. 375-8.

Within each of these dimensions relations may commonly involve all the constituent units within the federation, regional groupings of units, or be bilateral (i.e., between the federal government and one regional unit or between two regional units).

7.2 FORMS AND EXTENT OF INTERGOVERNMENTAL RELATIONS

An important element of intergovernmental relations that occurs within federations is carried out informally through various means of direct communication (e.g., by letter and telephone) between ministers, officials and representatives of different governments at various levels with each other.

In addition to these there are in most federations a range of more formal institutions to facilitate intergovernmental relations, such as those we have already noted in section 6.8 above relating to financial relations. These have usually taken the form of a variety of standing and ad hoc meetings involving ministers, legislators, officials and agencies of different governments. A noteworthy feature, especially in parliamentary federations where first ministers and cabinet ministers responsible to their legislatures tend to predominate within both levels of government, is the prevalence of "executive federalism," i.e., the dominant role of governmental executives (ministers and their officials) in intergovernmental relations. The institutions and processes of executive federalism have usually developed pragmatically rather than by constitutional requirement, but in such federations as Canada, Australia, Germany, India and Malaysia they range extensively from meetings of officials to councils of ministers and to first ministers' meetings.[2] Within some federations there have been well over five hundred such committee, council and conference meetings a year. These meetings have provided institutional processes for consultation, negotiation, cooperation and, on occasion, joint projects. Not uncommonly, where executive federalism has been the characteristic mode of intergovernmental relations, governments have each established their own internal specialized intragovernmental organizations to coordinate their relations with other governments within the federation.

An interesting development in Australia was the establishment in 1992 of the Council of Australian Governments to oversee the collaborative processes and particularly to make the operation of the Australian economic union more effective,

---

[2] While in most federations the institutions and processes for intergovernmental relations have developed pragmatically, in South Africa an Intergovernmental Relations Framework Act was enacted in 2005 (Act No. 13 of 2005). See *Intergovernmental Relations Framework Act: Evolution and Practice* (Pretoria: Department: Provincial and Local Government, Republic of South Africa, 2005)

but after an active period in its first few years its influence has varied with the emphasis put on its activities by the Australian prime minister. Another interesting development was the intergovernmental cooperative framework established in Canada in the form of the "Framework for Improving the Social Union for Canadians" signed by the federal government and nine of the provinces (but not including Quebec) on 4 February 1999. This was intended to commence a new era of federal-provincial cooperation, collaboration and information-sharing in creating and financing social programs and includes a dispute resolution mechanism. Proceeding with this framework without the participation of Quebec because of the difficulty of obtaining an agreement with the Quebec government of the day marked an implicit recognition, however, of the need for asymmetry in the relationships within the Canadian federation.

Among contemporary federations, executive federalism in intergovernmental relations is probably the most extensively developed in Australia and Germany, with the Bundesrat serving as the centrepiece in the latter. In India, the activation of the Inter-State Council (provided for in the 1950 constitution) recognized in the 1990s the increased importance of processes for formal intergovernmental relations within a federation marked by multiple political parties.

While executive federalism has not developed in Spain as far as in Australia, Canada and India, a Council of Autonomous Community Presidents was formed recently, and it has biannual meetings with the federal prime minister. Nevertheless, multilateral networks as opposed to bilateral relations between Madrid and the communities are still relatively underdeveloped. This may have been influenced by the bilateral laws governing relations with each community.

Where there has been a separation of legislative and executive powers within each government of a federation, as in the United States, the Latin American federations and Switzerland, channels for intergovernmental relations have been more dispersed. These have involved a variety of channels between executives, administrators and legislators in different governments often in crisscrossing patterns. A notable feature has been the extensive lobbying of federal legislators by various state and cantonal representatives.

Nevertheless, some presidential regimes have had strong executives. Notable examples are Russia under the Putin regime, some Latin American federations such as Mexico up to 2000, currently Venezuela, Nigeria since 1999, Ethiopia, and Pakistan in the early years under President Musharraf. In a number of these cases the presidential power has been derived from the dominance of a presidential party that is in control of the federal legislature.

An important factor affecting the character of intergovernmental relations within a federation is the character of the political party regime. Where a single party (or alliance) has dominated politics within both orders of government, as in India in the early decades with the Congress party, in Malaysia with the Alliance party, in Mexico up to 2000 with the predominance of the PRI, and currently in South Africa and Ethiopia, federal party leaders have had great influence over the party leaders and organizations in the constituent units. In these cases, many of the intergovernmental issues have been virtually dictated by the federal government or have been resolved through party channels. In federations where different parties predominate within different levels, as has often been the case in Canada, Australia, and in recent years India, the formal intergovernmental processes and institutions have been the major channels for negotiating cooperative arrangements.

The need for extensive intergovernmental relations has been further increased in those federations where there is a constitutional requirement that a considerable portion of federal legislation must be administered by the governments of the regional units. This has been a major factor contributing, for example, to the "interlocked federalism" for which Germany is especially noted.

As already noted in section 6.8, in most federations intergovernmental institutions and processes have been particularly important for the regular adjustment of financial arrangements and transfers.

In virtually every federation intergovernmental relations have had both vertical and horizontal dimensions. In addition to relations between the federal and constituent unit governments there have been inter-unit relations. These have often dealt with cross-boundary issues affecting neighbouring states or provinces, for example, jointly shared rivers, transportation routes or environmental issues. In addition there are often efforts by regional groupings of states or provinces to cooperate. Sometimes inter-unit efforts at cooperation have been extended even more broadly to encompass all the states or provinces within a federation to deal cooperatively with issues of wider scope without resort to the centralizing impact of relying on federal government action. Such efforts in Switzerland have been referred to as "federalism without Bern" and in the United States as "federalism without Washington." The confederal character of the decision making involved has sometimes limited the success of such arrangements, however. Nevertheless, similar proposals in Canada have recently been the focus of considerable attention. Furthermore, in 2003 the premiers in Canada established a new formal interprovincial Council of the Federation comprising the 13 premiers of the ten provinces and three territories not only to foster interprovincial cooperation but to enable a common stand in negotiations with the federal government. This precedent has influenced a similar development in Australia. In Switzerland similarly, the Conference of Cantonal Governments has for some time been playing an increasingly important role in collective negotiations with the federal government.

7.3 OTHER DEVICES FOR FLEXIBILITY AND ADJUSTMENT IN THE DISTRIBUTION OF POWERS

In most federations, the distribution of powers between the federal and regional unit governments is embodied in a relatively rigid constitution which is difficult to amend (see section 11.4). Indeed in most established federations comprehensive constitutional amendment has proved extremely difficult as the experience of such efforts in Canada, Switzerland, Germany and Austria has made clear. This has required the resort to a variety of devices for flexibility and adjustment.

In those federations such as the United States, Australia, India and Malaysia where the constitution sets out extensive areas of concurrent jurisdiction this has provided a degree of flexibility and cooperation in areas of shared jurisdiction. It should be noted, however, that concurrency can also contribute to intergovernmental competition and conflict when processes for partnership in these areas are not developed.

Another device for flexibility is that of intergovernmental delegation of powers. The earlier federations did not expressly provide for this and as a result courts have sometimes limited the scope for the delegation of legislative powers. Australia and most of the federations created later in the twentieth century enhanced their flexibility by including express constitutional provisions enabling delegation of legislative as well as administrative authority in either direction.

Yet another device for flexibility is the concept of "opting-out" or "opting-in" to the exercise by a government of certain legislative powers. Examples in the Canadian *Constitution Act, 1867* are section 94A enabling provincial legislation to override federal legislation on pensions and survivors' benefits, and section 94 relating to federal legislation for uniform property and civil rights applying in those provinces which assent. Another Canadian example of an "opting-in" provision is section 23(1)(a) of the *Charter of Rights and Freedoms* relating to certain minority educational rights which do not apply in Quebec until authorized by the Quebec legislative assembly (section 59). Elsewhere similar provisions available to all constituent units but enabling *de facto* asymmetry have existed in Spain and Belgium.

In a number of federations, the practice of formal intergovernmental (federal-state or interstate) agreements and accords has been developed. This has been a subject much discussed in recent decades in Canada where the Macdonald Commission advocated the inclusion of a provision allowing for the constitutional entrenchment of federal-provincial agreements. The notion of interstate agreements finds its origin in the United States constitution. The arrangement there permits two or more states to enter into an agreement for joint action, becoming effective upon receiving congressional consent. Interstate agreements have been used in a number of federations by the regional units as a way of taking joint action where there is a consensus without calling upon direct intervention by the federal government.[3]

---

[3] J. Poirier, "The Functions of Intergovernmental Agreements: Post-Devolution Concordats in a Comparative Perspective," *Public Law* (spring, 2001): 134–57.

7.4 COOPERATIVE VERSUS COMPETITIVE FEDERALISM

The unavoidability of interdependence and the need for intergovernmental institutions and processes to deal with this has led to an emphasis on "cooperative federalism" within most federations. But equally significant is the concept of "competitive federalism." In many federations, but particularly in Germany during the past decade as the internal interlocking relationships of the federation have come under critical review, there has been considerable debate about the relative merits of "cooperative" and "competitive" federalism.[4] Analysis indicates that there are benefits and costs associated with each approach.

"Cooperative federalism" contributes to the reduction of conflict and enables coordination, but when it becomes "interlocking federalism," to the extent experienced for example in Germany, it may lead to what Scharpf has called the "joint decision trap" which reduces the autonomy and freedom of action of governments at both levels.[5] Furthermore, where "executive federalism" predominates, it may limit the role of legislatures. Nevertheless, virtually every federation has found that it is impossible to isolate the activities of the different levels of government in a federation into watertight compartments. Given the unavoidability of overlaps of jurisdiction, cooperative federalism in the form of intergovernmental collaboration has proved necessary in all federations. The question remains, however, to what degree such intergovernmental cooperation may, if extensive, limit the opportunity for autonomous action and initiative by each order of government.

Advocates of "competitive federalism" argue that competition between governments in a federation may actually produce beneficial results for citizens. For example, Albert Breton in his supplementary note to the Macdonald Commission Report in Canada argues that just as economic competition produces superior benefits compared to monopolies or oligopolies, so competition between governments serving the same citizens is likely to provide citizens with better service.[6] He equates "cooperative federalism" with collusion directed at serving the interests of governments rather than of citizens. Competition among governments may

---

[4] Ralf Thomas Baus, Raoul Blindenbacker, and Ulrich Karpen, eds., *Competition versus Cooperation: German Federalism in Need of Reform – A Comparative Perspective* (Baden-Bade: Nomos Verlagsgesellschaft, 2007).

[5] F. Scharpf, "The Joint Decision Trap: Lessons from German Federalism and European Integration," *Public Administration* 66 (autumn 1988): 238–78.

[6] Albert Breton, "Supplementary Statement," in Royal Commission on the Economic Union and Development Prospects for Canada, Macdonald Commission, *Report*, vol. 3 (Ottawa: Supply and Services Canada, 1985), pp. 486–526. On competitive federalism, see also Daphne A. Kenyon and John Kincaid, eds., *Competition among States and Local Governments: Efficiency and Equity in American Federalism* (Washington, D.C.: The Urban Institute Press, 1991).

take vertical (federal-state) or horizontal (inter-state or inter-provincial) forms. In the case of the latter, advocates of competition often criticize equalization arrangements because they suppress competition, thus producing Länder inefficiencies. But it must be noted that, while competition does not necessarily equate with conflict, "competitive federalism" to excess, as Canadian experience indicates, can lead to intergovernmental conflict and acrimony and have a divisive impact within a federation.

It should be noted that virtually all federations combine elements of cooperation and competition. Thus, for instance, while the culture of cooperation has been important in Switzerland, there is considerable tax competition among the cantons. Federations generally are characterized simultaneously by elements of cooperation, collaboration, coordination, collusion, competition and conflict coexisting and changing over time. The extent to which elements of cooperation or of competition prevail among governments within different federations has varied, however. In some, such as Switzerland, Germany and South Africa, there is a strong "culture of cooperation" which in some respects has been enshrined as a principle in the constitution. In others, such as Canada, Australia, India, Brazil, Nigeria, Comoros, Mexico and St. Kitts and Nevis, intergovernmental relations have to varying degrees tended to be competitive and conflictual, although all of them have found some measure of cooperation unavoidable. The differences have tended to reflect the divisions within their societies and the character of party politics.

7.5 IMPLICATIONS FOR THE DEMOCRATIC CHARACTER OF FEDERATIONS

Excessive "cooperative federalism" may undermine the democratic accountability of each government to its own electorate, a criticism frequently voiced about executive federalism in Germany, Australia and Canada. But while, as noted above, there is some democratic value in competition among governments to serve their citizens better, competition to excess can be harmfully divisive. As is usually the case in federations, the need for balance seems to be the keynote. It has usually been found that there needs to be a combination of cooperation to avoid the harmful effect of conflict in areas of interdependence, and of competitive bargaining among governments, each aiming through autonomous action to serve better the interests of its citizens.

In these circumstances, most federations have attempted to reinforce the direct democratic accountability of their representatives in intergovernmental negotiations through the development of internal procedures, processes and legislative committees within each level of government rather than by restricting intergovernmental collaboration.

Chapter 8

Symmetry and Asymmetry in Federations

8.1 POLITICAL AND CONSTITUTIONAL ASYMMETRY DISTINGUISHED

Two kinds of asymmetry among regional units may affect the operation of federations. One, which is characteristic of all federations and might be described as *political* asymmetry, arises from the impact of cultural, economic, social and political conditions affecting the relative power, influence and relations of different regional units with each other and with the federal government. The other, which exists in some but not all federations and which might be labelled *constitutional* asymmetry, refers specifically to the degree to which powers assigned to regional units by the constitution of the federation are not uniform.

8.2 POLITICAL ASYMMETRY

Political asymmetry among full-fledged constituent units exists in every federation.[1] Among the major factors are variations in population, territorial size, economic character, and resources and wealth among the regional units. Table 8 (in chapter 4) gives an indication of the variation in population between the largest and smallest units within the federations in descending order of the ratio between the largest and smallest regional units. The impact of this factor lies in the relative power and influence within these federations of the larger regional units, especially

---

[1] C.D. Tarlton was the first to draw attention to this feature. See C.D. Tarlton, "Symmetry and Asymmetry as Elements of Federalism: A Theoretical Speculation," *Journal of Politics*, 27:4 (1965): 861–74.

where one or two dominate, and in the relative powerlessness of the smallest member units. Both can be a source of internal resentment and tension in the political dynamics within federations. A particularly serious source of tension has existed in those federations where a single unit has contained over half the federation's population, almost invariably a source of instability. Examples have already been noted in section 4.3 above. They include Jamaica (with 52 percent of population) within the short-lived West Indies Federation 1958–62, East Pakistan with 54 percent within Pakistan prior to its secession (and Punjab Province with 56 percent of the population within Pakistan after that), Russia within the former USSR, the Czech Republic within Czechoslovakia prior to the separation of 1992, Serbia within Serbia and Montenegro with 92 percent, the Flemish Region with 58 percent within the current Belgian federation, the Bosniac-Croat Federation as an entity within Bosnia and Herzegovina with 61 percent, Grande Comore within Comoros with 51 percent, Chuuk within Micronesia with 50 percent, and St. Kitts within St. Kitts and Nevis with 76 percent. Each of these cases has created serious tensions. Examples where two member provinces or states have had a preponderant influence within a federation include Abu Dhabi and Dubai in the UAE (combined population 67 percent), Ontario and Quebec in Canada (combined population 62 percent), Oromia and Amhara in Ethiopia (combined population 61 percent), and New South Wales and Victoria in Australia (combined population 59 percent).

By contrast with these instances of relatively large and dominant regional units within federations, as table 8 indicates, most federations also contain among their full-fledged regional units some very small ones. Most notable in terms of the population ratio between largest and smallest units are India, the European Union, Ethiopia, Belgium, Canada and Switzerland. In some federations, the desirability of reducing the asymmetry in the size of the constituent regions has led to pressures for the redrawing of unit boundaries, as in Nigeria (where the number of units has been progressively increased from 3 regions to 36 states and one territory) or in Pakistan in 1956 (where the number of provinces was reduced from 4 provinces to 2). Among other federations where the constituent units have been reshaped are Germany during the early years of the West German Republic and in East Germany at the time of reunification. In Belgium, the federalization process of the past three decades has included the delineation of the Flemish, Walloon and Brussels Regions and of the Dutch-, French- and German-speaking Communities. Most recently, South Africa in the 1990s reconstituted its regional structure into 9 provinces. Asymmetry in terms of the territorial size and per capita wealth of regional units within individual federations are other factors that have reinforced the picture of unit political asymmetry among the units within federations generally.

These asymmetries are politically significant for two reasons. First, they affect the relative capacity of different regional units to exercise their constitutionally assigned powers. Second, they affect the degree of a regional unit's influence within those institutions of the federal government in which representation is based on population (such as the first chambers of the legislature, to which in parliamentary federations the federal executive is responsible).

Generally speaking, some political asymmetry has existed in every federation, but where it has been extreme it has been a source of tension and instability. Furthermore, political asymmetry has often induced efforts at corrective measures. These have included moderating the political influence of larger regional units at the federal level by establishing a federal second legislative chamber with representation weighted to favour smaller regional units, and assisting less wealthy regional units by redistributive equalization transfers (see section 6.7 and table 14).

8.3 CONSTITUTIONAL ASYMMETRY

Constitutional asymmetry refers specifically to differences in the status or legislative and executive powers assigned by the constitution to the different regional units.

As indicated in the introduction and in table 2, and noted in chapter 4, many federations have a variety of units with relationships to the federation substantially different from that of the full-fledged units of regional government. These have taken the form of federal capital districts, federally administered territories, or peripheral federacies and associated states.

In most federations the formal constitutional distribution of legislative and executive jurisdiction and of financial resources applies symmetrically, however, to all the *full-fledged member states*. Nevertheless, there are some instances where the constitution explicitly provides for constitutional asymmetry in the jurisdiction assigned to full-fledged member states. Where this has occurred the reason has been to recognize significant variations among the full-fledged constituent units relating to geographic size and population or to their particular social and cultural composition and economic situation.

There have been basically three approaches to establishing constitutional asymmetry in the distribution of powers within federal systems. One has been to increase from the norm the federal authority (i.e., to reduce regional autonomy) in particular member states for certain specified functions within the federal system. Such arrangements have existed in India and the short-lived Federation of Rhodesia and Nyasaland (1953–63).

The second approach has been to increase from the norm the jurisdiction of particular member states (i.e., to increase regional autonomy). The most sustained example of this approach has been the concessions made to the Borneo states when they joined the Malaysian federation in 1963. Certain matters which come under federal government jurisdiction elsewhere in the Malaysian federation, such as native laws, communications, shipping and fisheries, were made matters of exclusive state or concurrent jurisdiction in Sabah and Sarawak. Other matters,

such as immigration, remained under federal authority, but in these the approval
of a Borneo state is required when a policy is applied to one of those states. In
India there have been similar adjustments in constitutional jurisdiction applied to
the state of Jammu and Kashmir and to some of the newer small states that contain distinct ethnic groups. Canada from the beginning has had a measure of
constitutional asymmetry, principally related to denominational and linguistic
guarantees in education, the use of French in the legislature and the courts, and
the civil law.

TABLE 16: Constitutional Asymmetry of Full-Fledged Constituent Units in
Federal Systems

Symmetrical Units	*Asymmetrical Units*
Argentina	Belgium
Australia	Bosnia-Herzegovina
Austria	Canada
Brazil	Comoros
Ethiopia	European Union
Germany	India
Mexico	Malaysia
Micronesia	St. Kitts and Nevis
Nigeria	Spain
Pakistan	
South Africa	
Switzerland	
United Arab Emirates	
United States	
Venezuela	

Note: There are large variations in the degree of asymmetry in the federations listed in
the second column.

There is a third constitutional approach for permitting asymmetry in the jurisdiction and powers exercised by certain member states. That is one in which the
constitution is formally symmetrical in giving all the member states the same
jurisdiction, but includes provisions that permit member states in certain cases to
"opt in" or "opt out" of these assignments. These provisions enable governments
to take up the full exercise of their autonomy at different speeds. Such arrangements retain the formal symmetrical application of the constitutional distribution
of powers to all member states, but provide specific means for accommodating
within that framework a *de facto* asymmetry among member states in the exercise
of these powers. In Canada sections 94 and 94A of the *Constitution Act, 1867* and

section 23(1)(a) of the *Charter of Rights and Freedoms* in the *Constitution Act, 1982* have been such constitutional provisions. Thus, at a practical level, Quebec as a province within Canada has enjoyed a degree of legislature asymmetry when compared with other provinces (exemplified by the Quebec Pension Plan) and administrative asymmetry (it collects it own income tax, for example). The Meech Lake Accord 1987 and the Charlottetown Agreement 1992, which were proposals for a comprehensive revision of the Canadian constitution, contained provisions for more asymmetry relating to Quebec, but these were not enacted. The Spanish approach has been to recognize variations in the pressures for autonomy in different regions by granting to each Autonomous Community its own statute of autonomy tailored to is particular set of compromises negotiated between Madrid and the regional leadership. These agreements are nonetheless set within a framework in which it is anticipated that eventually there will be less asymmetry among them.

Among the examples of federal systems not yet mentioned which have exhibited some degree of constitutional asymmetry in the application of jurisdiction are the European Union, Russia and Belgium. The European Union, in negotiating the accession of each new member, has often had to make particular concessions. Furthermore, in order to get agreement upon the adoption of the Maastricht Treaty, the European Union found it necessary to accept a measure of asymmetry in the full application of that treaty, most notably in the cases of Britain and Denmark. Perhaps the most complex current example of constitutional asymmetry within a federal political system occurred in the variety of powers which the 89 component units (such as republics, oblasts, okrugs, etc.), constituting the Russian Federation were able to negotiate during the Yeltsin presidency. Within a formally symmetrical constitutional framework, many of the constituent units within Russia concluded bilateral treaties providing for asymmetrical treatment. Under the Putin presidency there has, however, been a policy to cancel these treaties and to return to more symmetrical arrangements. In the Belgian Federation, constitutional asymmetry exists not only in the differences in jurisdiction of the three territorial constituent Regions and the three non-territorial constituent Communities, but also in the interrelation between Regional Councils and Community Councils, since the Flanders Region and the Flemish Community have merged their institutions. Bosnia and Herzegovina consists of two entities, one of which is itself a federation (the Bosniac-Croat Federation) and the other is the unitary Republic of Srpska.

Two of the micro-federations, Comoros and St. Kitts and Nevis, have established asymmetric constituent units by arranging that the largest island (Grande Comore in the former and St. Kitts in the latter), unlike the other islands does not have its own separate legislative assembly, that purpose being served by the federal assembly. In a small federation this arrangement reduces institutional duplication and complexity, but in both cases it has contributed to internal tensions.

An important factor influencing the powers and autonomy that member states in a federation are able to exercise is the constitutional allocation of financial resources. As the extensive literature on fiscal federalism has invariably emphasized, where there has been initial symmetry in the constitutional allocation of financial resources in federations it has often produced sharp variations in the wealth and fiscal capacities of their member states. Consequently, in many federations there have been efforts to reduce the corrosive effect on unity of such disparities and to enhance federal cohesion by formal schemes for the redistribution and equalization of resources among the member states (see section 6.7 for details). Thus, redistributive asymmetrical transfers have been employed to make the fiscal capacities of the member states more symmetrical. In the case of Spain, furthermore, two quite distinct financial arrangements have been established for the 15 "common" Autonomous Communities and the two *foral* Autonomous Communities of the Basque Country and Navarre (see section 6.2).

Proposals for constitutional asymmetry have sometimes, most notably in Canada, raised the question whether greater autonomy of jurisdiction for some member states should affect the representation of those states in the federal institutions. For example, should representatives from the more autonomous member states be restricted from voting within the federal institutions on those matters over which the federal government does not have jurisdiction in their particular member state? A rational argument can be made for such a *quid pro quo*, and the issue has recently been intensely debated in Canada as a consideration if Quebec were to be granted significant asymmetric legislative authority. The issue has also been raised in the United Kingdom as a result of the implementation of Scottish devolution. There would, however, be serious complexities in trying to operate a system of responsible cabinet government if cabinets had to rely on different majorities according to the subject matter under deliberation. In any case, in no federation to date have adjustments actually been made in federal representation or voting by state or provincial representatives within the federal institutions on such grounds.

Clearly, constitutional asymmetry among the regional units within a federation introduces complexity. Nevertheless, some federations have found that the only way to accommodate the varying pressures for regional autonomy has been to incorporate asymmetry in the constitutional distribution of powers. The most notable of such cases are Malaysia, Canada, India and Belgium. In some other cases, asymmetry has proved useful as a transitional arrangement accommodating regions at different stages of political development. Examples are the arrangements within Spain for the various Autonomous Communities and the concept of a Europe of "variable geometry" proceeding at "varying speeds." In some cases, pressures for asymmetry have induced intense counter-pressures for symmetry, for example, in Canada and Spain, and these examples suggest that there may be limits beyond which extreme asymmetry may become dysfunctional. Nevertheless, in at least some federations it appears that the recognition of constitutional asymmetry has proved an unavoidable way of accommodating major differences between constituent units in the relative pressures for autonomy.

Chapter 9

Multilevel Federal Systems

9.1 MEMBERSHIP IN SUPRA-FEDERAL ORGANIZATIONS

A notable feature in the contemporary world is the membership of a number of federations within wider federal organizations. One particular example is the membership of Germany, Belgium, Austria and Spain in the European Union. Membership in the European Union, itself a hybrid which is predominately confederal in character but has some of the characteristics of a federation, has had implications for the internal relationships within those European Union member states which are themselves federations. Among the issues that have arisen has been the role of the regional units within each of these federations in negotiations with the institutions of the European Union. This has led to the establishment by regional units within the member federations of offices at the European Union capital in Brussels and to their direct representation in the Committee of Regions of the European Union. The result has been a new element of complexity in inter-governmental relations in these federations. The impact upon the federal-regional balance within each federation of the transfer of certain powers to Brussels has also on occasion become a contentious issue, most notably in Germany.[1] There it led to an important case before the German Constitutional Court. It should also be noted that concern about the impact of membership in the European Union upon the character of the Swiss federation has been a factor in the resistance within Switzerland to joining the European Union.

---

[1] R. Hbrek, "Germany," in A.L. Griffiths, ed., *Handbook of Federal Countries, 2005* (Montreal & Kingston: McGill-Queen's University Press, 2005), pp. 157–8.

Other illustrations of federations in wider supra-federation organizations are the membership of Canada, the United States, and Mexico (all three themselves federations) within the North American Free Trade Area (NAFTA), Malaysia in the Association of South East Asian Nations (ASEAN), and India and Pakistan (both at the time federations) in the South Asian Association for Regional Co-operation (SAARC). In each of these cases membership in the wider organization has had implications for the internal organization and balance within the member federations.

Traditionally, the analysis of federations has centred upon relations between their federal and state governments. But increasingly in the contemporary world, federal arrangements have taken on a multi-tiered character. It has been the effort to maximize citizen preferences or reduce their frustrations that has led to the establishment of multiple levels of federal organization each operating at a different scale for performing most effectively their particular functions.[2] The resulting multi-tiered federal systems have created a more complicated context for the operation of individual federations participating in these wider forms of federal organization.

9.2 THE PLACE OF LOCAL GOVERNMENTS

While considering the trend to multi-tiered federal systems, it should be noted that there has been increasing attention given also to the role of local governments within federations.[3] Traditionally, the determination of the scope and powers of local governments was left in federations to the intermediate state governments. The importance and autonomy of the tier of local government has varied enormously from federation to federation being perhaps most prominent in Switzerland and the United States and least in Australia. Furthermore, in some federations intergovernmental relations directly between federal and local governments have been considerable, whereas in others (including Canada) such relations have been funnelled through the provinces or states as intermediaries. It is worth noting that there have been efforts in some federations, notably Germany, India (since constitutional amendments in 1992), Nigeria (in its 1999

---

[2] J.R. Pennock, "Federal and Unitary Government: Disharmony and Reliability," *Behavioral Science*, 4:2 (1959): 147–57.

[3] See, for instance, N.Steytler, ed., *The Place and Role of Local Government in Federal Systems* (Johannesburg: Konrad-Adenauer-Stiftung, 2005); J.Kincaid and G.A. Tarr, eds., *A Global Dialogue on Federalism*, vol. 1: *Constitutional Origins, Structure and Change in Federal Countries* (Montreal & Kingston: McGill-Queen's University Press, 2005), pp. 438–9.

constitution) and Switzerland in the new constitution of 1999, to recognize formally in the constitution of the federation the position and powers of local governments. Brazil, Venezuela and South Africa are notable in that their constitutions fully recognize local governments as a full-fledged third order of government within the federation. Indeed in both Brazil and South Africa there have been efforts recently to emphasize local governments at the expense of the states or provinces. In Brazil the first Lula administration clearly favoured the cities over the states with new transfers, in part because his party's power base was in the cities. In South Africa there has been some consideration even of abolishing the provinces or at least characterizing the Republic as a case of "hour-glass" federalism in which the national and local spheres each weigh more than the provinces.[4] In Australia, although local governments fall within state jurisdiction, representation for local governments was formally included in the Council of Australian Governments established in 1992 to improve collaboration on economic development policies.

---

[4] Department: Provincial and Local Government, Republic of South Africa, *Policy process on the system of Provincial and Local Government: Background: Policy questions, process and participation* (Pretoria: Department of Provincial and Local Government, 2007).

Chapter 10

The Representative Institutions of Federal Governments

10.1 THE IMPORTANCE OF SHARED FEDERAL INSTITUTIONS AS A FOCUS FOR UNITY

There are two essential aspects in the design and operation of any federation. One is the recognition of diversity through a constitutional distribution of powers which enables the self-rule of the constituent units in specified areas of jurisdiction; the other is the shared institutions of federal government which enable common action and provide the glue to hold the federation together. With respect to the shared institutions of federal government, experience in federations generally suggests that to obtain the confidence of the citizens in the different units, two criteria must be met: (1) representativeness within the institutions of the federal government of the internal diversity within the federation, and (2) effectiveness in federal government decision making.

The shared institutions of a federation are different in character from those in a confederation. In a confederation the common institutions are composed of delegates appointed by and accountable to the *constituent governments*. In a federation the executive and first legislature chamber in the common institutions are composed of representatives directly elected by and accountable to the *citizens*, and in exercising its legislative and taxing powers the federal government normally acts directly on the citizens, paralleling the direct relationship of the regional governments to their electorates. In this way they minimize the apparent "democratic deficits" and technocracy that have characterized contemporary confederal political systems. In the latter, major central institutions are not directly elected but are composed of officials and ministers who serve as delegates of the constituent governments. This "indirect" relationship with the electorate of the central confederal institutions has tended in practice to create difficulties for generating public support and loyalty for confederal institutions, a problem that has become apparent, for instance, in the European Union.

10.2 INSTITUTIONS BASED ON THE SEPARATION OF POWERS OR PARLIAMENTARY PRINCIPLES

Generally the federal government institutions within federations fall into one of two basic categories: those embodying the separation of executive and legislative powers and those involving the fusion of executive and legislative powers in a parliamentary executive responsible to the popularly elected house of the federal legislature. The distinction between these alternatives is significant because the form of these institutions has a major impact on the political dynamics within a federation.[1]

Each of these forms of executive-legislature relationship has a differing democratic premise. The separation of executive and legislative powers with fixed terms for each is directed at limiting the possible abuse of power. It is a further extension of the principle of dispersing powers among multiple decision-making centres which is implicit in the concept of federation itself. In federations incorporating the separation of the executive and the legislature, power is not only divided *between* federal and regional governments but also divided *within* each order of government. By contrast, the fusion of executive and legislative power in parliamentary systems is based instead on the democratic notion that by placing the executive within the legislature and making it continuously responsible to the legislature which is itself democratically controlled in elections, coherent but controlled and accountable federal policies will be possible. In federations incorporating this latter arrangement authority is *divided* between the federal and regional governments, but within each order power is *concentrated* in a parliamentary fusion of executive and legislature.

One form of executive-legislature relationship embodying the principle of the separation of powers is the presidential-congressional form exemplified by the United States in which the president and the two houses of Congress are each elected directly for a fixed term. The Latin American federations — Argentina, Brazil, Mexico and Venezuela — have all adopted this model as has Nigeria in its current constitution. Another form is the collegial executive in Switzerland where the executive is a Federal Council elected by the federal legislature but for a fixed

---

[1] K. LeRoy and C.Saunders, eds., *Legislative, Executive and Judicial Governance in Federal Countries*, Forum of Federations and International Association of Centres of Federal Studies, A Global Dialogue on Federalism, vol. 3 (Montreal & Kingston, McGill-Queen's University Press, 2006).

term, and constitutes a collegial group, rather than a single person. In this latter form the presidency rotates annually among the members of the Federal Council.

There are two types of parliamentary executives: those modelled closely on the pattern of the majoritarian British institutions at Westminster, as found, for example, in Canada, Australia, India and Malaysia, and those following European traditions of responsible cabinet government, usually with coalitions, as found in Austria, Germany, Belgium and Spain. Some federations in each of these two variants of parliamentary government are constitutional monarchies, e.g., Canada, Australia, Malaysia, Belgium and Spain, while some are republics with presidents elected either directly or by an electoral college, as in Austria, Germany and India. Despite these variations, basically common to all these parliamentary federations is a fusion of powers in which the federal cabinet is chosen from the members of the federal legislature and is accountable to it for its continued existence if office.

There is a third category which might be called the hybrid presidential-parliamentary form of executive. Russia is an example of a federation incorporating this form in which a directly elected president with some significant executive powers is combined with a parliamentary cabinet responsible to the federal legislature. Pakistan is also an example. The constitution of 1973 provided for a president elected by the parliament and the leader of the majority party or majority coalition to be elected prime minister by the National Assembly. After General Musharraf took power in a military coup in 1999, he organized a referendum in 2002 to elect himself president for five years and then issued a legal framework order to amend the constitution. As president he chairs the National Security Council where most decision making is concentrated. That Council is comprised of the military chiefs, the prime minister and the cabinet. South Africa provides another variant closer to the parliamentary model. There the leader, as in parliamentary systems is drawn from parliament and to hold office depends on its continued confidence, but the leader is described as a president rather than a prime minister and plays not only the role of government leader but also that of head of state. Once elected, the president ceases to be a member of parliament, although most of the ministers must be members of parliament. France was an earlier non-federal example of a presidential-parliamentary hybrid form of executive.

The examples of the basic forms of executive-legislature relationship are set out in table 17, which refers not only to the institutions of the federal governments but also to those of the regional governments in each federation.

10.3 THE SIGNIFICANCE FOR THE REPRESENTATIVENESS AND EFFECTIVENESS OF FEDERAL GOVERNMENTS

These various forms of federal government institutions have had a differing impact upon the dynamics of federal politics affecting particularly the representativeness and effectiveness of their federal governments.

TABLE 17: Forms of Executives and Legislatures in Federations

Federation (current constitution)	Federal Executive-Legislature Relationship	Head of Federal Government	Head of Federation	Bicameral or Unicameral Federal Legislature	State/Provincial Executive-Legislature Relationship	Head of Regional Government	Head of Regional State
A) Separated Executive (Presidential or Fixed Term Collegial)							
United States (1789)	Separated: President-Congress	President[1]	President[1]	Bicameral	Separated: Governor-legislature	Governor[1]	Governor[1]
Switzerland (1848, 1999)	Separated: Fixed-term collegial executive	President[2]	President[2]	Bicameral	Separated: Fixed-term collegial executive	President of cantonal council[3]	President of cantonal council[3]
Mexico (1917)	Separated: President-Congress	President[1]	President[1]	Bicameral	Separated: Governor-legislature	Governor[1]	Governor[1]
Brazil (1988)	Separated: President-Congress	President[1]	President[1]	Bicameral	Separated: Governor-legislature	Governor[1]	Governor[1]
Argentina (1994)	Separated: President-Congress	President[1]	President[1]	Bicameral	Separated: Governor-legislature	Governor[1]	Governor[1]
Venezuela (1999)	Separated: President-Congress	President[1]	President[1]	Unicameral	Separated: Governor-legislature	Governor[1]	Governor[1]
Nigeria (1999)	Separated: President-Congress	President[1]	President[1]	Bicameral	Separated: Governor-legislature	Governor[1]	Governor[1]

	Fused: responsible government/cabinet	Prime Minister / Chancellor	Monarch / President	Bicameral	Fused: responsible cabinet	Premier / Chief Minister	Lieutenant Governor / Governor
B) Fused Executive							
Canada (1867)	Fused: responsible government	Prime Minister	Monarch (Governor General)	Bicameral	Fused: responsible cabinet	Premier	Lieutenant Governor[4]
Australia (1901)	Fused: responsible cabinet	Prime Minister	Monarch (Governor General)	Bicameral	Fused: responsible cabinet	Premier	Governor[5]
Austria (1920)	Fused: responsible cabinet	Chancellor	President	Bicameral	Fused: responsible cabinet	Governor	Governor
Germany (1949)	Fused: responsible cabinet	Chancellor	President[6]	Bicameral	Fused: responsible cabinet	Minister President (or Mayor)	Minister President (or Mayor)
India (1950)	Fused: responsible cabinet	Prime Minister	President[6]	Bicameral	Fused: responsible cabinet	Chief Minister	Governor[7]
Malaysia (1963)	Fused: responsible cabinet	Prime Minister	Yang di Pertuan Agong[8]	Bicameral	Fused: responsible cabinet	Chief Minister	Hereditary ruler or Governor[9]
Spain (1978)	Fused: responsible cabinet	Prime Minister[10]	Monarch	Bicameral	Fused: responsible cabinet	President of governing council[11]	President of governing council[11]
Belgium (1993)	Fused: responsible cabinet	Prime Minister	Monarch	Bicameral	Fused: responsible collegial executive	President of executive	President of executive
Ethiopia (1995)	Fused: responsible cabinet	Prime Minister	President	Bicameral	Fused: responsible cabinet	President of region	President of region

... continued

TABLE 17 (*continued*)

	Federation (current constitution)	Federal Executive-Legislature Relationship	Head of Federal Government	Head of Federation	Bicameral or Unicameral Federal Legislature	State/Provincial Executive-Legislature Relationship	Head of Regional Government	Head of Regional State
C) Mixed Executive	Pakistan (1973)	Fused: responsible cabinet	Prime Minister	President[12]	Bicameral	Fused: responsible cabinet	Chief Minister	Governor[13]
	Russia (1993)	Fused: responsible cabinet	Prime Minister	President[1]	Bicameral	Fused: responsible cabinet	Governor[14]	Governor[14]
	South Africa (1996)	Fused: responsible cabinet	President[15]	President[15]	Bicameral	Fused: responsible cabinet	Premier[16]	Premier[16]

Notes:

[1] Directly Elected
[2] Annual rotating chairman of Federal Council
[3] Some directly elected, some elected by cantonal legislature, some elected by cantonal executive
[4] Appointed by monarch on advice of federal prime minister
[5] Appointed by monarch on advice of state government
[6] Elected by electoral assembly of federal and state legislators
[7] Appointed by president on advice of Union Government
[8] Selected for five-year term from among hereditary rules of nine Malay states
[9] Hereditary rules in nine states, governors in four states appointed by state legislative assemblies
[10] Titled President of Government
[11] Elected by Legislative Assembly from among its own members
[12] President (normally elected by Parliament) chairs National Security council, where most decision-making authority is vested
[13] Appointed by President
[14] Elected in constituent units, but President has power to dismiss under certain conditions
[15] Elected by National Assembly; appoints the cabinet
[16] Elected by provincial legislature

They have, for instance, affected the relative roles and effectiveness of their federal executives and legislatures. The presidential-congressional form in the United States has given both the president and the two houses of Congress prominent roles and has limited the excessive dominance by any one body by the checks and balances on each other. It has, however, been prone to deadlocks and impasses, especially when different parties control the presidency and the houses of Congress.

The Swiss form of the separation of executive and legislative powers has provided, by contrast with the presidential systems, the collegial Federal Council traditionally with an opportunity for inclusive representativeness through multi-party maximum coalitions embracing in their membership most of the major parties in the legislature. This has, however, resulted in prolonged and lengthy decision-making processes. Nevertheless, it has meant that when decisions are reached they have generally had wide public support.

The parliamentary forms of executive found in the other federations, especially Canada and Australia, have tended to provide more cohesive and decisive federal governments than in the US model, but at the price of entailing strong party discipline, executive dominance and a more majoritarian emphasis by comparison with those embodying the separation of powers principle. On the other hand, in multi-party situations where coalitions of federal parties have become the norm as in many European federations and India, decisive decision making has been sacrificed but a less majoritarian representativeness has been achieved.

The presidential-parliamentary hybrid, as exemplified by the Russian federation, aims at the best of both worlds but in practice seems often to have fluctuated between strong and weak presidentialism. In the Yeltsin period it was characterized by complexity and tensions between the two arms of the federal government, but under the Putin regime the executive has reasserted a dominant role. With the term limit on Putin's presidency, the possibility of his successor naming Putin as prime minister may mark another significant shift towards a less dominant president.

The different forms have also affected the capacity for regional representativeness within the executive of the federal government. In terms of balancing regional and minority interests within the executive, the U.S. presidential form is limited basically to two individuals: the president and the vice-president. While most presidential candidates have taken regional balance into account in selecting their vice-presidential running mates, this has provided only a rudimentary opportunity for regional or other balancing. In other presidential systems internal political diversity has often required not only the president and the vice-president to come from different constituent units but also, as in Nigeria, that the Cabinet include a member from every state; but even in such cases, the president has usually proved to be the dominant figure. The collegial form in Switzerland consciously avoided emphasizing a single individual as president. Although limited to seven members, the Federal Council has in practice exhibited a much better opportunity to ensure representation not only of the major political parties but also of the different language and religious groups and of major cantons. In this respect it is an important vehicle for expressing within the federal executive the Swiss proportionality syndrome (i.e., the insistence upon proportional representativeness of different groups in the composition of every federal body). The various parliamentary executives in other federations have typically all been widely representative. The "proportionality syndrome" in federal cabinet composition has been strong not only in Canada but in virtually all the parliamentary federations, although party distribution within the federal legislature may moderate or constrain the scope of representation that is possible. In the Belgian case, the constitution (article 99) actually requires equality in the numbers of French-speaking and Dutch-speaking ministers (excluding the prime minister). The Russian presidential-parliamentary hybrid has enabled some representativeness in the parliamentary portion of the executive, but this has been hampered by the complex and not always clear party distribution in the Duma.

The form of executive has also affected the capacity of the federal executive to generate federal consensus. The U.S. presidential form provides a strong personal focus upon the president as federal leader. Furthermore, the need to capture the support of a majority in the Electoral College in presidential elections has encouraged electoral campaigns aimed at aggregating the widest range of possible support from different groups. On the other hand, the frequency of presidential-congressional impasses, particularly when the presidency and the houses of Congress are dominated by different parties, has often emphasized political divisions and has had a corrosive impact on consensus within the federation. The collegial form of federal institutions in Switzerland has contributed to federal cohesion by inducing political processes that have emphasized maxi-coalitions and inclusiveness. On the other hand, the time taken to produce decisions through these processes has on occasion produced a measure of public frustration. The increasing success of the People's Party led by Christoph Blocher in federal elections since 1999 has, however, recently introduced a more adversarial element into Swiss politics.

The parliamentary federal executives, where based on single-party majorities or on stable coalitions (the latter being typical of the European federations), have generally contributed to cohesion. But where cabinets are based upon the support of a simple majority in the federal legislature, they tend often to be perceived as less inclusive of the variety of regional interests and minorities than in the Swiss example and to leave significant regions or groups feeling themselves inadequately represented. Canadian experience in this respect, such as when Pierre Trudeau's parliamentary majority from 1980 to 1984 included no Members of Parliament from the three most western provinces, is but one example. Furthermore, in those parliamentary federations where a multiparty system develops but stable coalitions are not achieved, the resulting federal government instability may seriously undermine federal cohesion. The experience of Pakistan prior to the secession of

East Bengal is an example, and the tensions within Belgium from time to time is another. The development in India of a multiparty system with strong regional parties has led to a gradual recognition of the importance of power-sharing to reconcile conflict and of the need to make coalition governments work rather than merely toppling them.

As noted in chapter 7, the form of executive within both federal and regional levels of government has also had a significant impact upon the character and processes of intergovernmental relations in federations. In the USA the presidential-congressional system at the federal level, together with the parallel separation of powers between governors and legislators in the states, has meant the dispersal of power within each tier of government. This has made necessary multiple channels of federal-state relations involving executives, officials, legislators and agencies interacting not only with their opposite numbers but in a web of criss-crossing relationships which one American scholar has characterized as "marblecake federalism."[2] Within this complex set of processes, Congress, and its various committees and sub-committees, have played a particularly significant role because of their part in approving the variety of specific grant-in-aid programs.

The collegial form of executive within governments at both levels in Switzerland has also led to the dispersed conduct of intergovernmental relations. Two other factors have contributed to the character of intergovernmental relations in Switzerland. One is the arrangement whereby the Swiss cantons are responsible for the administration of much federal legislation and therefore are extensively consulted by different branches of the federal government concerning proposed legislation. Second, an additional channel of intergovernmental communication between legislators arises from the provisions enabling dual membership in cantonal and federal legislatures. About one-fifth of the legislators in each federal house have in practice usually fallen into this category.

In the other federations where parliamentary responsible cabinets have operated within governments at both levels, a common prevailing characteristic has been the executive predominance in intergovernmental relations (see also section 7.2). "Executive federalism" has been most marked in Germany, Australia and Canada, but is also a major characteristic of intergovernmental relations in India, Malaysia, Austria, Belgium and Spain. This is a natural outcome of the existence within both levels of a governmental form in which dominant cabinets and strong party discipline have been induced by the requirement of continuous support by their respective legislatures.

The presidential-parliamentary hybrid in Russia would appear so far to have led to executive dominance in intergovernmental relations due to the weakness of

---

[2] Morton Grodzins, "The Federal System," in A. Wildavsky, ed., *American Federalism in Comparative Perspective* (Boston: Little Brown, 1967), p. 257.

the legislators. An interesting feature affecting intergovernmental relations in Russia is the constitutional provision that each regional unit is represented in the federal second chamber, the Federation Council, by two representatives, one chosen by the legislature of the constituent unit and the other by the executive body of the that unit. In South Africa the provincial delegations in the central second chamber, the National Council of Provinces, also include representatives of both the provincial legislatures and executives.

10.4 THE IMPACT OF ELECTORAL SYSTEMS AND POLITICAL PARTIES

The particular electoral system employed for the institutions of federal government has also had an impact on the representativeness and effectiveness of these federal institutions. In the USA, Canada, India and Malaysia, single-member constituency plurality electoral systems have been employed for the popularly elected first house of the federal legislature. In Switzerland, Austria and Belgium various forms of proportional representation have been used for elections to the lower house of the federal legislature. Germany employs a mixed system with half the members of the Bundestag elected by proportional representation from party lists and the other half by plurality votes in single-member constituencies. Australia has used the single-member preferential voting system for its House of Representatives.

These differing electoral systems have shaped the processes for generating federal cohesion, the representation of regional and minority views, and the relative stability of governments. In federations with single-member plurality electoral systems, the inherent overrepresentation of swings in voting patterns has made them highly sensitive to shifts in electoral opinion. In the United States and (until recently) Canada, this system has also for the most part provided stable single-party majorities. However, the inherent overrepresentation of pluralities has been at the expense of representativeness, with minority parties tending to be underrepresented. Furthermore, by favouring regionally concentrated parties, single-member plurality electoral systems have, as in Canada, often heightened regional splits in parliamentary representation over-representing the regional concentrations in actual voting. On the other hand, in some cases, such as India, the degree of social diversity has produced a pattern requiring coalition governments. Those federations employing proportional representation electoral systems have reflected voting distribution much more accurately, although since they do not exaggerate voting shifts, they are less sensitive to changes. Furthermore, they have tended to encourage multiparty systems. As a result, party coalitions have been the norm for federal governments in many of these countries and particularly Switzerland, Austria, Belgium and Germany.

In some federations where both houses of the federal legislature have directly elected members, different electoral rules or terms apply to the two houses. An example is Australia, where members of the House of Representatives are elected on the basis of preferential voting for three-year terms and senators are elected by proportional representation for six-year terms. Other examples of differing electoral rules or of terms for the two houses occur in Argentina, Brazil, Mexico, Nigeria, Switzerland and the United States.

An important factor in the dynamic of any federation is the character and role of its political parties. These tend to be influenced by both institutional characteristics, particularly the executive-legislature relationship and the electoral system, and by the nature and characteristics of the diversity in the underlying society. There are four aspects of political parties that may particularly affect the operation of a federation: (1) the relationship between the party organizations at the federal level and provincial or state party level, (2) the degree of symmetry or asymmetry between federal and provincial or state party alignments, (3) the impact of party discipline upon the representation of interests within each level, and (4) the prevailing pattern of political careers.

In terms of party organization, the federal parties in the United States and especially Switzerland have tended to be loose confederations of state or cantonal and local party organizations. This decentralized pattern of party organization has contributed to the maintenance of non-centralized government and the prominence in their federal legislatures of regional and local interests. In the parliamentary federations, the pressures for effective party discipline within each government in order to sustain the executive in office have tended to separate federal and provincial or state branches of parties into more autonomous layers of party organization. This tendency appears to have been strongest in Canada. The ties between federal and regional branches of each party have remained somewhat more significant, however, in such parliamentary federations as Germany, Australia and India. In the case of Belgium, the federal parties have in fact become totally regional in character, with each party based in a region or distinct linguistic group.

In virtually all of these federations the prevailing alignment of parties in different regions has often varied significantly from region to region and from federal politics. These variations in the character of party competition and predominance in different regional units have usually been the product of different regional economic, political and cultural interests. Consequently, these regional variations in prevailing parties have contributed further to the sense of regional identification and distinctiveness within these federations.

The pressure or absence of strong party discipline in different federations has also had an impact upon the visible expression of regional and minority interests within the federal legislatures. Where parliamentary institutions have operated, the pressure has been to accommodate regional and minority interests as far as possible behind closed doors within party caucuses so that the visible façade is one of cabinet and party solidarity. This contrasts with the shifting alliances and visibly varying positions much more frequently taken by legislators in federal legislatures where the principle of the separation of powers has been incorporated. Regional and minority concerns are more openly expressed and deliberated in the latter cases, although that has not necessarily meant that they are translated any more effectively into adopted policies.

An area that illustrates the contrasting representational patterns in different federations is the variation in the normal pattern of political careers. In some federations, most notably the United States and Switzerland, the normal pattern of political careers is progression from local to state or cantonal and then to federal office. Presidential candidates in the USA, for instance, have usually been selected from among governors or senators rooted in their state politics. By contrast, in Canada few major federal political leaders have been drawn from the ranks of provincial premiers, and it is the norm for Canada's most ambitious politicians to fulfill their entire careers at one level or the other, either in federal or in provincial politics. The political career patterns in most of the other parliamentary federations fall between these extremes, examples of the links between provincial experience and filling positions of federal office being more frequent in such federations as Germany, Australia and India than in Canada.

Federations have varied in having many parties, two or more major parties, or one dominant party, and these have significantly affected the functioning and character of their operation as federations. Among those with multiparty systems, especially regionally based parties, coalition governments seeking interparty compromises have been typical; Belgium, Brazil, Austria, Germany, India in recent decades, and Switzerland provide prime examples. Examples of federations characterized by two major parties holding power in different periods have been Australia and the United States. Until recently this was the pattern in Canada, although the impact of regional and minority parties has recently reduced the major parties to governing as minority governments. Spain has a competitive system of two major parties, but to form a government each must rely on the support of smaller regionally based parties. India in its early decades, Mexico until 2000, and South Africa currently have been dominated by one party prevailing within both orders of government and thus contributing to centralized policy making under the influence of the central party apparatus. Nigeria's recent post-military politics has seen the president's People's Democratic Party predominant at both levels and a fractured opposition, but charges that elections have not been free and fair have raised questions about the government's legitimacy. In Russia, President Putin has built up a strong presidential party from the formerly fractured party system of the Yeltsin period, and this has contributed to the reassertion of the federal government's strength. Argentina and Pakistan both have experienced volatile party politics, reflecting the primarily "presidential" character of their politics frequently punctuated by periods of military rule.

10.5 THE ROLE OF FEDERAL SECOND CHAMBERS

BICAMERALISM WITHIN FEDERATIONS

The principle of bicameralism has been incorporated into the federal legislatures of most federations. Debate over whether representation in the federal legislature should be in terms of the population or in terms of the states was intense at the time of the creation of the first modern federation, the United States. The issue was resolved at the Philadelphia Conference in 1787 by the Connecticut Compromise whereby a bicameral federal legislature was established with representation in one house, the House of Representatives, based on population, and representation in another house, the Senate, based on equal representation of states with senators originally elected by the state legislatures. This ensured that differing state viewpoints would not be simply overridden by a majority of the population dominated by the larger states.

Since then, most subsequent federations have adopted bicameral federal legislatures. Indeed, all eighteen federations listed in table 19, without exception, have bicameral federal legislatures. Two other contemporary federations, Bosnia and Herzegovina and Belau, also have bicameral federal legislatures. Currently, the only federations among the 25 listed in table 2 (in chapter 1) that do not have bicameral federal legislatures are the United Arab Emirates, Venezuela and three of the four small island federations, Comoros, Micronesia and St. Kitts and Nevis. Two other former federations which had unicameral legislatures were Pakistan (1956–73) and Serbia-Montenegro (1992–2006), neither of which proved stable.

While the European Union is a hybrid of confederal and federal institutions, it is worth noting that it, too, has bicameral legislative institutions. Both the European Parliament, representing the citizens, and the Council of Ministers, representing constituent governments, have certain co-decision powers. However, the Council, which in character corresponds to the second chambers in federations, plays the more predominant role within the European Union.

While most federations have found it necessary to establish bicameral federal legislatures, there is enormous variation among them in the method of selection of members, the composition, and the powers of the second chamber, and consequently its role. Table 18 sets out the variations of these elements that have existed in federal second chambers. Table 19 summarizes the particular combination of elements incorporated in eighteen federal second chambers.

SELECTION OF MEMBERS

There is considerable variety in the ways in which members of federal second chambers are elected or appointed. In seven federations, Australia since its inception in 1901, the United States since 1913, Switzerland (by cantonal choice eventually in all cantons), Argentina, Brazil, Mexico and Nigeria, members of the

TABLE 18: Variations in Selection, Composition, Powers and Role of Second
Chambers in Federations

Selection	Composition	Powers	Role
1. Appointment by federal government (no formal consultation) (e.g., Canada, Malaysia 63% of seats)	1. Equal "regional" representation (e.g., Canada for groups of provinces)	1. Absolute veto with mediation committees (e.g., Argentina, Brazil, Mexico, Switzerland, USA)	1. Primarily legislative chamber (e.g., Argentina, Australia, Brazil, Canada, India, Malaysia, Mexico, Switzerland, USA)
2. Appointment by federal government based on nomination by provincial governments (e.g., Canada: Meech Lake Accord proposal)	2. Equal state representation (e.g., Argentina, Australia, Brazil, Malaysia 37% of seats, Mexico 75% of seats, Nigeria, Pakistan 88% of seats, Russia, South Africa, USA)	2. Absolute veto on federal legislation affecting any state administrative functions (e.g., Germany, South Africa)	2. Combined legislative and intergovernmental role (e.g., Germany, South Africa)
3. Appointment ex officio by state governments (e.g., Germany, Russia 50% of seats, South Africa 40% of seats)	3. Two categories of cantonal representation (e.g., Switzerland: full cantons and half cantons)	3. Suspensive veto: time limit (e.g., Malaysia, South Africa except above, Spain)	3. Ultimate interpretation of constitution (e.g., Ethiopia)
4. Indirect election by state legislatures (e.g., Austria, Ethiopia, India, Malaysia 37% of seats, Pakistan, Russia 50% of seats, South Africa 60% of seats, USA 1789–1912)	4. Weighted state voting: four categories (e.g., Germany: 3, 4, 5 or 6 block votes)	4. Suspensive veto: matching lower house vote to override (e.g., Germany except above)	
5. Direct election by simple plurality (e.g., Argentina, Brazil, Mexico 75% of seats, USA since 1913)	5. Weighted state representation: multiple categories (e.g., Austria, India)	5. Deadlock resolved by joint sitting (e.g., India)	
6. Direct election by proportional representation (e.g., Australia, Nigeria, Mexico 25% of seats)	6. Additional or special representation for others including aboriginals (e.g., Ethiopia, India, Malaysia, Pakistan)	6. Deadlock resolved by double dissolution then joint sitting (e.g., Australia)	
7. Choice of method left to cantons or states (e.g., Ethiopia, Switzerland: Swiss choice direct election by plurality)	7. A minority of regional representatives (e.g., Belgium, Spain)	7. Money bills: brief suspensive veto (India, Malaysia), or no veto (Pakistan).	
8. Mixed (e.g., Belgium, Ethiopia, Malaysia, Mexico, Russia, South Africa, Spain)			

TABLE 19: Selection, Composition and Powers of Federal Second Chambers

Argentina	Senate: elected by direct vote; one-third of the members elected every two years to a six-year term; equal state representation; absolute veto.
Australia	Senate: direct election (by proportional representation); equal state representation; absolute veto (but followed by double dissolution and joint sitting).
Austria	Bundesrat: elected by state legislatures; weighted representation (range 12:3); suspensive veto (may be overridden by simple majority in lower house, the Nationalrat).
Belgium	Senate: combination of directly elected (40), indirectly elected by linguistic Community Councils (21), and co-opted senators (10); variable representation specified for each unit; equal competence with House of Representatives on some matters but on others House of Representatives has overriding power.
Brazil	Senado Federal (Senate): 3 members from each state and federal district elected by a simple majority to serve eight-year terms; one-third elected after a four-year period, two-thirds elected after the next four-year period; absolute veto.
Canada	Senate: appointed by federal government; equal regional representation for 4 regional groups of provinces (Ontario; Quebec; 4 western provinces; 3 maritime provinces) plus 6 for Newfoundland and one each for the 3 territories; absolute veto (legally) but in practice weakened legitimacy.
Ethiopia	House of Federation (Yefedereshn Mekir Bet): 71 members (63%) directly or indirectly elected by the states and 41 (27%) appointed on population and ethnicity. This body serves as the supreme constitutional arbiter. The House of Federation also plays a role in adjustments to taxing powers and to subsidies to the states. Members serve five-year terms. For members selected by states, directly or indirectly elected according to decision of state councils.
Germany	Bundesrat: state government ex officio delegations; weighted voting (3, 4, 5 or 6 block votes per state); suspensive veto on federal legislation overridden by corresponding lower-house majority, but absolute veto on any federal legislation affecting state administrative functions (60% of federal legislation reduced to about 40% by reforms in 2006); mediation to resolve differences.
India	Rajya Sabha (Council of States): elected by state legislatures (plus 12 additional representatives appointed by the President for special representation); weighted representation of states (range 31:1); veto resolved by joint sitting.

... continued

TABLE 19 (*continued*)

Malaysia	Dewan Negara (Senate): 26 (37%) elected by state legislatures plus 44 (63%) additional appointed representatives for minorities; equal state representation (for 37% of total seats); suspensive veto (six months).
Mexico	Camara de Senadores (Senate): 128 seats in total; 96 (3 per state) are elected by popular vote to serve six-year terms and cannot be re-elected; 32 are allocated on the basis of each party's popular vote; absolute veto.
Nigeria	Senate: each state has three seats while one senator represents the Federal Capital Territory. A total of 109 senators are directly elected for a four-year term; absolute veto (except taxation and appropriation bills resolved by joint sitting) with joint committees to resolve deadlocks.
Pakistan	Senate: 100 seats indirectly elected by provincial assemblies to serve 4-year terms. Of the 22 seats allocated to each province, 14 are general members, 4 are women and 4 are technocrats. Federally Administered Tribal Areas (FATAs) and the Capital Territory fill seats through direct election, with 8 seats given to the FATAs and 4 for the Capital Territory; no veto on money bills, budget, borrowing or audit of federal accounts.
Russia	Federation Council (Soviet Federatsii): Asymmetry of length of term and method of selection depending on the republic or region. Each unit has 2 representatives in the Federation Council, one elected by of the constituent unit legislature, the other appointed by the governor; dispute resolution by joint committee which may be overridden by two-thirds majority in lower house.
South Africa	National Council of Provinces (NCOP): 90 seats, consisting of 54 representing provincial legislatures and 36 representing provincial executives; equal provincial representation (6 legislators plus 4 executives per province); veto varied with type of legislation.
Spain	Senate: 208 members directly elected from the provinces and 51 appointed by parliaments of 17 Autonomous Communities; categories of 4, 3 or one directly elected senator(s) per province (sub-units of Autonomous Communities) supplemented by representation of one or more (related to population) appointed by each autonomous parliament; suspensive veto (2 months).
Switzerland	Council of States: in practice direct election (direct election by plurality; method chosen individually by all cantons); 2 representatives for full cantons and 1 for half cantons; absolute veto (mediation committees).
United States	Senate: direct election since 1913 (by simple plurality); equal state representation (six-year terms with one-third elected every two years); absolute veto (mediation committees).

federal second chamber are directly elected by the citizens of the constituent units. A feature unique to Switzerland is the provision enabling cantonal legislators to sit concurrently in both federal legislative houses, and in practice about one-fifth of the members of each federal house concurrently hold seats in a cantonal legislature, thus providing a channel for cantonal views to influence federal policy making. Originally in the USA (1789–1912), members of the federal second chamber were indirectly elected by the state legislatures. This is currently the case in Austria, India, Ethiopia and Pakistan for most members of the federal second chamber, and in Belgium, Malaysia, Russia, South Africa and Spain for a portion of the members. In Germany the members of the Bundesrat are delegates of their Land cabinets, holding office in the federal second chamber ex officio as members of their Land executive and voting in the Bundesrat in a block on the instructions of their Land governments. In Canada, senators are appointed by the federal prime minister and hold office until their retirement at 75. Although appointed to represent regional groups of provinces, senators have, however, as a result of the method of appointment, tended to display little accountability to regional interests and to vote instead generally on party lines. The adoption of an appointed Senate in Canada in 1867 was the result of a conscious rejection of an elected Senate because of the difficulties previously experienced in the pre-federation period when the elected second chamber claimed an equal mandate to the elected lower chamber in relation to cabinets. The federal second chambers in Belgium, Ethiopia, Malaysia, Russia and Spain have a mixed membership. In Belgium 40 senators are directly elected, 21 indirectly elected by the Flemish, French and German Community Councils, and 10 are co-opted (appointed by the directly elected senators). The Ethiopian House of Federation is composed of 71 members directly or indirectly elected from the regional states as determined by their council of the state, plus 41 apportioned on the basis of population and ethnicity. In Malaysia only 37 percent of the Senate seats are filled by indirect election by the state legislators, the remaining 63 percent being central appointees. In Russia half the members of the Federation Council represent the legislatures and half the members represent the executive bodies of the constitutional units, while in South Africa 60 percent represent the legislatures of the provinces and 40 percent the executives. The Spanish Senate has 208 directly elected members elected from the provinces (sub-units within the communities) and 51 representatives appointed by the parliaments of the Autonomous Communities.

In those federations where the members of the federal second chamber are directly elected, generally they tend to vote along party lines rather than strictly for the regional interests they represent. Where they are indirectly elected by state legislatures they are more likely to regard themselves as representing regional interests, although regional political party interests also can play a significant role. Where, as Germany, they are ex officio instructed delegates of the constituent governments, it is primarily the views of those governments that they represent and only indirectly those of the electorate. Where senators are appointed by the federal government, as in Canada and to a large extent in Malaysia, they have the least credibility as spokespersons for regional interests, even when they are residents of the regions they represent. Federal appointment does, however, provide a means of ensuring representation of some particular minorities and interests. It was for this reason that the Indian constitution provided for 12 such appointed members out of an overall total of 250 members in the Rajya Sabha, and the Malaysian constitution currently provides for 44 out of 70 senators to be appointed by the federal government. The mixed basis of selection of senators in Belgium and Spain embodies political compromises intended to obtain the benefits of the different forms of selection for members of the federal second chamber.

BASIS OF REGIONAL REPRESENTATION

In most federations representation in the popularly elected lower house is based on population, and it is in the second chamber that representation of the constitutional units, either equally or weighted to favour the smaller units, occurs. In a few instances, however, guarantees of minimum representation have been given also to smaller constituent units in the lower house. Examples can be found in Brazil and Canada, although the extra weighting for smaller units is less than in the second chambers.

While it is often assumed that equality of state representation in the federal second chamber is the norm in federations, in practice this is the case, however, for most of the seats in only nine of the federal second chambers listed in tables 18 (second column) and 19. In most other federations representation in the federal second chamber favours in some measure the smaller regional units or significant minorities, but states with larger populations do get more seats.[3] In the Malaysian Senate the seats filled by indirectly elected senators are equally distributed among the states, but the substantial proportion that are filled by centrally appointed senators have not followed a consistent pattern of balanced state representation; thus the net effect has been one of considerable variation in state representation. In most other federations the population of the units is a factor in their representation in the federal second chamber, although generally there is some weighting to favour the smaller units. There have been various degrees of weighting. In Switzerland there are two categories of representation in the Council of States: 20 cantons have 2 representatives and 6 "half-cantons" have only one

---

[3] On the consequences of equal senate representation in the United States, see Frances E. Lee and Bruce I. Oppenheimer, *Sizing Up the Senate: The Unequal Consequences of Equal Representation* (Chicago: University of Chicago Press, 1998). On the effect of disproportionate representation in Latin American federations, see E.L. Gibson, ed., *Federalism and Democracy in Latin American* (Baltimore: Johns Hopkins University Press, 2004), especially chapters 2, 3, 4, 5, 9 and 10.

each. In Germany the constitution (article 51) establishes four population categories of Länder having three, four, five or six block votes in the Bundesrat. In India, Austria and Spain the range of state representation is wider; for example, 31:1 in India and 12:3 in Austria. In Belgium the differential representation of each Community and Region in the Senate is specified in the constitution, but for some especially significant issues the constitution (article 43) requires majorities within both the French-speaking and Dutch-speaking members in the Senate (as well as within the Chamber of Deputies). Canada, as is the case with so much about its Senate, is unique among federations in basing Senate representation on regional groups of provinces with the four basic regions having 24 seats each, plus an additional 6 for the Province of Newfoundland and Labrador, and 3 for the three territories.

POWERS OF SECOND CHAMBERS RELATIVE TO FIRST CHAMBERS

Where there is a separation of powers between the executive and the legislature, as in the United States, Switzerland, Argentina, Brazil and Mexico, normally the two federal legislative houses have had equal powers (although in the United States the Senate has some additional powers relating to ratification of appointments and treaties). Where there are parliamentary executives, the house that controls the executive (invariably the popularly elected first chamber) inevitably has more power. In these federations the powers of the second chamber in relation to money bills are usually limited. Furthermore, in the case of conflicts between the two houses, provisions for a suspensive veto, for joint sittings where the members of the second chamber are less numerous, or for double dissolution have usually rendered the second chamber weaker (see table 18, column three, for examples). This has sometimes raised questions within parliamentary federations about whether their second chambers provide sufficient regional influence in central decision making. This concern is reinforced by the overriding strength of party discipline within parliamentary federations. Nonetheless, some of the federal second chambers in parliamentary federations, such as the Australian Senate and the German Bundesrat, have been able to exert considerable influence. The particular membership of the German Bundesrat, and the fact that its absolute veto over all federal legislation involving administration by the Länder has in practice until recently applied to more than 60 percent of all federal legislation, have been major factors in its influence.

ROLE OF FEDERAL SECOND CHAMBERS

The primary role of most of the federal second chambers in the federations reviewed in this study has been legislative, reviewing federal legislation with a view to bringing to bear upon it regional and minority interests and concerns. In a number of federations the federal second chambers also perform some other functions of a federal character, such as nominations for or giving consent to certain federal appointments (as in Germany and the United States), consent to treaties (as in the United States and Argentina) or approval of emergencies or the use of federal overriding powers (as in India and South Africa). In contrast to the others, the German Bundesrat performs an additional and equally important role of serving as an institution to facilitate intergovernmental cooperation and collaboration. It is able to do this because, unlike the other federal second chambers, as noted, it is composed of instructed delegates of the Land governments and because its suspensive veto power over all federal legislation and absolute veto over federal legislation affecting state legislative and administrative responsibilities give it strong political leverage. This model heavily influenced the South Africans in the design of their national second chamber in the constitution adopted in 1996, although some significant modifications were made to include representation of both executives and legislators from the provinces in the National Council of Provinces (NCOP). From time to time during the past two decades the reform of the Canadian Senate has been suggested. Various alternative models have been advocated, but while most Canadians agree that the Senate should be reformed, disagreement about the appropriate model has left it unreformed.

The Ethiopian House of Federation is unique among federal second chambers in having been assigned a role as the ultimate guardian of the constitution. It has the exclusive right and ultimate authority to interpret the constitution, and this indeed is its main function.

10.6 DO FEDERAL SECOND CHAMBERS CONSTRAIN DEMOCRACY?

Critics of federations have noted particularly that most federations, in establishing bicameral federal legislatures with second chambers weighted in differing degrees to favour smaller constituent units, have appeared to violate the cardinal principle of democracy based on "one person one vote." Consequently, they have characterized such federal second chambers as "demos-constraining."[4] To take just one example, in the United States Senate a single vote in Wyoming counts 65 times more than its equivalent in California. Such contrasts are replicated in many other federal second chambers. Brazil represents an extreme example where sena-

---

[4] A. Stepan, "Toward a New Comparative Politics of Federalism Multinationalism, and Democracy," in E.L. Gibson, ed., *Federalism and Democracy in Latin America* (Baltimore: Johns Hopkins Press, 2004), pp. 28–84; A. Stepan, "Electorally generated Veto Players in Unitary and Federal Systems," in E.L. Gibson ed., *op.cit.*, pp. 323–61; G. Tsebelis, *Veto Players: How Political Institutions Work* (Princeton: Princeton University Press, (2002).

tors representing 43 percent of the federal population control over 74 percent of the Senate vote. Argentina is another case where the disproportion representing the smaller constituent units has had a marked influence on federal policies. Of course, as the differing composition and powers of federal second chambers outlined in tables 18 and 19 indicate, there are considerable variations among federal second chambers in the degree to which they operate as "veto players" and are "demos-constraining" in character. The federal second chambers of the United States, Switzerland, the Latin American federations and Germany (the latter because of the special character of the Bundesrat) have tended to be strong veto players, while those in most parliamentary federations, where cabinets have been responsible to the popularly elected house, have normally been weaker (although in Australia the Senate has some significant veto powers). Consequently, it is appropriate to place federal second chambers, depending on their composition and powers, on a continuum in terms of their character as "veto-players" constraining democratic majorities.

It should be added that while federal institutions may place some limits upon majoritarian democracy, democracy more broadly understood as liberal democracy may actually be expanded by federalism. Democracy and governmental responsiveness can be enhanced within federations because multiple levels of government maximize the opportunity for citizens' preferences to be achieved, because they establish alternative arenas for citizen participation and because they provide for governments that are smaller and closer to the people. In this sense, federations are potentially "demos-enabling" and hence might be described as "democracy-plus."

Furthermore, from a liberal-democratic point of view, by emphasizing the value of checks and balances and dispersing authority to limit the potential tyranny of the majority, federal second chambers contribute to the protection of individuals and minorities against abuses.[5] This is, however, a question of balance and in some cases like Brazil and Argentina the disproportionate representation of the smaller constituent units may have been carried too far.[6] The checks on democratically elected majorities imposed by federal second chambers have often pushed federations in the direction of "consensus democracy," contributing to the accommodation of different groups within diverse and multicultural federations, and have added to the vitality and recognition in federal policy making of the distinct peoples in their various constituent units.[7]

---

[5] J. Madison, A. Hamilton and J. Jay, *The Federalist Papers* (1788; reprint with editor's introduction, New York: Penguin Books, 1987), no. 9.

[6] See footnote 4.

[7] A. Liphart, *Patterns of Democracy: Government Forms and Performance in Thirty-Six Countries* (New Haven: Yale University Press, 1999).

Chapter 11

Constitutional Supremacy in Federations

11.1 THE CONSTITUTION AS SUPREME LAW

Since an essential characteristic of federations is the constitutional distribution of powers between two or more orders of government, an important feature in the design and effective operation of any federation is ensuring the supremacy of the constitution as the source of governmental authority for each order of government. A recognition of the supremacy of the constitution over all orders of government and a political culture emphasizing the fundamental importance of respect for constitutionality are therefore prerequisites for the effective operation of a federation. If these are lacking, a federation is likely to deteriorate to a situation where one or other order of government subordinates the other thereby undermining the basic constitutional coordinacy that is an essential feature of federations.

The constitutions of most federations therefore explicitly or implicitly declare the supremacy of the constitution. This helps to explain why judicial review by the courts, discussed below, has been an important element in the operation of most federations. Other important implications flow from the principle of constitutional supremacy in federations. These relate to the processes of constitutional amendment, the role of constitutional bills of rights, and provisions, if any, for formal secession.[1]

---

[1] J. Kincaid and G.A. Tarr, eds., *Constitutional Origins, Structure and Change in Federal Countries*, Forum of Federations and International Association of Centres for Federal Studies, *A Global Dialogue on Federalism*, vol. 1 (Montreal & Kingston: McGill-Queen's University Press, 2005).

Federal constitutions have varied in terms of their detail. Most of the federations created before the middle of the twentieth century contain less detail, laying out the basic features and principles. Those created since the middle of the twentieth century tend to extend to much more detail. The Indian constitution as adopted in 1950, for instance, contained 395 articles and 9 schedules, running to 291 pages. While the more recent constitutions have thereby attempted to reduce conflicts over their interpretation, they have tended to be less flexible than the older shorter constitutions.

In some federations, generally those established by a devolutionary process, the basic elements of the state or provincial constitutions are included in the federal constitution; Canada and India are examples. In others, generally those established by aggregating previously separate states (e.g., Switzerland, Australia, Brazil and Mexico), the federal constitutions have set out only a few minimum principles which the state constitutions must meet, otherwise leaving it to the constituent units to adopt their own constitutions. Nevertheless, in matters relating in any way to the relationship between federal and constituent unit governments, the ultimate supremacy of the federal constitution over all governments has always been prescribed in federations.

11.2 PROCESSES FOR CONSTITUTIONAL ADJUDICATION AND JUDICIAL REVIEW

Given the unavoidability of overlaps and interdependence between governments within federations and the consequent likelihood of intergovernmental competition and conflict, most federations have found the need for processes to adjudicate disputes and resolve conflicts. Disputes may arise over interpretation of the exact scope of power assigned to each order of government by the constitution, from conflicts of laws passed by different governments in areas of concurrent jurisdiction, from non-governmental bodies challenging the legal jurisdiction of a government, and from challenges that a law contravenes a constitutionally established right. A fundamental question that arises is whether electoral or judicial processes should be the primary means for dealing with such disputes and conflicts. Most federations have in fact relied on a combination of these processes. Ultimately, through the periodic elections that occur within both levels of government in federations, electorates have had the opportunity where there is a conflict between governments to express and support their preferences by voting parties in or out of power in each level of government. In the case of Switzerland, in addition to elections at each level of government, the electorate plays a major adjudicating role through the operation of the legislative referendum. In this process, any federal legislation that is challenged by 50,000 citizens or 8 cantons must be submitted to a direct popular vote in a referendum. As a result, this referendum process becomes the adjudicative process for ruling on the validity of federal legislation. An interesting by-product of this constitutional procedure is the inducement that it provides for interparty compromise and cohesion within the federal government and legislature in order to ensure the maximum possible breadth of support, thereby reducing the risk of a successful challenge through the legislative referendum process.

In addition to elections within each level of government, most federations have also relied upon the courts to play a major adjudicating role. In this role, courts have performed three functions: (1) impartial constitutional interpretation, (2) adaptation of the constitution to changing circumstances (especially where constitutional amendment is difficult), and (3) resolution of intergovernmental conflicts.

11.3 SUPREME COURTS AND CONSTITUTIONAL COURTS

Two types of courts for ultimate constitutional jurisdiction may be found among federations. One is a supreme court serving as the final adjudicator in relation to all laws including the constitution. Examples are the Supreme Courts of the United States, Canada, Australia, India, the four Latin American federations, Malaysia, Nigeria, Pakistan, Comoros, Micronesia, Belau and the High Court in St. Kitts and Nevis. The other is a constitutional court, specializing in constitutional interpretation, which is the pattern followed in Germany, Austria, Russia, Bosnia and Herzegovina, the United Arab Emirates, Belgium and Spain. A third approach is that found in Switzerland involving a limited tribunal. Under the unique Swiss arrangement, the Federal Tribunal may rule on the validity of cantonal laws but not of federal laws. The validity of federal laws is determined instead through the instrument of the legislative referendum referred to above.

Ethiopia is unique among federations in making the federal second chamber, the House of Federation, composed of members representing the states, as the sole guardian of the constitution. It has the exclusive right (article 62(1)) and ultimate authority (article 83) to interpret the constitution, and that is its main function. The constitution (article 62(2)) provides for a Council of Constitutional Inquiry to advise the House of Federation on constitutional matters, but the House is not bound by the Council's advisory opinions.

If courts are to be accepted within a federation as impartial and independent adjudicators, there appear to be two requirements: (1) independence from influence on the court by any particular level of government, and (2) proportional representativeness of membership on the court. The first of these raises the issue of the method and security of appointment. In relation to the second of these issues, in most federations some provision is made either by constitutional requirement or in practice for the constituent unit governments to have a role in the appointment of judges adjudicating the constitution. In the USA, Argentina, Brazil and Mexico, appointments to the Supreme Court rest solely with the President but require ratification by the Senate, where the state electorates are equally represented. In Canada and Australia, constitutionally the power to appoint judges to the Supreme Court lies solely with the federal government, but by convention provincial or state governments are consulted. In Malaysia the federal cabinet has had the last word in the appointment of Supreme Court judges but has been required by the constitution to consult certain bodies before making the appointments. Although appointments to the Supreme Court in India are nominally made by the president in consultation with the Supreme Court, in a series of judgments between 1981 and 1998 the Supreme Court wrested from the executive the power to make these appointments. In Germany the Bundesrat representing the Länder appoints half the members of the Constitutional Court and the Bundestag the other half. In both cases two-thirds majorities are required (for the Bundesrat in plenary session and for the Bundestag in the Judicial Elections Committee). In Spain the Constitutional Court is composed of 12 members of whom 4 are elected by Congress, 4 by the Senate, 2 are appointed on the proposal of the Government Council, and 2 are appointed on the proposal of the General Council of Judicial Power. On the other hand, in Belgium the members of the ultimate adjudicating Court of Arbitration are simply elected by the multiparty Federal Assembly. In Russia the 19 judges of the Constitutional Court are appointed by the Federation Council (federal second chamber) on the recommendation of the President. The members of the Nigerian and Pakistan Supreme Courts are appointed by the President, but in Pakistan an attempt by the President to remove the Chief Justice in 2007 met with such public opposition that this became a major destabilizing factor within the federation. In most federations, in the interest of ensuring independence there is also provision for strong tenure, making it difficult to remove judges during their term of office.

The issue of proportionality in the composition of these ultimate adjudicating courts has also been an issue in most federations. This has been particularly so in Canada in relation to regional representation (especially of Quebec with its civil law tradition differing from the common law tradition prevailing elsewhere in Canada), in Switzerland where the three official languages are represented, and in Belgium where strict legal requirements are laid down for linguistic balance in the membership of the Court of Arbitration.

An important factor affecting the role of judicial review in federations is whether the character of the legal system is based on common law or civil law.[2] The United States and most of the federations that evolved from former British colonies (such

[2] K. LeRoy and C. Saunders, eds., *Legislative, Executive and Judicial Governance in Federal Countries*, Forum of Federations and International Association of Centres for Federal Studies, *A Global Dialogue on Federalism*, vol. 3 (Montreal & Kingston: McGill-Queen's University Press, 2006), p. 348.

as Australia, India, and Malaysia) have common law legal systems, while most of the European and Latin American federations have civil law systems. Canada, South Africa and Nigeria have mixed legal systems, although in the field of public law they are predominately common law in character. In civil law systems, legislative codes are the predominant source of law, and the courts in their interpretation tend to be more limited in their scope. In the common law federations, the law derives from either legislation or judicial decisions with the latter having precedential value, and in these federations judicial review has come to be a major element in the operation of their constitutions.

The question is sometimes raised, especially in common law federations, whether federation as a form of government results ultimately in rule by judges rather than by elected representatives. There is some element of truth in this and it is reinforced where the judges also interpret a set of fundamental individual and collective rights in the constitution. This has sometimes led to the advocacy of the popular election or recall of judges, although that has not yet been applied to the most senior constitutional court in any federation. To be noted is the Swiss alternative referred to above, of the legislative referendum to determine the validity of federal laws. In this process the electorate becomes the adjudicating umpire. It should also be noted that, generally speaking, the extent to which the role of courts as adjudicators becomes prominent depends on the extent to which problems fail to be resolved by other methods of adjustment and conflict resolution through intergovernmental agreements, mediation procedures between the federal legislative chambers (as in the USA, Germany and South Africa), governmental changes induced by elections, and formal constitutional amendments. The South African constitution, in order to minimize intergovernmental litigation, uniquely provides (section 41(3)) that "all spheres of government must exhaust every reasonable effort to resolve any disputes through intergovernmental negotiation," and the courts can refer a dispute back to the governments if they consider that substantial efforts have not been made in this regard (section 41(4)).

11.4 CONSITUTIONAL AMENDMENT PROCEDURES

In federations it is the constitution that defines the authority of each of the orders of government so that neither level is constitutionally subordinate to the other. It follows that the written constitution, at least in those respects defining and affecting the relative powers of the orders of government, must not be unilaterally amendable by just one order of government, since that would potentially subordinate the other order of government to it. But providing for special procedures to amend the constitution raises the issue of balancing the requirements for both rigidity and flexibility in the operation of the constitution in a federation. Some element of rigidity is required to safeguard the protections built in for regional and minority interests in the constitutional structure of the federation. This is

necessary since a sense of regional or minority insecurity generally tends to undermine federal cohesion. At the same time it is important that as conditions change,
the federation is sufficiently flexible to adapt. Too rigid a constitutional structure
may seriously weaken the ability of the federation to respond to and accommodate changing internal economic, social and political pressures and external
international conditions. What is required, then, in the constitutions of federations is a balance between rigidity and flexibility.

One common means of achieving such a balance has been to provide for different amendment procedures for different parts of the constitution, with amendment
of those aspects of the constitution that establish its fundamental federal character requiring the involvement of both orders of government, but the procedure for
amending other portions of the constitution being more flexible. For instance,
federal legislatures are often free to amend those institutions of federal government that do not affect the representation or influence of the constituent units,
and constituent units are usually free to amend their own constitutions within the
limits permitted by the federal constitution. This is typical of most federations,
but particularly notable examples are the constitutions of India and Canada, both
with a variety of amendment processes for different parts of the federal constitution. Following this pattern, when the Canadian *Constitution Act, 1982* (sections
38–49) added procedures for amending the Canadian constitution, five different
procedures were actually set out for amending different parts of the constitution.
These involve varying degrees of rigidity: (1) a "normal" procedure requiring the
assent of Parliament and two-thirds of the legislatures of the provinces containing
at least half the total population of all the provinces, (2) a procedure requiring the
assent of Parliament and the unanimous consent of the provincial legislatures for
a select number of constitutional provisions, (3) a bilateral procedure for amendment of provisions relating to some but not all provinces, (4) amendments by
Parliament alone for provisions not affecting the provinces, and (5) amendments
by provincial legislatures of provincial constitutions.

In most federations, while the federal legislature is assigned the power to initi-
ate constitutional amendments, approval of amendments to those portions of the
constitution relating to the distribution of powers and the integrity of the constituent units requires approval both in the federal legislature, often by special
majorities, and by a majority of the legislatures or of referendums in the constituent units. Approval by both federal houses of legislature by special majorities is
required in the United States, India, Malaysia, Argentina, Brazil, Mexico, Ethiopia (in a joint sitting), Nigeria, Pakistan and Russia. In South Africa a special
majority of the National Assembly is required. A simple majority in both federal
houses is required in Switzerland and Canada. In the unicameral federal legislatures of St. Kitts and Nevis and the United Arab Emirates, but not in Venezuela,
special majorities are also required.

In addition, in most federations such amendments require approval by a special majority of constituent unit legislatures. Examples are the USA, Canada,

Nigeria and Russia. In some a simple majority of state legislatures is required, as in India and Mexico. In Switzerland and Australia, instead of approval by constituent legislatures, a referendum with a double majority consisting of an overall majority and majorities in a majority of constituent units is required. A referendum with a special majority both federally and in Nevis is required in St. Kitts and Nevis for constitutional amendments. A simple federal majority in a referendum is required in Venezuela and in some special cases in Russia. Major amendments in Malaysia affecting the Borneo states require the concurrence of those states. Some federations, such as Argentina, Comoros, Belau, and in certain circumstances Russia, involve a special constituent assembly or constitutional convention procedure. In the United States, a convention called on the application of two thirds of the state legislatures is an alternative constitutional amendment procedure, but has almost never been invoked.

Brazil, Germany, Austria, Malaysia (for most amendments), South Africa, Pakistan and the United Arab Emirates stand out as federations requiring only special majorities in the federal legislature for constitutional amendments affecting the federal character of the federation, thus leaving the constituent units to depend on their representation in the federal second chamber to protect their interests in the processes of constitutional amendment.

Some special points may be noted about constitutional amendment procedures in the United States, Australia, Switzerland, Germany, South Africa, Austria, Belgium and Spain. The amendment processes in both the United States and Australia have in practice proved relatively rigid. In the United States, after the first 10 amendments made in 1791, over the two centuries since there have been only 17 further successful amendments to the constitution. In Australia over a century, of 42 proposed amendments sent to referendum only 8 have achieved the necessary double majorities for adoption. Switzerland in 1891 instituted two different procedures: one for total revision of the constitution and one for partial revision. Although attempted on a number of occasions, until 1999 the former had never been successfully used. In 1999, after more than three decades of efforts to undertake a comprehensive revision of the Swiss constitution, a total revision was finally achieved. But to improve its chances of adoption this revision involved few substantive changes and was characterized in the referendum for approval as simply a modernization of the language of the constitution. Even then the outcome was relatively close with only 59 percent voting in favour and with majorities in 12 of the full cantons and 2 of the half cantons out of the 20 full cantons and 6 half cantons. On the other hand, the procedure for partial revision has proved remarkably flexible. It has been used successfully more than 110 times since 1891. There is also in Switzerland an initiative process for constitutional amendments which has frequently been employed.

Germany requires only special majorities in the two federal houses for constitutional amendments, but the Bundesrat is composed of instructed state government delegates so that endorsement by a special majority in the Bundesrat is equivalent to consent by that majority among the Land governments. In practice this procedure has proved relatively flexible, producing 46 constitutional amendments during the first 50 years, including a strengthening of the legislative and financial roles of the federal government in 1967–69 and the reunification of Germany in 1990.

In South Africa the level of approval in Parliament required varies with the nature of the constitutional amendment, but the highest threshold requires approval of three-quarters of the National Assembly and 6 of the 9 provinces in the National Council of Provinces (composed of provincial delegates voting as a provincial block).

In Austria, partial constitutional amendments require passage in the lower house (Nationalrat) of the federal legislature by a two-thirds majority with at least half of the membership of the chamber present, but one-third of the membership of either federal house may demand a total revision of the constitution requiring a referendum at which a majority of the population decides the matter.

The Belgian procedure for constitutional amendment (article 131) involves only a two-thirds majority in the federal parliament, and does not involve the Regions or Communities. Most of the detailed provisions relating to its federal features do, however, require a complex process which involves a special election, special majorities in each federal house, and in many areas (relating to amendments to the distribution of powers or to the Court d'Arbitrage) special legislation supported by a majority of each of the two major linguistic groups in Parliament.

In Spain the initiating of constitutional amendments lies normally with the government, Congress or Senate, although there is provision for an Autonomous Community Assembly to propose constitutional amendments. Ratification is by a majority of three-fifths of the members of each federal chamber or, where the chambers disagree, by an absolute majority in the Senate and a two-thirds vote in the Congress. If one-tenth of the members of either house request it, this is followed by a referendum. A total revision of the constitution or a partial revision of certain specific portions of the constitution are more rigidly entrenched, requiring a two-thirds majority in each federal chamber and ratification by referendum.

Typically, most federations make a special attempt to protect the integrity of their constituent units by provisions in the constitution requiring the consent of a constituent unit for any modification of its boundaries. India is, however, an exception to this pattern, as noted above in section 4.6 of chapter 4.

A few federal constitutions include provisions prohibiting the abolishing of the federal system. Examples are Germany and Brazil. In a series of cases the Indian Supreme Court has imposed a similar limit on the power of constitutional amendment. In Australia there has been a division of opinion on whether the formal constitutional amendment process could be used to abolish the federal system.

As a result of the requirements described above, the constitutions of most federations have in practice proved relatively rigid concerning the features essential to their federal structures. Swiss and German experience points to the value of incremental partial constitutional revisions as opposed to efforts at comprehensive constitutional revision in achieving adaptation. The failure in Canada of several efforts at comprehensive constitutional revision of its federal features during the past forty years confirms this. The general rigidity of most constitutions of federations has made other forms of adjustment to achieve flexibility and adaptability all the more important. Consequently, there has been a heavy reliance in virtually all federations upon other forms of adjustment, including judicial review, financial transfer arrangements, and intergovernmental collaboration and agreements.

11.5 THE ROLE OF CONSTITUTIONAL BILLS OF RIGHTS

Federations are essentially a territorial form of political organization. Thus, as a means of safeguarding distinct groups or minorities, they do this best when those groups and minorities are regionally concentrated in such a way that they may achieve self-government as a majority within a regional unit government. Examples are the many largely unilingual and uniconfessional cantons within Switzerland, the predominantly French-speaking majority in Quebec within Canada, the various linguistic majorities in the different Indian states following the reorganization of the states along linguistic lines, the distinctive populations of the Borneo states in Malaysia, the predominantly Flemish and French-speaking Regions and Communities within Belgium, and the populations of the historical Regions of the Basque Country, Catalonia and Galicia within Spain. In each of these cases, the primary safeguard for groups which are a minority within the federation is through their control as a majority in a self-governing regional unit having guaranteed constitutional powers within the federation.

But populations rarely in practice are distributed into neat watertight territorial regions. In virtually all federations some intra-unit minorities within the regional units of government have been unavoidable. Where significant intra-region minorities have existed, three types of solutions have been attempted.

The first has been to redraw the boundaries of the constituent units to coincide better with the location of the linguistic and ethnic groups. Examples are the separation of the Jura from the canton of Bern to create a new canton in Switzerland, the major reorganization of state boundaries in India in 1956 and some subsequent further revisions, and Nigeria's evolution by stages from 3 regions to 36 states. While such revisions may produce more internally homogeneous and coherent regional units of government, experience makes it clear that in redrawing boundaries it is extremely difficult to avoid leaving some intra-regional minorities.

A second approach has been to assign to the federal government a special responsibility as guardian for intra-regional minorities against possible oppression by a regional majority. The Canadian *Constitution Act, 1867* included such a provision (section 93(4) relating to minority education). In addition the federal government was given exclusive legislative authority over Indians and lands re-served for them (section 91(24)). In India the federal government has been given a more extensive power to give direction to state governments regarding the recognition within states of minority languages, the use within states of minority languages for education, and the establishment within states of regional legislative committees and development boards. Provision has also been made for a special officer reporting to the Union government on the operation of minority safeguards within the states. The *Constitution of Malaya, 1957*, which preceded the later Malaysian one, gave to the federal government the power to give directions to the state governments regarding Aboriginal Peoples and also specified that changes in the reservation of land for Malays required not only a special majority in the state assembly but approval by special majorities in the federal parliament. In Pakistan, prior to its separation, a similar role to that in India was assigned to the federal government in relation to scheduled areas and tribes, and the authority to specify whether there would be joint or separate electorates was left under the 1956 constitution to the National Assembly to decide after consulting the provincial legislatures.

A third approach, and the most widely used one, has been to protect intra-regional minorities through embodying a set of fundamental citizens' rights in the constitution. In the United States this was not the original intention of the Bill of Rights, added to the constitution in the form of the first ten amendments ratified in 1791. These were intended to limit federal government action and did not initially apply to the states. The passage of the Fourteenth Amendment in 1868, following the civil war of 1861–65, however, led the Supreme Court in the process of judicial review, beginning in 1897 and particularly after World War II, to extend the protections of individual rights to apply also against state action. As set out in the constitution of the United States, all such protected rights are formulated as individual rights with no provision for group rights. Nevertheless, the right to equality proved crucial for desegregation within states.

Most subsequent federations have set out in their constitutions more extensive lists of rights protected from both federal and regional government action, although Australia and Austria have been notable exceptions. In some, but not all, of these federations special group rights have been included. Among the federations that have included in their constitutions a list of fundamental rights are Mexico (1917), Germany (1949), India (1950), Malaysia (1963), Spain (1978), Canada (added in 1982), Belgium (1993), Russia (1993), Brazil (1994), South Africa (1996), Nigeria (1999) and Switzerland (1999). Of these, the Basic Law of the Federal Republic of Germany lists numerous individual rights and some collective rights relating to trade unions, employee associations and university autonomy. On the other hand, the constitutions of such multi-ethnic federations as India, Malaysia, Nigeria, Canada and Belgium all make provision for some group rights.

As one of the most ethnically and linguistically diverse federations, India's constitution makes provision not only for fundamental individual rights but also for the recognition of 18 regional languages and for the recognition and protection of linguistic minorities (including their language and education), Anglo-Indians, and scheduled castes and tribes. This includes provision for a "special officer for linguistic minorities" and a national commission to investigate and monitor all matters relating to the rights and safeguards of the Scheduled Castes and Scheduled Tribes.

The Malaysian constitution similarly lists individual rights and also makes special provision for certain specified groups within the states. There are explicit arrangements on behalf of the Malays for the reservation of land, for quotas for permits and quotas for employment in the public services in the states. These guarantees have been intended to protect the Malays, who (although the majority) might otherwise, because of their relative education and economic backwardness, suffer in competition with other racial groups. Similar provisions extend to "natives" in the Borneo states, and additional safeguards have been provided for the variety of indigenous peoples in the Borneo states centring on the continued use of native languages and the protection of the Muslim religion and education.

In Canada, the *Charter of Rights and Freedoms* added by the *Constitution Act, 1982* not only includes a wide range of individual rights but also identifies minority language rights, the rights of Aboriginal Peoples, and rights related to the "preservation and enhancement of the multicultural heritage."

The Belgian constitution sets out fundamental individual rights and liberties and also constitutional guarantees for linguistic minorities. As a result, there are statutory guarantees concerning the use of language in administrative matters, in legislation, in the armed forces, in education, in labour relations, in the bilingual capital of Brussels and in the German-speaking Region.

The Spanish constitution of 1978 sets out a long list of civil, political and socioeconomic rights, most of which are individual rights. In terms of ethno-linguistic rights, the constitution specifies Castilian as the official language of Spain (article 3(1)) but also states (article 3(2)) that there may be other official languages in the respective Autonomous Communities, thus providing some measure of *de facto* territoriality to the language regime in Spain. Consequently, the Basque, Galician, Catalan and Valencian languages are co-official with Spanish.

The Swiss constitution until its amendment in 1999 was mainly concerned with the organization of government structures and with the distribution of powers between the orders of government. Concerns over rights (individual or collective) received very little treatment in the constitution. The constitution did recognize three official and four national languages and did specify that the Federal Tribunal must include representatives of all three official languages. But while the constitution contained little about rights, there evolved a number of unwritten principles relating to linguistic rights that came to take on considerable significance.

Three basic principles came to prevail considering language rights.[3] These were (1) the absolute equality of the Swiss languages, (2) cantons have general jurisdiction over language matters except where the constitution provides specific limits in favour of the federal government, and (3) the principle of "territoriality" prevails. This is interpreted to mean that "any canton or linguistic area is deemed to have the right to preserve and defend its own distinctive linguistic character against all outside forces tending to alter or endanger it."[4] The revised Swiss constitution adopted in 1999, while largely a modernization of the language of the previous constitution, does, however, now include a consolidation of fundamental rights (articles 6–32) as well as a statement of social goals (article 33).

The Ethiopian federation has ethnicity as its underlying organizing principle, clearly expressed in the preamble of the constitution. With more than 80 different ethnic groups and some 200 dialects, there are too many for each to have its own constituent unit within the federation. Consequently, although Amharic is the working language of the federal government, all Ethiopian languages enjoy equal recognition under the constitution.

In Australia and Austria the constitutions do not elaborate a set of fundament rights. Australia's constitution contains no general statement of individual or group rights, although there are specific references relating to the acquisition of property on just terms, trial by jury, freedom of movement between states, freedom of religion, protection against discrimination on the basis of state residence, and voting rights. Recent jurisprudence of the High Court indicating its willingness to "imply" certain rights from the provisions of the constitution has been the subject of considerable debate.

The Austrian constitution includes no list of rights of any kind, but there is a reference to minority group rights of the Croatian and Solvene minorities in article 7 of the *State Treaty of Austria, 1955* that was signed by the Allied powers and the Austrian government at the time the occupation of Austria was ended.

In a number of federations, including the United States and Canada, some state or provincial constitutions also grant more individual rights or minorities protections adding to those embodied in the federal constitution.

11.6 PROVISIONS FOR FORMAL SECESSION

Until recently, few federations anywhere have included in their constitution the recognition of a unilateral right of secession or explicit provisions for a formal

---

[3] Kenneth D. McRae, *Conflict and Compromise in Multilingual Societies: Switzerland* (Waterloo: Wilfrid Laurier University Press, 1983), p. 21.
[4] Ibid., 122.

process for secession. Indeed, the constitution of the former USSR was in its time unique in this respect, being the only constitution of a federation then making reference to a unilateral right of secession. Generally, three reasons have been offered for not including a unilateral right of secession in the constitutions of federations. First, it has been feared that the right to secede would weaken the whole system by placing a weapon of political coercion in the hands of the governments of the constituent units. Second, there has been anxiety that the possibility of secession would introduce an element of uncertainty and lack of confidence in the future, seriously handicapping efforts to build up federal economic development and unity. Third, theorists have argued that it would undermine the fundamental principle of coordinacy between levels of government in a federation: if a regional government acting alone had the unilateral right to leave the federation, or the federal government had the unilateral right to expel a regional unit, then the other level of government would be subordinated.

Consequently, secession has rarely been authorized by a federal constitution. Indeed, many federations have emphasized the "indissoluble" character of the federation and where necessary have enforced this by federal military action, of which the civil war in the United States in the 1860s was a prime example.

The current exceptions are the constitutions of Ethiopia, St. Kitts and Nevis, and Sudan, and the result of judicial review in Canada. The Ethiopian constitution with its emphasis on ethnic self-determination expressly provides for the constitutional right of secession (article 39(4)) by a procedure that includes as steps a two-thirds majority vote of the council of the respective state, a referendum organized by the federal government, and a majority vote in the referendum. To date, Eritrea in 1993 has been the only unit to gain *de jure* independence though this process. The St. Kitts and Nevis constitution (section 113) permits the secession of Nevis if two-thirds of the elected members of the Nevis Assembly approve such a bill and it is endorsed in a referendum on Nevis by two-thirds of all the votes cast. In 1998 such a referendum was actually held, but with 61.7 percent in favour it failed to achieve the necessary majority for secession. The Sudan peace agreement of 2005 provided for the possibility after a ten-year interim period of a referendum on the independence of Southern Sudan.

In Canada, the constitution contains no explicit reference to a right of secession, but in 1998 the Supreme Court of Canada admitted in a historic reference case that provinces did have the right to secede from Canada, but not unilaterally. It ruled that if the population of a province indicated by a clear majority in response to a clear question that they wished to secede (the measures of clarity were left unspecified), the rest of Canada would have an obligation to negotiate the terms of secession, taking into account the interests of all parties, including the province concerned, the rest of Canada and minorities within the particular province, and also the fundamental organizing principles of the constitution such as federalism, democracy, constitutionalism and the rule of law. Ultimately, secession would require that a constitutional amendment be negotiated, and this would require the agreement of the federal government. The judgement of the court left many issues open, but in attempting a balanced judgment that would not inflame passions among either federalists or Quebec secessionists, it did recognize the possibility within certain terms of the possibility of a non-unilateral secession.

It must be noted that the fact that virtually all other federations except Ethiopia, St. Kitts and Nevis and Sudan have made no explicit constitutional provision for a right of unilateral secession does not mean, however, that there have not been cases of actual unilateral succession or expulsion. It simply means that when secession has been attempted or has occurred, the process has invariably been extra-constitutional, expressing political pressures that have broken the constitutional mould. Examples will be taken up in chapter 13 below.

Chapter 12

Degrees of Decentralization and Non-centralization in Federations

12.1 CONCEPTUAL ISSUES IN MEASURING DECENTRALIZATION AND RELATIVE AUTONOMY

The concepts of decentralization and non-centralization are closely related. Some authors have preferred to use the term "non-centralization" to "decentralization" in relation to federations on the grounds that the latter implies a hierarchy with power flowing from the top or centre as exemplified by decentralization within unitary political systems, whereas the former infers a constitutionally structured dispersion of power and therefore better represents the character of a federation.[1] Nevertheless, since the term "decentralization" is in such widespread public use in referring to federations, the terms will be used interchangeably here.

While in ordinary language we may loosely compare differing degrees of decentralization within federations, the comparative measurement of decentralization or non-centralization is actually a complex issue. There are at least four problems in discussing the degree of decentralization (or centralization) within a political system: first, how to define what the concept of decentralization actually refers to; second, how to measure it; third, how to relate different indices of measurement to each other; and fourth, how to compare such measurements across countries or over time.

To begin with we must distinguish between decentralization of jurisdiction, i.e., the responsibilities exercised by each level of government, and decentralization

---

[1] Daniel J. Elazar, *Exploring Federalism* (Tuscaloosa: University of Alabama Press, 1987), pp. 34–6.

of decision making at the federal level, i.e., the degree to which the constituent units play a significant role in decision making at the federal level. The former, decentralization of jurisdiction, itself has two aspects to be distinguished: the *scope of jurisdiction* exercised by each level of government, and the *degree of autonomy* or freedom from control by other levels of government with which a particular government performs the tasks assigned to it. For example, in one sense Japan (a decentralized unitary state) is highly decentralized in terms of the administrative tasks performed by the prefectures and the local authorities, but in another sense it is relatively centralized in terms of the controls the central government exercises over these subordinate levels of government. Some federations allocate fewer responsibilities to their constituent states or provinces, but leave them with greater freedom and autonomy over the exercise of those responsibilities.

A major problem in any comparative assessment is that no single quantifiable index can adequately measure the scope of effective jurisdictional decentralization and the degree of autonomy of decentralized decision making within a political system. Among the multiple indices (although not all of equal weight) that need to be considered in any such assessment are legislative and administrative decentralization, financial decentralization, decentralization to non-governmental agencies, constitutional limitations, and the character of federal decision making.[2] Each of these indices is discussed below.

LEGISLATIVE DECENTRALIZATION

• The formal allocation by the constitution of legislative powers to each level of government gives an indication of the scope of decentralized jurisdiction. In comparing such allocations in different federations, however, it should be noted that the relative lengths of the lists of heads of federal or state powers do not by themselves give a full picture, because individual heads of power may vary in relative significance. Furthermore, account must be taken of the degree to which in practice constitutionally assigned powers are actually fully or only partially exercised by the governments to which they are assigned. Nevertheless, the constitutional allocation of legislative jurisdiction is one major indicator of the scope of jurisdictional decentralization.

• Account must be taken also of the degree of autonomy with which a government may exercise the legislative jurisdiction assigned to it by the constitution. In this respect the extent of exclusive jurisdiction and the extent of concurrent or shared responsibilities set out in the constitution is significant.

---

[2] See, for instance, L. Thorlaksen, "Comparing Federal Institutions: Power and Representation in Six Federations," *West European Politics*, 26:2 (2003): 1–22.

- Another aspect of the autonomy of legislative decentralization is the extent to which constituent units are bound by international treaties negotiated by the federal government in areas that normally come under the jurisdiction of the constituent units. In some federations international treaties may create a limitation on state autonomy (e.g., USA and Australia), but in others such federal treaties in areas normally under state jurisdiction require implementing state or provincial legislation or the consent of the provincial or state government (e.g., Canada, Germany and Austria) or non-binding consultation of state governments (e.g., India and Malaysia). The Belgian federation goes the farthest in giving constituent units specific powers to negotiate international treaties in areas of their own competence.

ADMINISTRATIVE DECENTRALIZATION

- The allocation of administration responsibilities assigned by the constitution or developed through delegation or intergovernmental agreements is another relevant index of the scope of jurisdictional decentralization. While in many federations the constitutional allocation of administrative responsibilities broadly corresponds to the constitutional legislative jurisdiction, there are many exceptions to this. Indeed, in most European federations their constitutions require a substantial portion of federal laws to be administered by the states. Thus, in these cases these federations are more decentralized administratively than legislatively. The same arrangement has also been applied in the European Union.
- The relative sizes of the public services of each level of government is another indicator of the scope of decentralization of decision making, particularly in relation to administrative responsibilities, although it provides little indication of the degrees of autonomy.
- In assessing the degree of autonomy in the exercise of administrative jurisdiction, one needs to take account of the extent to which one level of government may be dependent on another for implementing its policies (especially where a federal government is dependent upon constituent governments for this) and the degree to which the level of government that has legislative responsibilities may, as in Germany, give directions to the government that is administering its legislation. It is significant, for example, that in Switzerland, however, the cantons have extensive autonomy in how they implement federal laws for which the constitution has given them administrative responsibility, thus emphasizing the decentralized character of that federation. In other federations, where administration of federal laws is delegated by the choice of the federal government rather than by constitutional requirement, the terms of the arrangement (including financial terms) and the directives of the federal government may limit the degree of autonomy with which the delegated administration is performed.

FINANCIAL DECENTRALIZATION

- Federal government revenues before transfers as a percentage of all government revenues (federal-provincial-local) provide one measure of the scope
of financial centralization or decentralization. Since this relates to own-source
revenues directly raised by each level of government and excludes transfers,
it also provides a measure of the degree of their financial autonomy. Table 9
in chapter 6 above provides a comparative tabulation of federations in descending order, from the more centralized to the more decentralized in this
respect.

- Federal government expenditures after transfers as a percentage of all government expenditures (federal-provincial-local) give a measure of the scope of
centralization or decentralization of expenditure and of the administration of
programs and delivery of services. Since these include expenditures funded
by transfers, however, they are not a good indicator of the degree of financial
autonomy. Furthermore, the cost of different responsibilities does not by itself indicate their importance. Those functions involving delivery of services
are generally more expensive than those that are primarily regulatory. Nevertheless, table 10 in chapter 6, which provides a comparative tabulation of
expenditures after transfers, gives another measure of relative decentralization.

- The size and character (whether conditional grants, unconditional grants or
shares of federal taxes) of transfers from one level of government to another
gives some indication of the degree of dependency or autonomy with which
levels of government perform their responsibilities. Table 11 in chapter 6
provides a comparative tabulation indicating intergovernmental transfers as
a percentage of provincial or state revenue, and tables 12 and 13 indicate the
significance of conditional and unconditional transfers affecting the degree
of dependence or autonomy in different federations.

- The extent to which one level of government may and actually does use its
spending power to act or influence activities in areas of responsibility constitutionally assigned to other levels of government must also be taken into
account in assessing both the scope and the degree of autonomy applying to
decentralization within a particular political system.

- Access of constituent units to public borrowing is another indicator of the
degree of financial autonomy. Provided their governments are not mired in
debt, the autonomy of constituent units is enhanced when they have direct
and unhindered access to borrowed funds. Federations differ widely in terms
of the formal or practical ability of constituent units to borrow. In some federations (e.g., Austria, India and Malaysia) the federal constitution limits
foreign borrowing to the federal government. In the United States there are
balanced budget requirements in many states. In Australia the constitutionally established intergovernmental Loan Council is a coordinating body with
binding authority upon both levels of government. Such cases contrast with

other federations, including Canada, where constituent units have substantial and unhindered access to both domestic and international borrowing.

UNFUNDED MANDATES

In some federations, such as the United States, "unfunded mandates" may introduce an element of federal government control. These are federal actions requiring state and local government activity that are not accompanied by funding to cover the costs of the activity. This has been described as leading to the emergence of "fend-for-yourself federalism" in the United States.[3] The increase of this practice since 1945, coupled with the increase in federal pre-emption of state and local government authority, federal laws and actions pre-empting the ability of state and local governments to take action or generate policies on their own, and reductions in federal aid and support levels has produced a common assessment of the federal role in relation to states and local governments as "less money and more regulations".

DECENTRALIZATION TO NON-GOVERNMENTAL AGENCIES

- The scope and extent of decentralization to non-governmental agencies as opposed to other levels of government is also relevant in judging the character and scope of decentralization within a political system.

CONSTITUTIONAL LIMITATIONS

- Constitutional prohibitions (e.g., constitutional stipulations of individual or collective rights such as the Canadian *Charter of Rights and Freedoms*) prohibiting certain activities by any level of government must also be taken into account in measuring the extent of non-centralization.
- In some federations the extent of the autonomy of both levels of government (e.g., Switzerland) or of the states (e.g., some states in the USA) may be subject to the checks and balances of citizen-initiated referendums and initiatives.

THE CHARACTER OF FEDERAL DECISION MAKING

- In addition to the above indicators that provide various measures of decentralization and non-centralization in terms of the scope and autonomy of

---

[3] Christopher Hoene, "Unfunded Mandates in the U.S. and fend-for-yourself federalism," *Federations* 6:1 (February/March2007):31-2.

jurisdiction, the extent to which federal decision making requires involvement of other levels of government in a co-decision-making process (e.g., the role federal second chambers such as the German Bundersrat) is another measure of the degree to which policy making is decentralized. A related factor here too is the political party structure and the degree to which federal parties are distinct from or dependent upon provincial or state party structures, or control provincial or state party organizations.

The assessment of the degree of decentralization within a political system is further complicated by difficulties of quantification when measuring powers, degrees of dependency or autonomy, relative roles in areas of overlap and interdependence, or influence upon other governments. In many federations where the distribution of responsibilities among provincial or state governments is not uniform, one needs also to take account of differences (i.e., asymmetry) in the powers assigned or exercised by different constituent units and in the resources and expenditures available to them noted in chapter 8 above.

Thus, it is clear that attempting to measure with any precision the degree of decentralization (or centralization) within political systems is complicated and difficult and at the very least requires reference to multiple indices with some effort to weigh their relative importance.

12.2 A COMPARATIVE ASSESSMENT

Given the complex issues identified in the preceding section, a comparative assessment of the degree of decentralization in different federations would require intensive and extensive research in terms of the various indices noted above. Much of this research has yet to be undertaken by comparative scholars. Nonetheless, it is possible to make two sets of broad objective generalizations.

First, as noted in section 5.4 in chapter 5 above, the particular areas of legislative jurisdiction that are centralized or decentralized vary from federation to federation in order to meet the particular economic, demographic and social conditions of each federation. Thus, to take Canada as one example, it is less decentralized than Switzerland in relation to language policy and culture and to citizenship, but it is more decentralized in other areas. Canada is less decentralized than Germany regarding banking and broadcasting but more decentralized in a large number of other areas. In comparison with the United States, Canada is less decentralized regarding banking and criminal law but more decentralized in many other areas. Also, while Canada is more decentralized than most federations in many areas of jurisdiction, on the other hand, when it comes to the participation of its provincial governments in federal policy making, there is less constitutional provision for this than in most other federations. The Canadian example is just one illustration of the variations in the areas and forms of decentralization that has existed among federations.

The second broad generalization is that, while it is difficult to arrive at a ranking of federations in terms of overall decentralization because of the different indices that have to be taken into account (as described in section 12.1 above), nevertheless, it is possible to arrive at some general assessments.

For this purpose the tables in chapter 6 (tables 9, 10, 11, 12 and 13) provide a broad basis, although account must also be taken of the other criteria noted in section 12.1 above. Table 10, which compares federal-state-local expenditures (after transfers), gives a general indication of the relative cost of the functions performed by each order of government in the various federations. There, the federations in descending order of centralization would rank Malaysia as highly centralized, Brazil, Nigeria, Australia, Mexico, Austria, Spain, South Africa, Russia, the United States and, India in the middle range, and Belgium, Germany, Canada and Switzerland as the most decentralized.

This ranking has to be moderated when a number of other factors are considered. Germany, for instance, ranks where it does in that table because of the extensive administrative decentralization that affects the expenditure levels, but this indicator does not reflect sufficiently the high degree of legislative centralization. Furthermore, table 9 showing the distribution of federal-state-local revenues before transfers indicates that in terms of taxing powers, as contrasted with expenditure, federal governments are somewhat more dominant in comparative terms in Nigeria, South Africa, Mexico, Russia, Australia, Germany and India. Furthermore, tables 11, 12 and 13 indicate the differing degrees to which constituent units are dependent upon transfers from their federal governments and particularly upon conditional transfers. Taken together, the financial tables point to Canada and Switzerland as clearly the most decentralized federations.

When not only the financial figures but all the various criteria outlined in section 12.1 above are taken into account, we may broadly rank federations in practice on a continuum of descending centralization as follows: most highly centralized are Venezuela, Pakistan, Malaysia, Nigeria, Argentina, Mexico and Russia; relatively centralized are Brazil, Austria and Australia; moderately centralized are Germany, Spain, the USA and India; the most decentralized are Belgium, Canada and Switzerland. Of the four micro-federations, Comoros and Belau rank with the most highly centralized federations, and Micronesia and St. Kitts and Nevis with the relatively centralized federations.

12.3 MINIMUM FEDERAL POWERS

The preceding analysis in this study has indicated that there is an enormous variation among federations in terms of the degree of centralization or decentralization regarding both particular functions and in general. This raises the question whether experience elsewhere suggests that there is a minimum list of federal powers required if a federation is to be effective over the long term.

In addressing this question it should be noted that the essence of federal political systems is to reconcile diversity and unity within a single political system by assigning sovereignty over certain matters to the constituent provinces and sovereignty over other matters to the federal government, with each level of government responsible directly to its electorate. Any consideration of devolving additional powers to states or provinces must, therefore, also take account of what powers may be required for the federal government to fulfill its role effectively for the federation as a whole. Decentralization and devolution of powers that may be desirable to accommodate linguistic, cultural, historical and economic diversity or to enhance administrative efficiency will not by themselves hold a federation together. All federations need also a central focus of loyalty able to deal effectively with matters of common interest if the federation is to hold the loyalty of its citizens over the long term.

Experience in other federations suggests that although there have been many variations in the terms of the precise formulation, federal governments have generally been assigned the major responsibility for defence, international relations, currency and debt, and equalization, and the primary (although not exclusive) responsibility for management of the economy and the economic union.

Provinces or states have usually been given exclusive or major responsibility for education, health, natural resources, municipal affairs and social policy. Areas such as agriculture, environment, immigrant, language and culture have often been shared through some form of concurrency, legislative delegation or intergovernmental agreements. However, in some multicultural or multinational federations (e.g., Switzerland and Belgium) constituent governments have been given a primary responsibility for their own language policy and culture.

In addition, as noted in chapter 8, in a number of federations *de facto* and even *de jure* asymmetry in the powers of particular constituent units have affected the balance (e.g., Belgium, Malaysia, India, Spain and Canada).

Chapter 13

The Pathology of Federations

13.1 SIGNIFICANCE OF THE PATHOLOGY OF FEDERATIONS

Much of the comparative literature on federal systems and federations has concentrated on their establishment and operation. Furthermore, it is true that many federations continue to be remarkably effective and that many of the longest-standing constitutional systems anywhere in the world today are federations still operating basically under their original constitutions (e.g., United States 1789 (despite the civil war 1861–65), Switzerland 1848, Canada 1867 and Australia 1901).[1] A number of authors have attributed the prosperity, stability and longevity of such federations to the effectiveness of federation as a form of political organization.[2]

But the period since 1945 has seen not only the proliferation of federal systems and particularly federations, but also the failure of some of them. Significant examples have been the disintegration of federations in the West Indies (1962), Rhodesia and Nyasaland (1963), Yugoslavia (1991), and the USSR (1991); the splitting of Pakistan (1971), Czechoslovakia (1992) and Serbia and Montenegro (2006); the expulsion of Singapore from Malaysia (1965); and the civil war in Nigeria (1967–70) followed by alternating civilian and military rule. In any comparative review, account must therefore be taken of these failures, of other cases

---

[1] The new Swiss constitutions of 1874 and 1999, although total revisions, preserved the basic character of the federation established in 1848. In Canada, the *Constitution Act, 1982* added to but did not replace the *Constitution Act, 1867*.

[2] J.R. Pennock, "Federal and Unitary Government: Disharmony and Reliability," *Behavioral Science*, 4:2 (1959): 147–57; Martin Landau, "Federalism, Redundancy and System Reliability," *Publius: The Journal of Federalism*, 3:2 (1973): 173–95.

of serious stress in federations that have not failed, and of the literature examining the conditions and processes leading to the breakdown of federations where this has occurred.[3] An important point to note at the outset of any consideration of the pathology of federal systems is that the problems faced by them have arisen not so much because of the adoption of federation as a form of government but from the particular variant or variation of federal arrangements that was adopted. It should also be noted that it is not so much because they are federations that countries have been difficult to govern but because they were difficult to govern in the first place that they adopted federation as a form of government.

13.2 SOURCES OF STRESS

There are four factors that have contributed to stress within federations: (1) sharp internal social divisions, (2) particular types of institutional or structural arrangements, (3) particular strategies adopted to combat disintegration, and (4) political processes that have polarized internal divisions.

THE DISTRIBUTION AND CHARACTER OF INTERNAL SOCIAL DIVISIONS

Regional divergences of political outlook and interests are typical of all federations; that is usually why they adopted "federation" as a solution in the first place. But a number of factors may sharpen such differences. Among the sharpest divisive forces have been language, religion, social structure, cultural tradition and race. Where several of these have operated simultaneously to reinforce each other, as for instance in India, Malaysia, and particularly in Pakistan before its separation, Nigeria, Rhodesia and Nyasaland, Yugoslavia and the USSR, the internal cleavages have been accentuated. By contrast, in Switzerland linguistic, religious and economic differences among the cantons have tended to cut across each other, moderating the sharpness of internal differences. Other factors that have contributed to the sharpness of internal cleavages have been variations in the degree of economic development, and regional disparities in wealth accentuating regional resentment, especially when these have further reinforced linguistic, cultural and social differences among regions. On the other hand, in some instances moderating

---

[3] See, for instance, Thomas Franck, *Why Federations Fail: An Inquiry into the Requisites for a Successful Federation* (New York: New York University Press, 1966); Ronald L. Watts, "The Survival and Disintegration of Federations," in R. Simeon, ed., *Must Canada Fail?* (Montreal: McGill-Queen's Press, 1977), pp.42–60; Ursula K. Hicks, *Federalism: Failure and Success: A Comparative Study* (London: Macmillan, 1978); Robert A. Young, *The Secession of Quebec and the Future of Canada* (Montreal & Kingston: McGill-Queen's University Press, 1995), chapters 10 and 11.

factors that have emphasized the importance of maintaining unity have been the need for security from external threats (an important motivation in both Swiss and Canadian history but in both cases now much diminished in relative influence), and the significance of interregional trade and of the need for international leverage through united action in trade and investment negotiations and relations.

THE ROLE OF THE INSTITUTIONS AND STRUCTURES

Whether the stresses within a federation can be accommodated and resolved depends not only upon the strength and configuration of the internal divisions within the society in question but also upon the institutional structure of the federation. The way these institutions have channelled the activities of the electorate, political parties, organized interest groups, bureaucracies, and informal elites has contributed to the moderation or accentuation of political conflict. The function of federations is not to eliminate internal differences but rather to preserve regional identities within a united framework. Their function, therefore, is not to eliminate conflict but to manage it in such a way that regional differences are accommodated. But how well this is done has in practice depended not just on the adoption of a federal form of government but often upon *the particular form of the institutions* adopted within the federation.

Four institutional factors have been particularly critical. First, extreme disparity in the population, size and wealth of the constituent units has invariably contributed to stress, even leading in some cases to reorganization of the boundaries of the regional units, as in India and Nigeria. Almost invariably a source of extreme instability has been the situation within a federation where one regional unit has dominated through having a majority of the population. Examples are Prussia within the German confederation and subsequent federation up to the 1930s, Jamaica within the abortive West Indies Federation 1958–62, Northern Nigeria prior to the Nigerian civil war, East Pakistan prior to its secession, Russia prior to the breakup of the USSR in 1991, the Czech Republic within Czechoslovakia prior to its split in 1992, and Serbia with 92 percent of the population of Serbia and Montenegro. This is a continuing problem in the Belgian federation, where the Flemish Community represents 59.7 percent of the federal population, and in Pakistan under the 1973 constitution where the province of Punjab contains 55.6 percent of the total federal population.

Second, while regional distinctiveness is a basic factor leading to the adoption of federation as a form of government, the ability of the federal institutions to generate some sense of positive consensus is vital to their continued operation. Particularly critical is how regional groups are represented in the federal legislature, executive, civil service, political parties and life of the capital city. Where particular regional groups have had inadequate representation and influence in the federal institutions, the resulting alienation has directed itself into separatist movements, as in the cases of the East Pakistanis, the Singapore Chinese, the

Jamaicans in the West Indies Federation, and the black Africans of Nyasaland and Northern Rhodesia. A particularly dangerous situation is where parties operating at the federal level have become primarily regional in their focus so that there are no federal political parties serving as effective interregional bridges. This was a major factor in the instability within Pakistan prior to its split in 1971, in Nigeria prior to the outbreak of civil war in 1967, in the ultimate breakdown of the Yugoslavian federation in 1991, and in Czechoslovakia in the period before it was divided in 1992. In this respect one of the most ominous signs within the current Belgian federation is the regional character of all its political parties operating at the federal level and the difficulties of negotiating federal coalitions of these parties to bridge the divisions. Indeed, this situation reached crisis proportions following the 2007 elections. The recent signs of a similar trend in Canada in terms of the federal opposition parties and the difficulty of obtaining majority federal governments is therefore something of a danger signal.

Third, in most multicultural federations it has proved necessary to recognize as official the languages of major minority groups and to provide constitutional or political guarantees of individual and group rights against discrimination. Where the language of a major regional group has been denied recognition as a federal language, extreme bitterness and tension has resulted. Pakistan, Nigeria, India and Malaysia have provided examples of the intensity of resentment and pressure that can be aroused.

Fourth, where the particular distribution of powers has failed to reflect accurately the aspirations for unity and regional autonomy in a given society, there have been pressures for a shift in the balance of powers or, in more extreme cases, even for abandoning the federal system, as in overcentralized Pakistan or the ineffectual West Indies Federation. It has been to avoid this extreme result that some federations, such as Malaysia, have instituted and maintained a constitutional asymmetry in the distribution of powers.

Fifth is the special case of two-unit federations dealt with below in section 13.3.

STRATEGIES ADOPTED TO COMBAT DISINTEGRATION

Once stress within a federation has reached a certain level, the issue of the appropriate strategy to combat it usually comes to the fore. Broadly speaking, in this sort of situation one of two alternative strategies has been attempted. One is to reinforce the strength and power of the federal government in order to resist disintegration and to hold the federation together. Such a strategy, which in effect attempted to impose unity, clearly failed in Pakistan, Nigeria and Malaysia (in relation to Singapore). Indeed, where assimilationist or repressive measures have been adopted, these have usually exacerbated the situation and have often led to violence. An alternative strategy is to attempt to accommodate regional pressures by emphasizing further devolution. Such a strategy when carried out without any attempt to generate at the same time a focus of loyalty to the federation has also generally failed, as exemplified by the disintegration of the West Indies Federation, the Federation of Rhodesia and Nyasaland and Czechoslovakia. It would appear from these examples that where the *sole* focus has been exclusively on one or other of these two strategies this has failed. Other cases where secession movements have been successfully countered suggest that what is required is a strategy that combines *both* efforts to strengthen a federal focus of loyalty *and* an accommodation of the major concerns of disaffected regional groups. Also important is developing a culture of tolerance and accommodation that is reinforced by policies and symbols that give the different groups within the federation a sense of belonging. Federations such as Switzerland, Canada and India have found that embracing diversity as a federal value has enhanced unity. Yet a further factor has been the importance of inspired political leadership such as that of Ghandi and Nehru in India and Mandela in South Africa.

POLARIZING POLITICAL PROCESSES

The preceding survey indicates that there is no single condition, institutional arrangement or strategy that has by itself generated stress or led to all the examples of disintegration in federations. In each case, crises have been the product of a cumulative combination of factors. What does appear to be common is the resulting development of processes of a polarizing character. Where different kinds of social cleavages have reinforced each other, where federal institutions have been unable to moderate or have even exacerbated these cleavages, where political strategies have involved an emphasis upon either federal unity at the expense of regional accommodation or regional accommodation at the expense of federal unity, and where negotiations have repeatedly failed to produce solutions, there has usually resulted a decline in the support for compromise and a cumulative political polarization within the federation. In such situations, political conflict has usually taken on the character of a contest with very high stakes in which each side becomes convinced that only one side can win — and that at the expense of the other. Once such a situation of emotional confrontation and mounting frenzy has developed, it has often taken only a relatively insignificant incident to trigger an act of unilateral secession or expulsion, resulting in civil war or disintegration of the federation.

It is worth noting that the character of separatist movements may affect the nature of the polarizing process. Where such movements have resorted to violence or terrorist activities as in Spain, Sudan or Sri Lanka, the resulting reaction to this has often increased the polarization and resistance to separation. On the other hand, where separatist movements have respected the democratic rules of the game, as in Canada and Belgium, federations have survived long periods even with separatist parties in power within constituent units, in part because they have accepted that they had no democratic mandate to separate.

13.3 THE SPECIAL PROBLEM OF TWO-UNIT FEDERATIONS

A set of cases worthy of special examination is that of federal systems and federations composed of only two constituent units.

The experience of bipolar or dyadic federal systems is not encouraging. Pakistan prior to the secession of East Pakistan in 1971, Czechoslovakia prior to its segregation in 1992 and Serbia and Montenegro prior to its splitting in 2006 have provided examples of the difficulties that arise in bipolar federations. Another relevant case was the bipolar racial and ideological Malaysia-Singapore relationship within the Malaysian federation which culminated in Singapore's expulsion after only two years. All four of these cases resulted in the end in the splitting of these federations. Another example of the difficulties arising in a federation composed of only two constituent units is St. Kitts and Nevis. While it continues to survive as a federation, it has experienced severe pressures in Nevis for secession. Indeed, the particular difficulties of dyadic federations and unions have generally been recognized.[4] Although constitutionally the Belgian federation consists of six units — three Communities and three Regions — the fundamentally bipolar Flemish-French character of its federal politics has been a source of severe political tensions. To date, however, a major factor discouraging separation has been the existence of Brussels with its French-speaking majority, as the capital within Flanders.

The problem within two-unit federations usually has been that insistence upon parity in all matters between the two units has tended to produce impasses and deadlocks. This is because there is no opportunity for shifting alliances and coalitions among the constituent units, which is one of the ways in which multi-unit federations are able to resolve issues. Furthermore, since invariably one of the two units is less populous than the other (e.g., West Pakistan, Slovakia and Montenegro) that unit has usually been particularly conscious of the continuous need to insist upon equality of influence in federal policy making, while the larger unit (and in the case of Czechoslovakia, the wealthier unit) has developed a sense of grievance over the constraints imposed upon it in order to accommodate the smaller unit. The resulting cumulatively intensifying bipolarity in these examples led ultimately to their terminal instability. Such tendencies would appear likely to be accentuated in a two-unit confederation, since it is a normal characteristic of confederations that each member unit possesses a veto on all major policy decisions in the confederation. The existence of mutual vetoes where there are only two units is a recipe for repeated impasses and deadlocks contributing to cumulatively sharpening frustrations. Thus, the application of the European Union

---

[4] See, for instance, Ivo Duchacek, "Dyadic Federations and Confederations," *Publius: The Journal of Federalism*, 18:2 (1998): 5–31.

Maastricht model, which despite its difficulties works for a confederation of 27 member states, is likely to be much less workable when applied to a confederation of two units.[5]

The case of three-unit federations is almost as problematic as that of two-unit federations, especially where one of the three units possesses a majority of the federal population. This was the case in the Nigerian federation of the 1950s and early 1960s which ultimately broke down in a civil war. Subsequently, Nigeria has been divided into a progressively larger number of units, now 36. Where there are only three constituent units almost invariably there has developed a feeling on the part of one of the units that the other two have allied to impose their interests, and this has had a corrosive impact upon relations within the federation. Other cases where this has been apparent are the disintegration of the short-lived three-unit federation of Rhodesia and Nyasaland (1953–63) and the difficulties that arose when East African political leaders attempted to establish a three-unit federation of Kenya, Uganda and Tanganyika (before it became Tanzania) in 1963–64. Comoros, a federation of three islands, has in recent years experienced considerable tensions. As a general rule it would appear that federations composed of only two or three constituent units are likely to experience terminal instability.

13.4 PROCESSES AND CONSEQUENCES OF DISINTEGRATION

While the constitutions of nearly all federation have explicitly or implicitly prohibited unilateral secession by member units (see section 11.6 in chapter 11), these constitutional restrictions have seldom prevented sufficiently alienated regional groups from taking matters into their own hands and acting extraconstitutionally. Once a regional unit has declared its own unilateral secession, a federal government is faced with the dilemma whether to enforce the constitution of the federation upon the unwilling region or simply to accept the secession as a political fact even if unconstitutional. In the past, most independent (i.e., non-colonial) federations have chosen the former course, fearing that once the secession of one member unit is accepted there will be nothing to prevent other member units from separating whenever they wish or at least using such a threat as a lever against the federal government. Consequently, in a number of cases the result of a unilateral declaration of secession has been a civil war in which the federal government (or in the case of Switzerland, the then confederal government) has imposed continued federation either successfully, e.g., United States (1861–65), Switzerland (1847) and Nigeria (1967–70), or unsuccessfully,

---

[5] Peter M. Leslie, *The Maastricht Model: The Canadian Perspective on the European Union* (Kingston: Institute of Intergovernmental Relations, Queen's University, 1996).

e.g., Pakistan (1971) and Yugoslavia (1991–95). The breakup of the USSR also led to some incidences of violence, and within the successor Russian federation bitter fighting in Chechnya followed an attempt at secession. One interesting case that did not involve violence was that of Western Australia which, dissatisfied with its place in the federation, in 1933 voted by a majority in a referendum to secede from the Australian federation. The Australian federal government, however, stood firm and refused to implement the separation of Western Australia (as did the United Kingdom Parliament when subsequently petitioned by the state of Western Australia to permit secession). The federal government instead responded to the concerns and grievances of Western Australia by establishing a system of special financial assistance to claimant states based on advice by a Commonwealth Grants Commission instituted in 1933.

While secessions have usually been contested and have often led to violent conflict, there have been some cases of peaceful secession from federations.[6] Two of these, which led ultimately to the disintegration of the West Indies Federation (1962) and the Federation of Rhodesia and Nyasaland (1963), occurred in colonial federations. In these cases it was the imperial government in the United Kingdom that not only accepted secession but held the ring to ensure that there was no violence. Among independent federations the only cases of peaceful separation during the past half-century have been in Malaysia, Czechoslovakia, and Serbia and Montenegro. The first of these in 1965 was not really a case of unilateral secession but of unilateral expulsion by the federal government reacting to the troublesome political dynamics that had followed Singapore's inclusion in the Malaysian federation two years earlier. The Czechoslovakian separation, which came into effect on 1 January 1993, occurred largely because it was the climax of a gradual but accelerating process of polarization in which the regionally based political parties within each of the two units found it politically profitable to engage in mutual antagonism, conflict and disagreement, and ultimately to effect the breakup of the federation without an election or referendum on the issue.[7] The splitting of Serbia and Montenegro without violence in 2006 was in part facilitated by the hopes held out by the European Union for their eventual individual membership in the EU.

Elsewhere, the general experience has been that once the separation of one unit has been conceded, other regional units have raised similar demands which have led to further disintegration. This was the pattern both in the West Indies and in Rhodesia and Nyasaland. Moreover, resentments aroused at the time of separation

---

[6] For an analysis of these cases in detail, see R.A. Young, *The Secession of Quebec*, chapters 10 and 11; and R.A. Young, *The Breakup of Czechoslovakia*, (Kingston: Institute of Intergovernmental Relations, Queen's University, Research Paper no. 32, 1994).

[7] Young, *The Breakup of Czechoslovakia*, p. 145. ·

or dissolution have tended to persist. They have usually discouraged, for a considerable subsequent period, creation of a looser form of association between the separating territories, because whenever secession has occurred it has inevitably been accompanied by sharp political controversies that were not easily forgotten. Furthermore, the unscrambling of federations has made necessary the allocation of assets and liabilities among successor states, and rarely has this been achieved without adding further to the resentments felt by one or both sides. In this respect the least negative examples have been the expulsion of Singapore from Malaysia and the separation of Czechoslovakia. Yet in both cases, despite professions about the desirability of continued economic linkages after separation, in practice for a considerable subsequent period, economic ties fell far below expectations. Generally it is clear that the separation of units from federations, even in the few cases where it has been managed peacefully, has exacted a high price in economic costs, diplomatic and defensive ineffectiveness, and lasting bitterness between the groups involved.

In some countries where there has been pressure for devolution, the establishment of a federation has been resisted for fear that it would simply be the first step towards ultimate secession, a fear that has often been expressed recently in both the United Kingdom and Sri Lanka. It should be noted, however, that while the risk of secession has often been associated with federations, historically separatist movements have occurred in many unitary countries as well. Among notable examples have been the separation of Ireland from the United Kingdom early in the twentieth century, the Basque insurgency under Franco in Spain, the lengthy civil wars in South Sudan, and the current insurgency of the Tamils in Sri Lanka. Where societies contain distinctive diverse groups, imposing unity within a unitary system has, if anything, proved less successful than a federal solution.

13.5 POST-CONFLICT SITUATIONS

Most federations have emerged peacefully from a period of negotiations aimed at creating a federation involving the aggregation of separate units or the devolution of autonomous powers to constituent units. That has not universally been the case, however. Some federations have been created in post-conflict situations or have survived periods of internal conflict. Among the mature federations, Switzerland, India and the United States serve as examples. Switzerland became a federation after the preceding confederation erupted in the brief Sonderbund civil war of 1847, but the very brevity of that conflict and the compromises between the war's winners and losers that were embodied in the new federal constitution of 1848 moderated the intensity of the feelings aroused by the civil war. The independence of India in 1947 occurred under emergency conditions marked by the violence of partition with Pakistan and the need for rapid integration of the princely states, but the drafting of the new federal constitution by the Constituent Assembly, 1947–

49, occurred in a period that was not marked by internal strife. The adoption of a federal constitution by the United States took place a full decade after the War of Independence, but more than seventy years later the USA did experience a prolonged and bitter civil war, 1861–65. Although the federal military forces ultimately triumphed, the war and the period of reconstruction imposed on the South, 1865–76, left a sense of southern alienation that took a long time to heal. Among more recent emergent federations, a number have been created or re-established after periods of civil war: Mexico in 1917, Argentina and Venezuela on a number of occasions, Nigeria 1967–70, and Ethiopia 1991 and 1998–2000. Typically, such conflicts have left these societies deeply divided, and it has taken a considerable period for reconciliation to be achieved.

In recent years there have been a number of attempts to resolve conflicts by creating a federation.[8] Notable examples have been Bosnia and Herzegovina, Sudan, Iraq and the Democratic Republic of the Congo. In addition, proposals have been advanced for federal solutions in Sri Lanka, Nepal and the Philippines as a way of ending insurgencies. These efforts have all been fraught with difficulties because of the absence of the necessary conditions for establishing an effective federation. As a consequence, it is not surprising that Bosnia and Herzegovina remains under international tutelage and that Sudan, Iraq and the Democratic Republic of the Congo, although formally committed to federal institutions, have not consolidated their operation as federations. The lack of mutual trust and accommodation and of an acceptance of the rule of law and constitutionality has made it difficult to obtain agreement on federal solutions or to operate federal institutions that require an emphasis upon trust, accommodation and constitutionality. Where these requisites for an effective federation are lacking, the challenge is how to achieve them in the atmosphere of distrust and hostility aroused by the preceding conflict. All too often, insufficient attention has been given to the need to establish the necessary conditions. The dilemma is how these conditions are to be created in situations that are already permeated by the antagonisms aroused by conflict.

---

[8] See, for instance, David Cameron, "Making Federalism Work," in M.E. Bouillon, D.M. Malone and B. Rowswell, eds., *Iraq: Preventing A New Generation of Conflict* (Boulder, Col.: Lynne Rienner Publication, 2007), pp. 153–5.

Chapter 14

Conclusions

14.1 IMPLICATIONS DRAWN FROM THIS COMPARATIVE STUDY

In drawing implications from this comparative analysis of federations, we must keep in mind the comments at the outset about the benefits and limits of comparisons among federations. Comparisons do help draw attention to crucial issues and to possible alternatives illustrated by the experience of other federations. But we need also to recognize the limits to the applicability of comparisons and particularly to the transferability of institutions to differing circumstances and contexts. Above all, it is important to recognize that it is not simply in the examples of different institutional structures that the comparisons may lead to useful conclusions; rather, it is in coming to understand the way in which underlying social, economic and political conditions, and federal institutions and political processes have interacted with each other within federations.

What we can learn from federations that have succeeded and from the pathology of other federations is that even more important than their formal structures has been the public acceptance of the basic values and processes required for federal systems. These include the explicit recognition and accommodation of multiple identities and loyalties within an overarching sense of shared purposes and objectives. Efforts to deny or suppress the multiple identities within a diverse society have almost invariably led to contention, secession or civil war. An essential element therefore in any federation encompassing a diverse society has been the acceptance of the value of diversity and of the possibility of multiple loyalties expressed through the establishment of constituent units of government with genuine autonomous self-rule over those matters most important to their distinct identity. At the same time, equally important has been the recognition of the benefits within even a diverse society to be derived from shared purposes and objectives providing the basis for the parallel processes of shared-rule.

This comparative study has made clear that within the general category of federal political systems, and indeed within the more specific category of federations, there has been a considerable variety in the patterns of social conditions accommodated and an enormous range in the institutional arrangements and political processes adopted. All these systems have attempted, many with considerable success, to combine elements of autonomous self-rule for the constituent units in certain matters and an overarching shared-rule in other matters in order to reconcile the desire for both distinctive diversity and united action. But the variations among them also make it clear that there is no single pure ideal form of federation that is applicable everywhere. Federations have varied greatly in their institutional design and in their operation to meet their own particular conditions and context. A further implication that may be drawn from some of the more recent examples is that political leaders should not be constrained to traditional arrangements or theories about federalism but should be ready to consider more imaginative and innovative ways of applying pragmatically the spirit of federalism as a way of combining unity and diversity. At the same time, it may be possible to draw lessons or inspiration from practice in other federations, particularly in relation to identifying potential dangers to be averted, desirable objectives to be attained, and appropriate and inappropriate processes for achieving those objectives. But ultimately, while bearing these in mind, each federation, if it is to be effective and long-lasting, will have to direct its efforts at pragmatically accommodating the particular conditions and "realities" of its own society.

We can conclude by noting that the experience of federal systems has taught us five major lessons. *First*, as the mature federations illustrate as a group, federal systems *do* provide a practical way of combining through representative institutions the benefits of both unity and diversity. For instance, the United States (1789), Switzerland (1848), Canada (1867), and Australia (1901) are among the longest continually operating constitutional systems anywhere in the world today. Furthermore, the United Nations annual Index of Human Development, issued in recent years, ranking some 174 countries in terms of quality of life based on a weighted average of life expectancy, adult literacy, school enrolment and per capita gross domestic product, has consistently ranked four federations — Australia, Canada, the United States and Switzerland — among the top ten countries in the world, with four others — Belgium, Austria, Spain and Germany — not far behind.[1] Furthermore, a number of recent empirical studies, including those of Arendt Lijphart, Ute Wachendorfer-Schmidt and John Kincaid, have indicated that federal

---

[1] United Nations Development Programme, *Human Rights Report* (New York: Oxford University Press, 2006).

political systems have on balance generally actually facilitated political integration, democratic development and economic effectiveness better than non-federal systems.[2]

Second, as the pathology of federations has illustrated, it is also clear, however, that federal systems are not a panacea for humanity's political ills. Account must therefore also be taken of the pathology of federal systems and of the particular types of federal structural arrangements and societal conditions and circumstances that have given rise to problems and stresses within federal systems.

Third, the degree to which a federal political system is effective depends very much upon the extent to which there is acceptance of the need to respect constitutional norms and structures, and an emphasis upon the spirit of tolerance and compromise. Where these are lacking, as for instance currently in Sri Lanka, Iraq and Sudan, it has usually been futile to advocate federal solutions unless the necessary conditions are also established.

Fourth, the extent to which a federal system can accommodate political realities depends not just on the adoption of federal arrangements but on whether the particular form or variant of federal institutions that is adopted or evolved gives adequate expression to the demands and requirements of the particular society. There is no single, ideal federal form. Many variations are possible. Examples have been variations in the number and size of the constituent units, in the form and scope of the distribution of legislative and executive powers and financial resources, in the degree of centralization or non-centralization, in the character and composition of their central institutions, and in the institutions and processes for resolving internal disputes. Ultimately, federalism is a pragmatic, prudential technique, whose applicability may well depend upon the particular form in which it is adopted or adapted, or even upon the development of new innovations in its application.

Fifth, some commentators, such as Daniel Elazar,[3] have questioned whether federations composed of different ethnic groups or nations are workable, or simply run the risk of suffering civil war. While these possibilities exist, the persistence of federal systems despite their difficulties in such multi-ethnic or multinational countries as Switzerland, Canada, India and Malaysia indicates that with

---

[2] Arend Lijphart, *Democracies: Patterns of Majoritarian and Consensus Government in Twenty-One Countries,* (New Haven: Yale University Press, 1984), and *Patterns of Democracy: Government Forms and Performance in Thirty-Six Countries*, (New Haven: Yale University Press, 1999); Ute Wachendorfer-Schmidt, ed., *Federalism and Political Performance.* (London & New York: Routledge, 2000); and John Kincaid "Federalism and Democracy; Comparative Empirical and Theoretical Perspectives," (forthcoming in M. Burgess, ed., *Federalism and Democracy*).

[3] D. J. Elazar, "International and Comparative Federalism," *PS: Political Science and Politics,* 26:2 (1993): 190–5.

appropriately designed institutions, federal systems can be sustained and prosper in such countries. In a number of significant cases where ethnic nationalism has been a crucial issue, federal devolution has in fact reduced tension by giving distinct groups a sense of security through their own self-government, thereby paradoxically contributing to greater harmony and unity.

While federal political systems are not universally appropriate, in many situations in the contemporary world they may be the only way of combining, through representative institutions, the benefits of both unity and diversity. Experience does indicate that countries with a federal form of government have often been difficult to govern; but it has usually been because they were difficult countries to govern in the first place that they have adopted federal political institutions.

14.2 FEDERALISM AND LIBERAL-DEMOCRATIC VALUES

The question is sometimes raised whether a federal system, by limiting the range of issues on which a majority within the polity may ultimately rule, is undemocratic. If democracy is interpreted simplistically, solely as majority rule, there is no question that a federal system by limiting the jurisdiction of the federal government and establishing constituent units of government with autonomous jurisdiction over some matters does place constitutional limits upon the scope of decision making by an overall majority within the polity. Federal systems with their constitutional distributions of authority and resources, normally adjudicated by courts, are clearly a form of limited constitutional government.

On the other hand, in another sense it can be argued that federal systems enhance democratic majority rule by giving constituent groups who are in a majority within their own region the opportunity to decide matters of regional interest by majority rule. In this sense, federalism represents "democracy plus," since it provides for majority rule relating to issues of shared interest throughout the polity, *plus* majority rule within autonomous units of self-government dealing with matters of particular regional interest.

At a more fundamental level the congruence of federal and liberal-democratic values should be noted. Liberal-democracy is not based solely on majority rule but also emphasizes constitutionalism and the rule of law, respect for minorities and the dispersal of political power. Thus, liberal-democratic values are a precondition for an effective federal political system that depends upon respect for constitutional norms and the rule of law, respect for regional minorities, and a spirit of tolerance and compromise. Federalism, in turn, on balance enhances liberal-democratic values by ensuring the democratic legitimacy of both the federal and the constituent unit governments, each directly elected by and accountable to its own electorate, and by checking autocracy through the dispersal of legitimate power among multiple centres of decision making within the polity.

Appendix A

The Distribution of Powers and Functions in Selected Federations: A Comparative Overview

The purpose of this appendix is to provide a comparative overview of the constitutional distribution of powers in 12 federations (as originally published in R.L. Watts, *Comparing Federal Systems,* 2nd edition (1999), pp. 125–30). Information in this table is based on a reading of constitutional texts, academic interpretive texts and other sources. The tables indicate whether legislative authority for a subject matter is Federal (F), State (S) or Concurrent (C). Where different aspects of a matter are assigned exclusively to the federal and to the state governments this is indicated by the notation FS. The legend at the bottom of each page explains the notations for variations or exceptions to these standard classifications. A space left blank indicates that the matter is not explicitly referred to in the constitution or that the power to legislate in that area rests with the residual authority (indicated in the first line of the table). The content and allocation of some subjects are often more complex than might appear from the table, and reference to the constitutional documents themselves should be made for greater detail.

The Distribution of Powers and Functions in Federal Systems: A Comparative Overview

	Canada (1867)	United States (1789)	Switzerland (1848/1999)	Australia (1901)	Germany (1949)	Austria (1929)	India (1950)	Malaysia (1963)	Belgium (1993)	Spain (1978)	Czechoslovakia (1968)	Pakistan (1962)
BASIC FEATURES												
Residual Power	F	S	S	S	S	S	F	S	F	FS*	S	S
Enumeration of State Powers	YES	NO	SOME	NO	NO	YES	YES	YES[a]	YES[a]	YES[a]	NO	NO
Delegation of Legislative Authority	NO	NO	YES	YES	YES	NO	YES	YES		YES		YES
SCOPE OF POWERS												
Finance and Fiscal Relations												
Taxation												
Customs/Excise	F	F/C	F	F	F	F	F/FS	F[a]	C	F	F	F
Corporate	FS	C	F	C	C	F	F	F	C	F	F	F
Personal Income	FS	C	FS	C	C	F	FS	F	C	FS[a]	F	FS
Sales	FS	C	F	C	C	F	FS	F[a]	Sr	F	S	F
Other			FS						F	FS[a]		
Equalization	F		F								F	
Debt and Borrowing					FS							
Public Debt of the Federation	F	F	F	F	F	F	F	F	F	F	F	F
Foreign Borrowing	FS	FS	FS	C	FS	F	F	F	FScr	FS	FS	FS
Domestic Borrowing	FS	FS	FS	C	FS	FS	FS	FS	FScr	FS	FS	FS

Legend:

F = federal power

S = state (provincial/canton/Länd/autonomous community)

C = concurrent power (federal paramountcy except where denoted C[s] which denotes provincial paramountcy)

c = "Community" power

r = "Regional" power

* = 5 of the 17 sub-national orders of government retain residual powers, for the others the residual powers are federal

[a] = asymmetrical application of powers

The Distribution of Powers and Functions (continued)

	Canada (1867)	United States (1789)	Switzerland (1848/1999)	Australia (1901)	Germany (1949)	Austria (1929)	India (1950)	Malaysia (1963)	Belgium (1993)	Spain (1978)	Czechoslovakia (1968)	Pakistan (1962)
International Relations												
Defence	F	FS	F	FS	F	F	F	F	F	F	F	F
Treaty Implementation	F(1)	F	FS	F	FS	F(1)	F(2)	F(2)S	ScrF	F	F	F(2)
Citizenship	F	F	FS	F	F	FS†	F	Fᵃ	F	F	F	F
Immigration (into federation)	C	C	F	C	F	F	F	Cᵃ	F	F	F	F
Immigration (between regions)			C		C†							
Functioning of Economic Union												
"Trade and Commerce"	F	F	F	F	C†	F	F	F	Sc	F	F	F
External Trade	F	F	F	C	F		F	Fᵃ	Sr	F	C	F
Inter-state Trade	F	F	F	C	C		F	Fᵃ				
Intra-state Trade	S	S		S	C		SC	Fᵃ				
Currency	F	F	F	F	F	F	F	F	F	F	F	F
Banking	FS(3)	C	F	C	C†	F	F	F	F	F	C	FS
Bankruptcy	F	FS		C		F	C	Fᵃ	F	F		
Insurance	FS	FS	FS	C	C	F	F		F	F		FS

Legend:

F = federal power

S = state (provincial/canton/Land)

C = concurrent power (federal paramountcy except where denoted Cˢ which denotes provincial paramountcy)

c = "Community" power

r = "Regional" power

a = asymmetrical application of powers

† = federal legislation in this field administered by the states

This page:

(1) = requires implementing legislation or consent of provincial or state governments

(2) = requires consultation (non-binding of state governments)

(3) = banking is exclusively federal but savings and credit unions are provincial

The Distribution of Powers and Functions (continued)

	Canada (1867)	United States (1789)	Switzerland (1848/1999)	Australia (1901)	Germany (1949)	Austria (1929)	India (1950)	Malaysia (1963)	Belgium (1993)	Spain (1978)	Czechoslovakia (1968)	Pakistan (1962)
Transportation and Communications												
Roads and Bridges	S	FS	FS	FS	FC†	FS	FS	F[a]	Sr	SF		
Railways	FS	FS	F	FS	C†	F	F	FS	F	S		S
Air	F	F	F	FS	FC†	F	F	F[a]	Sr	SF		F
Telecommunications	FS	FS	F	C	F	F	F	F	F	F	C	F
Postal Services	F	F	F	C	F	F	F	F	F	F	C	F
Broadcasting	F	F	F	C	SC†		F	F	Sc	F	C	F
Agriculture and Resources												
Agriculture	C	S	F	SC	C†	F†	SC	SC[a]	Sr	S	C	
Fisheries	FS	S	F	FS	C†		FS	FS[a]	Sr	S*F		FS
Mineral Resources	FS	S		S	C†	F	FS	FS	Sr	F	F	
Nuclear Energy	F	FS	F	C	C	F	F	F	F	F		F

Legend:

F = federal power

S = state (provincial/canton/Länd)

C = concurrent power (federal paramountcy except where denoted C[s] which denotes provincial paramountcy)

c = "Community" power

r = "Regional" power

[a] = asymmetrical application of powers

* = fishing in inland waters

† = federal legislation in this field administered by the states

Note: Italics denote *de facto* distribution of powers and functions

The Distribution of Powers and Functions (*continued*)

	Canada (1867)	United States (1789)	Switzerland (1848/1999)	Australia (1901)	Germany (1949)	Austria (1929)	India (1950)	Malaysia (1963)	Belgium (1993)	Spain (1978)	Czechoslovakia (1968)	Pakistan (1962)
Social Affairs												
Education and Research												
Primary and Secondary Education	S	S	C†S	S	S	FS	CS	F[a]	Sc	FS[*]	S	
Postsecondary Education	S	FS	FC†S	FS	C†[**]	F	FCS	F[a]	Sc	F		
Research and Development		FS	F	FS	SC†	FS	FCS	F[a]	FSc			FS
Health Services								F				
Hospitals	SF	SF	S	FS	C†	C†	S	F[a]	Sc	FS[*]		
Public Health and Sanitation	S	S	C†	S	C†	FS	S	FC	Sc	S		
Labour and Social Services			FS		C	F	S	F			C	
Unemployment Insurance	F	FS	C†	C	C	F	S	F[a]	F	F		
Income Security	FS		FC	C	C	s	CS	F[a]	F	F		
Social Services	SF	SF	C†	C	C†	F	CS	C	Sc	FS		C
Pensions	C[s]	C	C†	C	C†S	FS	C	F[a]S	F	F	F	FS

Legend:

F = federal power

S = state (provincial/canton/Länd)

C = concurrent power (federal paramountcy except where denoted C[s] which denotes provincial paramountcy)

c = "Community" power

a = asymmetrical application of powers

* = 6 of the 17 sub-national orders of government have jurisdiction over education and health

** = enumerated as a framework legislation jurisdiction whereby the federal government may enact general principles only

† = federal legislation in this field administered by the states

Note: Italics denote *de facto* distribution of powers and functions

The Distribution of Powers and Functions (*continued*)

	Canada (1867)	United States (1789)	Switzerland (1848/1999)	Australia (1901)	Germany (1949)	Austria (1929)	India (1950)	Malaysia (1963)	Belgium (1993)	Spain (1978)	Czechoslovakia (1968)	Pakistan (1962)
Law and Security												
Civil Law	S	S	F	FS	C[†]	FS[*]	C	F[a]S	F	F		FS
Criminal Law	F	S	F	S	C[†]	FS[*]	C	F				S
Organization of Courts	FS	FS	S	FS	C[†]	F	FS	F[a]				
Internal Security (police)	FS	FS	C	SF	C[†]S	FS	FS	F	F	FS[a]	C	
Prisons	FS	FS	S	S	C[†]	F	S	F		F		S
Other Matters												
Language	FS		FS				FS	F	FSc	FS		
Culture	FS		C[†]					FS	Sc	FCS[a]	S	
Aboriginal Affairs	F	F		C	C[†]		FS	C				
Environment	FS	FS	F[†]S	FS		FS		F[a]	Sr	C		FS
Municipal Affairs	S	S	S	S	S	S	S	F[a]S	FSr	FS		

Legend:

F = federal power

S = state (provincial/canton/Länd)

C = concurrent power (federal paramountcy except where denoted Cˢ which denotes provincial paramountcy)

c = "Community" power

[a] = asymmetrical application of powers

[†] = federal legislation in this field administered by the states. Legislation regarding criminal law and organization of the courts is in practice predominantly federal in Germany.

[*] = states may legislate in the fields of criminal and civil law if necessary to dispose of an item within the scope of their legislative competence (Article 15, paragraph 9)

Selected Readings

Agranoff, Robert, ed., "Federal Evolution in Spain," *International Political Science Review*, 17:4 (1996): 385–401.

———, ed., *Accommodating Diversity: Asymmetry in Federal States*, Series of the European Centre for Research on Federalism Tuebingen, vol. 10. (Baden-Baden: Nomos Verlagsgesellschaft, 1999).

———, "Autonomy, Devolution and Intergovernmental Relations," *Regional and Federal Studies*, 14:1 (2004): 25–65.

Ahmad, Ehtisham and Giorgio Brosio, eds., *Handbook of Fiscal Federalism* (Cheltenham, UK, & Northampton, Mass., USA: Edward Elgar, 2006).

Alen, André, and R. Ergec, *Federal Belgium after the Fourth State Reform of 1993*, 2nd edn (Brussels: Ministry of Foreign Affairs, 1998).

Amoretti, Ugo, and Nancy Bermeo, eds., *Federalism and Territorial Cleavages* (Baltimore: Johns Hopkins University Press, 2004).

Anckar, Dag, "Lilliput Federalism: Profiles and Varieties," *Regional and Federal Studies*, 13:3 (2003): 107–24.

Anderson, George, *Federalism: An Introduction* (Don Mills, ON: Oxford University Press, 2008).

Arora, B., and D.V. Verney, eds., *Multiple Identities in a Single State: Indian Federalism in Comparative Perspective* (New Delhi: Konark Publishers, 1995).

Bakvis, Herman, and William M. Chandler, eds., *Federalism and the Role of the State* (Toronto: University of Toronto Press, 1987).

Baus, Ralf, Raoul Blindenbacher and Ulrich Karpen, eds., *Competition versus Cooperation: German Federalism in Need of Reform — A Comparative Perspective* (Baden-Baden: Nomos Verlagsgesillschaft, 2007).

Beer, Samuel H., *To Make a Nation: The Rediscovery of American Federalism* (Cambridge, MA: Belknap Press, Harvard University, 1993).

Bird, Richard A., *Federal Finance in Comparative Perspective* (Toronto: Canadian Tax Foundation, 1986).

_____, "A Comparative Perspective on Federal Finance," in K.G. Banting, D.M. Brown, and T.J. Courchene, eds., *The Future of Fiscal Federalism* (Kingston: School of Policy Studies, Institute of Intergovernmental Relations, John Deutsch Institute for the Study of Economic Policy, Queen's University, 1994).

Bird, Richard, and Thomas Stauffer, eds., *Intergovernmental Fiscal Relations in Fragmented Societies* (Bâle: Helbing and Lichtenhahn, Institut du Fédéralisme, 2001).

Blindenbacher, Raoul and Arnold Koller, eds., *Federalism in a Changing World: Learning from Each Other* (Montreal & Kingston: McGill-Queen's University Press, 2003).

Boadway, Robin, and Anwar Shah, *Intergovernmental Fiscal Transfers: Principles and Practice* (Washington, DC: The World Bank, 2007).

Boeckelman, K.A., and J. Kincaid, eds., *Federal Systems in the Global Economy,* Special Issue of *Publius: The Journal of Federalism,* 26:1 (1996).

Burgess, Michael, *Comparative Federalism: Theory and Practice* (London: Routledge, 2006).

_____, ed., *Multinational Federations* (London: Routledge, 2007).

Burgess, Michael, and Alain-G. Gagnon, eds., *Comparative Federalism and Federation: Competing Trends and Future Directions* (Hemel Hempstead: Harvester Wheatsheaf, 1993).

Bzdera, A., "A Comparative Analysis of Federal High Courts: A Political Theory of Judicial Review," *Canadian Journal of Political Science,* 26:1 (1993): 3–29.

Cairns, Alan, "The Governments and Societies of Canadian Federalism." *Canadian Journal of Political Science,* 10:4 (1977): 695–725.

Cameron, David, "Making Federalism Work," in M.E. Bouillon, D.M. Malone, and B. Rowswell, eds., *Iraq: Preventing a New Generation of Conflict* (Boulder, CO: Lynne Rienner Publishers, 2007).

Colomer, Josep M., "The Spanish 'State of Autonomies': Non-Institutional Federalism," in Paul Heywood, ed., *West European Politics,* Special Issue on "Politics and Policy in Democratic Spain: No Longer Different?," 21:4 (1998): 40–52.

De Villiers, Bertus, ed., *Evaluating Federal Systems* (Cape Town: Jutta, 1994).

Duchacek, Ivo, *Comparative Federalism: The Territorial Dimension of Politics,* rev. edn (Lanham: University Press of America, 1987).

_____, ed., "Bicommunal Societies and Politics," *Publius: The Journal of Federalism,* Special Issue, 18:2 (1988).

Elaigwu, J. Isawa, *The Politics of Federalism in Nigeria* (Jos: Aha Publishing House, 2005).

_____, ed., *Fiscal Federalism in Nigeria: Facing the Challenges of the Future* (Jos: Aha Publishing House, 2007.

Elazar, Daniel J., *Exploring Federalism* (Tuscaloosa, AL: University of Alabama Press, 1987).

_____, "International and Comparative Federalism," *PS: Political Science and Politics,* 20:2 (1993): 190–5; also in D. Elazar, *Federalism and the Way to Peace* (Kingston:

Institute of Intergovernmental Relations, Reflections Paper no. 13, 1994), pp. 159–170.

_____, ed., *Federal Systems of the World: A Handbook of Federal, Confederal and Autonomy Arrangements*, 2nd edn (Harlow: Longman Group, 1994).

_____, *Federalism and the Way to Peace* (Kingston: Institute of Intergovernmental Relations, Queen's University, 1994).

_____, *Federalism: An Overview* (Pretoria: HSRC, 1995).

_____, ed., "New Trends in Federalism," *International Political Science Review*, Special Issue, 17:4 (1996).

Fiseha, Assefa, *Federalism and the Accommodation of Diversity in Ethiopia: A Comparative Study* revised edition (Nijmegen: Wolf Legal Publishers, 2007).

Forsyth, Murray, *Unions of the States: The Theory and Practice of Confederation* (Leicester: Leicester University Press, 1981).

_____, ed., *Federalism and Nationalism* (Leicester: Leicester University Press, 1989).

Forum of Federations, *Intergovernmental Relations in Federal Countries* (Ottawa: Forum of Federations, 2001).

_____, *Handbook of Federal Countries 2005*, ed. A.L. Griffiths (Montreal & Kingston: McGill-Queen's University Press, 2005).

Franck, T., *Why Federations Fail: An Inquiry into the Requisites for a Successful Federation* (New York: New York University Press, 1966).

Friedrich, Carl J., *Trends of Federalism in Theory and Practice* (New York: Praeger, 1968).

Gagnon, A.-G., and J. Tully, eds., *Multinational Democracies* (Cambridge: Cambridge University Press, 2001).

Galligan, Brian, *A Federal Republic: Australia's Constitutional System of Government* (Oakleigh, Melbourne: Cambridge University Press, 1995).

Gana, Aaron T., and Samuel G. Egwu, eds., *Federalism in Africa*, vol. 1: *Framing the National Question* (Trenton, NJ: Africa World Press, 2003).

Ghai, Yash, ed., *Autonomy and Ethnicity: Negotiating Competing Claims in Multi-Ethnic States* (Cambridge: Cambridge University Press, 2004).

Gibson, Edward L., ed., *Federalism and Democracy in Latin America* (Baltimore: Johns Hopkins University Press, 2004)

He, Bargang, Brian Galligan, Takshi Inoguchi, eds., *Federalism in Asia* (Cheltenham, UK & Northampton, Mass, USA: Edward Elgar, 2007).

Hicks, Ursula K., *Federalism: Failure and Success: A Comparative Study* (London: Macmillan, 1978).

Hrbek, R., ed., *Political Parties and Federalism: An International Comparison* (Baden-Baden: Nomos Verlagsgesellschaft, 2004).

Hueglin, Thomas O., and Alan Fenna, *Comparative Federalism: A Systematic Inquiry* (Peterborough, ON: Broadview, 2006).

International Social Science Journal, Special Issue: *Federalism*, no. 167 (2001).

Jeffery, C., ed., *Recasting German Federalism* (London & New York: Pinter, 1999).

Jeffrey, C., and D. Heald, eds., *Money Matters: Territorial Finance in Decentralized States.* Special Issue: *Regional and Federal Studies*, 13:4 (2003).

Kincaid, John, "From Cooperative to Coercive Federalism," *Annals of the American Academy of Politics*, 509 (1990): 139–52.

Kincaid, John, and G. Alan Tarr, eds., *A Global Dialogue on Federalism,* vol. 1: *Constitutional Origins, Structure, and Change in Federal Countries,* (Montreal & Kingston: Published for the Forum of Federations and the International Association of Centers for Federal Studies by McGill-Queen's University Press, 2005).

King, Preston, *Federalism and Federation* (London: Croom Helm, 1982).

Knop, K., S. Ostry, R. Simeon and K. Swinton, eds., *Rethinking Federalism: Citizens, Markets and Governments in a Changing World* (Vancouver: UBC Press, 1995).

Lalande, Gilles, *In Defence of Federalism: The View for Quebec* (Toronto: McClelland & Stewart, 1978).

Landau, Martin, "Federalism, Redundancy and System Reliability," *Publius: The Journal of Federalism*, 3:2 (1973): 173–95.

Lazar, H., H. Telford, and R.L. Watts, eds., *The Impact of Global and Regional Integration on Federal Systems: A Comparative Analysis* (Montreal & Kingston: McGill-Queen's University Press, 2003).

Lee, Frances E., and Bruce I. Oppenheimer, *Sizing Up the Senate: The Unequal Consequences of Equal Representation* (Chicago: University of Chicago Press, 1998).

LeRoy, Katy, and Cheryl Saunders, eds., *A Global Dialogue on Federalism,* vol. 3: *Legislative, Executive, and Judicial Governance in Federal Countries* (Montreal & Kingston: Published for the Forum of Federations and the International Association of Centers for Federal Studies by McGill-Queen's University Press, 2006).

Leslie, Peter M., *The Maastricht Model: The Canadian Perspective on the European Union* (Kingston: Institute of Intergovernmental Relations, Queen's University, 1996).

Lister, F.W., *The European Union, the United Nations and the Revival of Confederal Governance* (Westport, CT: Greenwood, 1996).

Livingston, W.S., *Federalism and Constitutional Change* (Oxford: Clarendon Press, 1956).

Madison, James, Alexander Hamilton and John Jay, *The Federalist Papers* (1788; reprint with editor's introduction, New York, Penguin Books, 1997).

Maiz, R., "Democracy, Federalism and Nationalism in Multinational States," in W. Sefran and R. Maiz, eds., *Identity and Territorial Autonomy in Plural Societies* (London: Frank Cass, 2000).

Majeed, Akhtar, Ronald L. Watts, and Douglas M. Brown, eds., *A Global Dialogue on Federation,* vol. 2: *Distribution of Powers and Responsibilities in Federal Countries* (Montreal & Kingston : Published for the Forum of Federations and the International Association of Centers for Federal Studies by McGill-Queen's University Press, 2006).

Michelmann, Hans, J., ed., *Global Dialogue on Federalism.* vol. 5: *Foreign Relations in Federal Countries.* Montreal & Kingston: Published for the Forum of Federations and the International Association of Centres of Federal Studies by McGill-Queen's University Press, forthcoming 2008).

Milne, David, "Equality or Asymmetry: Why Choose?" in R.L. Watts and D.M. Brown, eds., *Options for a New Canada* (Toronto: University of Toronto Press, 1991), pp. 285–307.

Moreno, Luis, *The Federalization of Spain* (London: Frank Cass, 2001).

Nathan, R.P., "Defining Modern Federalism," in H.N. Scheiber, ed., *North American and Comparative Federalism: Essays for the 1990s* (Berkeley: University of California Press, 1992), pp. 89–99.

Obinger, Herbert, Stephan Leibfried, and Francis G. Castles, *Federalism and the Welfare State: New World and European Experiences* (Cambridge: Cambridge University Press, 2005).

Olson, David M., and C.E.S. Franks, eds., *Representation and Policy Formation in Federal Systems* (Berkeley: Institute of Governmental Studies Press, 1993).

Orban, E., *Le Fédéralisme: Super ÉTAT Fédéral? Association d'États Souverains?* (Quebec: Hurtubise HMH Ltée, 1992).

Ostrom, Vincent, "Can Federalism Make a Difference?" *Publius: The Journal of Federalism*, 3:3 (1974): 197–238.

_____, *The Political Theory of a Compound Republic* (Lincoln: University of Nebraska Press, 1986).

Pagano, M.A., ed., *The Global Review of Federalism, Publius: The Journal of Federalism*. Special issue 32:2 (2002).

Patterson, S., and A. Mughan, eds., *Senates: Bicameralism in the Contemporary World* (Columbus: Ohio State University Press, 1999).

Pennock, J.R., "Federal and Unitary Government: Disharmony and Reliability," *Behavioural Science*, 4:2 (1959): 147–57.

Riker, William H., "Federalism," in Fred I. Greenstein and Nelson W. Polsby, eds., *Handbook of Political Science: Government Institutions and Processes*, vol. 5 (Reading, MA: Addison Wesley, 1975), pp. 93–172.

Russell, Peter H., *Constitutional Odyssey: Can Canadians Become a Sovereign People?* 3rd edn (Toronto: University of Toronto Press, 2004).

Saunders, Cheryl, *The Constitutional Framework: Hybrid, Derivative but Australian* (Melbourne: Centre for Constitutional Studies, University of Melbourne, 1989).

_____, "Constitutional Arrangements of Federal Systems," *Publius: The Journal of Federalism*, 25:2 (1995): 61–79.

Sawer, Geoffrey, *Modern Federalism* (London: C.A .Watts, 1969).

Scharpf, F., "The Joint Decision Trap: Lessons from German Federalism and European Integration," *Public Administration* 66 (1988): 238–78.

Shah, Anwar, ed., *A Global Dialogue on Federalism*, vol 4: *The Practice of Fiscal Federalism: Comparative Perspectives* (Montreal & Kingston: Published for the Forum of Federations and the International Association of Centers for Federal Studies by McGill-Queen's University Press, 2007).

Sharman, Campbell, ed., *Parties and Federalism in Canada and Australia* (Canberra: Federalism Research Centre, Australian National University, 1994).

Simeon, Richard, and I. Robinson, *State, Society and the Development of Canadian Federalism* (Toronto: University of Toronto Press, 1990).

Smiley, D.V., *The Federal Condition in Canada* (Toronto: McGraw-Hill Ryerson , 1987).

Smiley, Donald V., and Ronald L. Watts, *Intrastate Federalism in Canada* (Toronto: University of Toronto Press, 1985), ch. 4.

Smith, J., *Federalism* (Vancouver: UBC Press, 2004).

Stepan, A., "Federalism and Democracy: Beyond the US Model," *Journal of Democracy*, 10:4 (1999): 19–34.

Stepan, A., "Toward a New Comparative Politics of Federalism, Multinationalism and Democracy: Beyond Rikerian Federalism," in E.L. Gibson, ed., *Federalism and Democracy in Latin America* (Baltimore & London: Johns Hopkins University Press, 2004), pp. 28–84.

Stevenson, Garth, *Unfulfilled Union: Canadian Federalism and National Unity*, 3rd edn (Toronto: Gage, 1989).

Stewart, W.H., *Concepts of Federalism* (New York: University Press of America, 1984).

Steytler, N., ed., *The Place and Role of Local Governments in Federal Systems* (Johannesburg: Konrad-Adenauer-Stiftung, 2005).

Tarlton, C.D., "Symmetry and Asymmetry as Elements of Federalism: A Theoretical Speculation," *Journal of Politics*, 27:4 (1965): 861–74.

Tarr, G. Alan, Robert F. Williams, Josef Marko, eds., *Federalism, Subnational Constitutions, and Minority Rights* (Westport: Praeger, 2004).

Task Force on Canadian Unity, *A Future Together: Observations and Recommendations* (Ottawa: Minister of Supply and Services, 1979).

Ter-Minassian, Teresa, ed., *Fiscal Federalism in Theory and Practice* (Washington, D.C.: International Monetary Fund, 1997).

Thorlakson, L., "Comparing Federal Institutions: Power and Representation in Six Federations," *West European Politics*, 26:2 (2003): 1–22.

Tsebelis, G., *Veto Players: How Political Institutions Work* (Princeton: Princeton University Press, 2002).

Verney, Douglas V., "Federalism, Federative Systems, and Federations: The United States, Canada and India," *Publius: The Journal of Federalism*, 25:2 (1995): 81–97.

Vijapur, A.P., ed., *Dimensions of Federal Nation Building* (New Delhi: Manok Publications, 1998).

Watts, Ronald L., *New Federations: Experiments in the Commonwealth* (Oxford: Claredon Press, 1966).

_____, *Multicultural Societies and Federalism*, Studies of the Royal Commission on Bilingualism and Biculturalism, no. 8 (Ottawa: Information Canada, 1970).

_____, "Federalism, Regionalism and Political Integration," in D. Cameron, ed., *Regionalism and Supranationalism* (Montreal: Institute for Research on Public Policy, 1981), pp. 3–19.

_____, "Divergence and Convergence: Canadian and US Federalism," in H.N. Schreiber, ed., *Perspectives on Federalism: Papers from the First Berkeley Seminar on Federalism* (Berkeley: Institute of Governmental Studies, University of California, Berkeley, 1987), pp. 179–213.

_____, *Executive Federalism: A Comparative Analysis* (Kingston: Institute of Intergovernmental Relations, Queen's University, 1989).

_____, *The Spending Power in Federal Systems: A Comparative Study* (Kingston: Institute of Intergovernmental Relations, Queen's University, 1999).

_____, *The Historical Development of Comparative Federal Studies* (Kingston: Institute of Intergovernmental Relations, Queen's University, Working Paper, 2007 (1)).

Watts, Ronald L., and Douglas M. Brown, eds., *Options for a New Canada* (Toronto: University of Toronto Press, 1991).

Wheare, K.C., *Federal Government*, 4th edn (London: Oxford University Press, 1963).

Young, Robert A., *The Secession of Quebec and the Future of Canada*, Revised and expanded edition (Montreal & Kingston: McGill-Queen's University Press, 1998).

Zimmerman, Joseph, *Contemporary American Federalism: The Growth of National Power* (Leicester: Leicester University Press, 1992).

_____, "National-State Relations: Cooperative Federalism in the Twentieth Century," *Publius: The Journal of Federalism*, 31:2 (2001): 15–30.

* * *

Journals in which articles about federal systems regularly appear:

Federations (published quarterly by the Forum of Federations in English, French, Spanish and Russian).

Publius: The Journal of Federalism (published quarterly in English).

Regional and Federal Studies (published quarterly in English).

Queen's Policy Studies
Recent Publications

The Queen's Policy Studies Series is dedicated to the exploration of major public policy issues that confront governments and society in Canada and other nations.

Our books are available from good bookstores everywhere, including the Queen's University bookstore (http://www.campusbookstore.com/). McGill-Queen's University Press is the exclusive world representative and distributor of books in the series. A full catalogue and ordering information may be found on their web site (http://mqup.mcgill.ca/).

School of Policy Studies

Exploring Social Insurance: Can a Dose of Europe Cure Canadian Health Care Finance?
Colleen Flood, Mark Stabile, and Carolyn Tuohy (eds.), 2008
Paper ISBN 978-1-55339-136-4 Cloth ISBN 978-1-55339-213-2

Canada in NORAD, 1957–2007: A History, Joseph T. Jockel, 2007
Paper ISBN 978-1-55339-134-0 Cloth ISBN 978-1-55339-135-7

Canadian Public-Sector Financial Management, Andrew Graham, 2007
Paper ISBN 978-1-55339-120-3 Cloth ISBN 978-1-55339-121-0

Emerging Approaches to Chronic Disease Management in Primary Health Care,
John Dorland and Mary Ann McColl (eds.), 2007
Paper ISBN 978-1-55339-130-2 Cloth ISBN 978-1-55339-131-9

Fulfilling Potential, Creating Success: Perspectives on Human Capital Development,
Garnett Picot, Ron Saunders and Arthur Sweetman (eds.), 2007
Paper ISBN 978-1-55339-127-2 Cloth ISBN 978-1-55339-128-9

Reinventing Canadian Defence Procurement: A View from the Inside, Alan S. Williams, 2006
Paper ISBN 0-9781693-0-1 (Published in association with Breakout Educational Network)

SARS in Context: Memory, History, Policy, Jacalyn Duffin and Arthur Sweetman (eds.), 2006
Paper ISBN 978-0-7735-3194-9 Cloth ISBN 978-0-7735-3193-2
(Published in association with McGill-Queen's University Press)

Dreamland: How Canada's Pretend Foreign Policy has Undermined Sovereignty, Roy Rempel, 2006
Paper ISBN 1-55339-118-7 Cloth ISBN 1-55339-119-5
(Published in association with Breakout Educational Network)

Canadian and Mexican Security in the New North America: Challenges and Prospects,
Jordi Díez (ed.), 2006 Paper ISBN 978-1-55339-123-4 Cloth ISBN 978-1-55339-122-7

*Global Networks and Local Linkages: The Paradox of Cluster Development in an Open
Economy,* David A. Wolfe and Matthew Lucas (eds.), 2005
Paper ISBN 1-55339-047-4 Cloth ISBN 1-55339-048-2

Choice of Force: Special Operations for Canada, David Last and Bernd Horn (eds.), 2005
Paper ISBN 1-55339-044-X Cloth ISBN 1-55339-045-8

Force of Choice: Perspectives on Special Operations, Bernd Horn, J. Paul de B. Taillon, and
David Last (eds.), 2004 Paper ISBN 1-55339-042-3 Cloth 1-55339-043-1

New Missions, Old Problems, Douglas L. Bland, David Last, Franklin Pinch, and Alan Okros (eds.), 2004   Paper ISBN 1-55339-034-2 Cloth 1-55339-035-0

The North American Democratic Peace: Absence of War and Security Institution-Building in Canada-US Relations, 1867-1958, Stéphane Roussel, 2004
Paper ISBN 0-88911-937-6 Cloth 0-88911-932-2

Implementing Primary Care Reform: Barriers and Facilitators, Ruth Wilson, S.E.D. Shortt and John Dorland (eds.), 2004   Paper ISBN 1-55339-040-7 Cloth 1-55339-041-5

Social and Cultural Change, David Last, Franklin Pinch, Douglas L. Bland, and Alan Okros (eds.), 2004   Paper ISBN 1-55339-032-6 Cloth 1-55339-033-4

Clusters in a Cold Climate: Innovation Dynamics in a Diverse Economy, David A. Wolfe and Matthew Lucas (eds.), 2004   Paper ISBN 1-55339-038-5 Cloth 1-55339-039-3

Canada Without Armed Forces? Douglas L. Bland (ed.), 2004
Paper ISBN 1-55339-036-9 Cloth 1-55339-037-7

Campaigns for International Security: Canada's Defence Policy at the Turn of the Century, Douglas L. Bland and Sean M. Maloney, 2004
Paper ISBN 0-88911-962-7 Cloth 0-88911-964-3

Understanding Innovation in Canadian Industry, Fred Gault (ed.), 2003
Paper ISBN 1-55339-030-X Cloth 1-55339-031-8

Delicate Dances: Public Policy and the Nonprofit Sector, Kathy L. Brock (ed.), 2003
Paper ISBN 0-88911-953-8 Cloth 0-88911-955-4

Beyond the National Divide: Regional Dimensions of Industrial Relations, Mark Thompson, Joseph B. Rose and Anthony E. Smith (eds.), 2003
Paper ISBN 0-88911-963-5 Cloth 0-88911-965-1

The Nonprofit Sector in Interesting Times: Case Studies in a Changing Sector, Kathy L. Brock and Keith G. Banting (eds.), 2003
Paper ISBN 0-88911-941-4 Cloth 0-88911-943-0

Clusters Old and New: The Transition to a Knowledge Economy in Canada's Regions, David A. Wolfe (ed.), 2003   Paper ISBN 0-88911-959-7 Cloth 0-88911-961-9

The e-Connected World: Risks and Opportunities, Stephen Coleman (ed.), 2003
Paper ISBN 0-88911-945-7 Cloth 0-88911-947-3

Knowledge Clusters and Regional Innovation: Economic Development in Canada, J. Adam Holbrook and David A. Wolfe (eds.), 2002
Paper ISBN 0-88911-919-8 Cloth 0-88911-917-1

Lessons of Everyday Law/Le droit du quotidien, Roderick Alexander Macdonald, 2002
Paper ISBN 0-88911-915-5 Cloth 0-88911-913-9

Improving Connections Between Governments and Nonprofit and Voluntary Organizations: Public Policy and the Third Sector, Kathy L. Brock (ed.), 2002
Paper ISBN 0-88911-899-X Cloth 0-88911-907-4

Governing Food: Science, Safety and Trade, Peter W.B. Phillips and Robert Wolfe (eds.), 2001
Paper ISBN 0-88911-897-3 Cloth 0-88911-903-1

The Nonprofit Sector and Government in a New Century, Kathy L. Brock and Keith G. Banting (eds.), 2001   Paper ISBN 0-88911-901-5 Cloth 0-88911-905-8

The Dynamics of Decentralization: Canadian Federalism and British Devolution, Trevor C. Salmon and Michael Keating (eds.), 2001   ISBN 0-88911-895-7

Institute of Intergovernmental Relations

Canada: The State of the Federation 2005: Quebec and Canada in the New Century – New Dynamics, New Opportunities, vol. 19, Michael Murphy (ed.), 2007
Paper ISBN 978-1-55339-018-3 Cloth ISBN 978-1-55339-017-6

Spheres of Governance: Comparative Studies of Cities in Multilevel Governance Systems, Harvey Lazar and Christian Leuprecht (eds.), 2007
Paper ISBN 978-1-55339-019-0 Cloth ISBN 978-1-55339-129-6

Canada: The State of the Federation 2004, vol. 18, *Municipal-Federal-Provincial Relations in Canada*, Robert Young and Christian Leuprecht (eds.), 2006
Paper ISBN 1-55339-015-6 Cloth ISBN 1-55339-016-4

Canadian Fiscal Arrangements: What Works, What Might Work Better, Harvey Lazar (ed.), 2005
Paper ISBN 1-55339-012-1 Cloth ISBN 1-55339-013-X

Canada: The State of the Federation 2003, vol. 17, *Reconfiguring Aboriginal-State Relations*, Michael Murphy (ed.), 2005   Paper ISBN 1-55339-010-5 Cloth ISBN 1-55339-011-3

Canada: The State of the Federation 2002, vol. 16, *Reconsidering the Institutions of Canadian Federalism*, J. Peter Meekison, Hamish Telford and Harvey Lazar (eds.), 2004
Paper ISBN 1-55339-009-1 Cloth ISBN 1-55339-008-3

Federalism and Labour Market Policy: Comparing Different Governance and Employment Strategies, Alain Noël (ed.), 2004   Paper ISBN 1-55339-006-7 Cloth ISBN 1-55339-007-5

The Impact of Global and Regional Integration on Federal Systems: A Comparative Analysis, Harvey Lazar, Hamish Telford and Ronald L. Watts (eds.), 2003
Paper ISBN 1-55339-002-4 Cloth ISBN 1-55339-003-2

Canada: The State of the Federation 2001, vol. 15, *Canadian Political Culture(s) in Transition*, Hamish Telford and Harvey Lazar (eds.), 2002
Paper ISBN 0-88911-863-9 Cloth ISBN 0-88911-851-5

Federalism, Democracy and Disability Policy in Canada, Alan Puttee (ed.), 2002
Paper ISBN 0-88911-855-8 Cloth ISBN 1-55339-001-6, ISBN 0-88911-845-0 (set)

Comparaison des régimes fédéraux, 2ᵉ éd., Ronald L. Watts, 2002   ISBN 1-55339-005-9

Health Policy and Federalism: A Comparative Perspective on Multi-Level Governance, Keith G. Banting and Stan Corbett (eds.), 2001
Paper ISBN 0-88911-859-0 Cloth ISBN 1-55339-000-8, ISBN 0-88911-845-0 (set)

Disability and Federalism: Comparing Different Approaches to Full Participation, David Cameron and Fraser Valentine (eds.), 2001
Paper ISBN 0-88911-857-4 Cloth ISBN 0-88911-867-1, ISBN 0-88911-845-0 (set)

Federalism, Democracy and Health Policy in Canada, Duane Adams (ed.), 2001
Paper ISBN 0-88911-853-1 Cloth ISBN 0-88911-865-5, ISBN 0-88911-845-0 (set)

John Deutsch Institute for the Study of Economic Policy

The 2006 Federal Budget: Rethinking Fiscal Priorities, Charles M. Beach, Michael Smart and Thomas A. Wilson (eds.), 2007
Paper ISBN 978-1-55339-125-8 Cloth ISBN 978-1-55339-126-6

Health Services Restructuring in Canada: New Evidence and New Directions, Charles M. Beach, Richard P. Chaykowksi, Sam Shortt, France St-Hilaire and Arthur Sweetman (eds.), 2006   Paper ISBN 978-1-55339-076-3 Cloth ISBN 978-1-55339-075-6

A Challenge for Higher Education in Ontario, Charles M. Beach (ed.), 2005
Paper ISBN 1-55339-074-1 Cloth ISBN 1-55339-073-3

Current Directions in Financial Regulation, Frank Milne and Edwin H. Neave (eds.),
Policy Forum Series no. 40, 2005   Paper ISBN 1-55339-072-5 Cloth ISBN 1-55339-071-7

Higher Education in Canada, Charles M. Beach, Robin W. Boadway and R. Marvin McInnis
(eds.), 2005   Paper ISBN 1-55339-070-9 Cloth ISBN 1-55339-069-5

Financial Services and Public Policy, Christopher Waddell (ed.), 2004
Paper ISBN 1-55339-068-7 Cloth ISBN 1-55339-067-9

The 2003 Federal Budget: Conflicting Tensions, Charles M. Beach and Thomas A. Wilson
(eds.), Policy Forum Series no. 39, 2004
Paper ISBN 0-88911-958-9 Cloth ISBN 0-88911-956-2

Canadian Immigration Policy for the 21st Century, Charles M. Beach, Alan G. Green and
Jeffrey G. Reitz (eds.), 2003   Paper ISBN 0-88911-954-6 Cloth ISBN 0-88911-952-X

Framing Financial Structure in an Information Environment, Thomas J. Courchene and
Edwin H. Neave (eds.), Policy Forum Series no. 38, 2003
Paper ISBN 0-88911-950-3 Cloth ISBN 0-88911-948-1

*Towards Evidence-Based Policy for Canadian Education/Vers des politiques canadiennes
d'éducation fondées sur la recherche*, Patrice de Broucker and/et Arthur Sweetman (eds./
dirs.), 2002   Paper ISBN 0-88911-946-5 Cloth ISBN 0-88911-944-9

*Money, Markets and Mobility: Celebrating the Ideas of Robert A. Mundell, Nobel Laureate
in Economic Sciences,* Thomas J. Courchene (ed.), 2002
Paper ISBN 0-88911-820-5 Cloth ISBN 0-88911-818-3

The State of Economics in Canada: Festschrift in Honour of David Slater, Patrick Grady and
Andrew Sharpe (eds.), 2001   Paper ISBN 0-88911-942-2 Cloth ISBN 0-88911-940-6

The 2000 Federal Budget: Retrospect and Prospect, Paul A.R. Hobson and
Thomas A. Wilson (eds.), 2001   Policy Forum Series no. 37, 2001
Paper ISBN 0-88911-816-7 Cloth ISBN 0-88911-814-0

Our publications may be purchased at leading bookstores, including the Queen's
University Bookstore
(http://www.campusbookstore.com/), or can be ordered online from: McGill-
Queen's University Press, at
http://mqup.mcgill.ca/ordering.php

For more information about new and backlist titles from Queen's Policy Studies,
visit the McGill-Queen's
University Press web site at:
http://mqup.mcgill.ca/

Institute of Intergovernmental Relations
Recent Publications

Available from McGill-Queen's University Press:

Canada: The State of the Federation 2005: Quebec and Canada in the New Century – New Dynamics, New Opportunities, vol. 19, Michael Murphy (ed.), 2007
Paper ISBN 978-1-55339-018-3 Cloth ISBN 978-1-55339-017-6

Spheres of Governance: Comparative Studies of Cities in Multilevel Governance Systems, Harvey Lazar and Christian Leuprecht (eds.), 2007
Paper ISBN 978-1-55339-019-0 Cloth ISBN 978-1-55339-129-6

Canada: The State of the Federation 2004, vol. 18, *Municipal-Federal-Provincial Relations in Canada*, Robert Young and Christian Leuprecht (eds.), 2006
Paper ISBN 1-55339-015-6 Cloth ISBN 1-55339-016-4

Canadian Fiscal Arrangements: What Works, What Might Work Better, Harvey Lazar (ed.), 2005
Paper ISBN 1-55339-012-1 Cloth ISBN 1-55339-013-X

Canada: The State of the Federation 2003, vol. 17, *Reconfiguring Aboriginal-State Relations*, Michael Murphy (ed.), 2005   Paper ISBN 1-55339-010-5 Cloth ISBN 1-55339-011-3

Money, Politics and Health Care: Reconstructing the Federal-Provincial Partnership, Harvey Lazar and France St-Hilaire (eds.), 2004
Paper ISBN 0-88645-200-7 Cloth ISBN 0-88645-208-2

Canada: The State of the Federation 2002, vol. 16, *Reconsidering the Institutions of Canadian Federalism*, J. Peter Meekison, Hamish Telford and Harvey Lazar (eds.), 2004
Paper ISBN 1-55339-009-1 Cloth ISBN 1-55339-008-3

Federalism and Labour Market Policy: Comparing Different Governance and Employment Strategies, Alain Noël (ed.), 2004   Paper ISBN 1-55339-006-7 Cloth ISBN 1-55339-007-5

The Impact of Global and Regional Integration on Federal Systems: A Comparative Analysis, Harvey Lazar, Hamish Telford and Ronald L. Watts (eds.), 2003
Paper ISBN 1-55339-002-4 Cloth ISBN 1-55339-003-2

Canada: The State of the Federation 2001, vol. 15, *Canadian Political Culture(s) in Transition*, Hamish Telford and Harvey Lazar (eds.), 2002
Paper ISBN 0-88911-863-9 Cloth ISBN 0-88911-851-5

Federalism, Democracy and Disability Policy in Canada, Alan Puttee (ed.), 2002
Paper ISBN 0-88911-855-8 Cloth ISBN 1-55339-001-6, ISBN 0-88911-845-0 (set)

Comparaison des régimes fédéraux, 2ᵉ éd., Ronald L. Watts, 2002   ISBN 1-55339-005-9

Health Policy and Federalism: A Comparative Perspective on Multi-Level Governance, Keith G. Banting and Stan Corbett (eds.), 2002
Paper ISBN 0-88911-859-0 Cloth ISBN 1-55339-000-8

Comparing Federal Systems, 2nd ed., Ronald L. Watts, 1999   ISBN 0-88911-835-3

**The following publications are available from the Institute of Intergovernmental Relations, Queen's University, Kingston, Ontario K7L 3N6
Tel: (613) 533-2080 / Fax: (613) 533-6868; E-mail: iigr@qsilver.queensu.ca**

Open Federalism, Interpretations Significance, collection of essays by Keith G. Banting, Roger Gibbins, Peter M. Leslie, Alain Noël, Richard Simeon and Robert Young, 2006
ISBN 978-1-55339-187-6

First Nations and the Canadian State: In Search of Coexistence, Alan C. Cairns, 2002 Kenneth R. MacGregor Lecturer, 2005   ISBN 1-55339-014-8

Political Science and Federalism: Seven Decades of Scholarly Engagement, Richard Simeon, 2000 Kenneth R. MacGregor Lecturer, 2002   ISBN 1-55339-004-0

The Institute's working paper series can be downloaded from our website www.iigr.ca

Marquis Book Printing Inc.

Québec, Canada
2008